Jews and American politics

Doubleday & Company, Inc.
Garden City, New York
1974

STEPHEN D. ISAACS

Jews and American politics

ISBN: 0-385-08494-3
Library of Congress Catalog Card Number 73–10969
Copyright © 1974 by Stephen D. Isaacs
All Rights Reserved
Printed in the United States of America
First Edition

This book is a project of the Washington *Post* and portions of it first appeared there in slightly different form.

For my parents

Contents

Contents

Foreword

AFTER HUNDREDS OF INTERVIEWS, this writer has been left with one salient impression: the Jews who are so actively involved in American politics fear that the rest of society misunderstands them. Many of these Jews were at first reluctant to grant interviews—apparently afraid that this writer was gathering information for a new and more invidious version of *The Protocols of the Learned Elders of Zion*. But once they talked, once they took the chance that it was not, they leaped at the opportunity at long last to explain and justify themselves to the *goyim*, the more than two hundred million persons in this nation who are not Jews. They, and not this writer, are the real authors of this book.

In that regard, the writer has occasionally printed their remarks more fully than might a volume of pure political science or sociology. The purpose has been to give the flavor of their thinking, to allow them to explain what they are like and how they came to hold the attitudes they do.

Three definitions were necessary to the writing of this book.

The first was that this book would be based on an essentially "Jewish" view of history; that is, it is men who make events, and not so much the other way around. The Jewish concept of politics in America, if one can attempt to synthesize it, is much like the one the late sociologist C. Wright Mills described this way: "Although we are all of us within history we do not all possess equal powers to make history."

Second was the old question of who is a Jew. Under rabbinic law, a Jew is one whose mother is Jewish or who has been converted to Judaism. To most people, however, a Jew is a person whom others regard as a Jew—whose name sounds Jewish, whose associations are with Jews. For the purposes of this book, only those persons who regard themselves as Jews are considered to be Jews, whether or not they meet the standards of the chief rabbi of Israel or the standards of Main Street.

Third, and most difficult, was the definition of Jewry. Some people consider Jewry strictly a religion. Some consider it a race. Others view Jews as members of an ethnic group. Still others consider Jewry a "religious civilization." This writer views America's Jews as a unique blend of Jewish religion and Jewish and American history and tradition; in short, as an ethnoreligious culture. The definition is crucial because, at times, this book might seem to emphasize to a fault familial and generational influences. The writer has tried to tread that delicate line between legitimate social comment and what some might consider racism. Perhaps more important than the author's own views is the fact that those in politics—Jews and non-Jews —view the Jews as an ethnic culture and treat them as a bloc in their planning of strategy, campaign literature, speeches, pleas for contributions, polls, and judgments. While the Jews of America—politically oriented and involved or not—may see this land as the first where they could be considered as men and women before they were considered to be Jews, viewed through the crusted and cynical lenses of the professional politician, that concept is still an illusion.

I

"Pray for the welfare
of the government…"

Jews' hyperactivity in politics

GLASSWARE SPARKLED, chandeliers glistened. The United States senator, trying to appear at ease, chatted to the left and right of him as if it was simply another night out for dinner. But from time to time he tried to study the thirty-nine other men around the long, elegant table in the Tent Room, the private dining room in Manhattan's Regency Hotel. It was Monday, January 5, 1970, and the South Dakota senator had not hobnobbed much with men like these. This was George S. McGovern's debut at trying to raise "big money" for his attempt to win the Presidency of the United States and he had a right to be nervous. The men seated around that table *were* big money. Indeed, *billions* of dollars in personal net worth was represented at the table. Laurence Tisch had invited his friends. The guests included financial giants such as Alfred P. Slaner, president of Kayser-Roth, the world's largest apparel manufacturer; Morris L. Levinson, president of Associated Products (Rival and Blue Mountain Dog Foods, 5-Day Deodorants, etc.); Preston Robert Tisch, Laurence's brother and president of the company that owns the Regency—the Loews conglomerate (which, besides hotels, controls theaters, real estate, Lorillard tobacco); Robert Bernstein, president of Random House, the publishing company; Saul P. Steinberg, the young board chairman of Leasco, a computer leasing giant; Arthur G. Cohen, board chairman of Arlen Realty (which owns, among other things, E. J. Korvettes); R. Peter Straus, a member of the Macy's Department Store family and president of Straus Communications, Inc., and Meshulam Riklis, chairman of the board of the Rapid-American Corporation (International Playtex, B.V.D., Schenley Industries).

Larry Tisch, Loews's board chairman, has assembled his friends as a favor to Henry Kimelman. Kimelman is a Virgin Islands millionaire who first met McGovern socially in late 1967 at the home of Washington lawyer Myer ("Mike") Feldman, who was also at the Regency that night. Kimelman had gradually become smitten with McGovern and ended up as his campaign's finance chief and principal angel—his loans totaled $390,000. Tisch, in consenting to host the dinner, emphasized to Kimelman that his doing so did not imply support for McGovern. (Tisch, indeed, was later to contribute to the Committee for the Re-Election of the President.)

After dessert, Larry Tisch stood. He thanked the men

for coming and said that, even though the next election was a long way off and he was endorsing no one at this point, he thought it never too early to start thinking about whom to support. Tisch introduced Mike Feldman, a veteran at working fund-raising circuits for candidates and White House counsel under the late President Kennedy.

McGovern, Feldman told the group, was the kind of Democrat they all could admire, the type of "liberal" candidate that their kind of people had always supported. He likened McGovern's early start for the nomination with John F. Kennedy's, noting that Kennedy, too, had been planning and traveling around the country to meet with people equally as long before the nominating convention, and he had been just as much of a long shot as McGovern at a comparable time. Among other things, Feldman briefly mentioned McGovern's position on Israel as being more moral than that of some of the other possible candidates who, he said, might back the defense of Israel only as long as that support would serve anti-Communist purposes. He told the group that, in time, they would find McGovern as good on Israel as their old friend Hubert Humphrey. According to several of those present, Feldman was inspiring. ("He was so good I actually believed, for a minute, that McGovern could win," said one guest.) Feldman then presented McGovern.

McGovern stood and, with his deceivingly shy and awkward smile, said he appreciated that they had all taken time to come to meet him. They should all know, he said, that even though he had not yet made a formal announcement, he definitely was a candidate for the Presidency. He said he supposed that the best way they could all get to know each other would be for him to answer questions. He remained standing and looked around the table. A slight, graying, carefully tailored man, seated several places to his right, rose. He spoke with a noticeable Hebrew accent in identifying himself as Meshulam Riklis—a name that McGovern, like most Americans, would not recognize. "Senator," Riklis asked, "just what is your position on Israel?"

The only hope for a just and permanent settlement in the Middle East, McGovern answered, looking down the table at Riklis, was not an imposed peace, but a negotiated one, worked out in a world forum like the United Nations.

With that answer, McGovern blew most of the traditional big money from Jews in 1972, money that was to go first to Hubert Humphrey, then later into the Republican campaign in unprecedented amounts. According to one man present, McGovern's mentioning the United Nations "was like waving a red flag in front of a bull." Riklis is reported to have demanded: What do you mean, the United Nations? How can you say such a thing considering the United Nations' record on Israel so far? He said that the United Nations had, time and again, voted against Israel's interests.

McGovern had not done his homework. He did not then know that the United Nations was anathema to Zionists and to Israelis. All McGovern knew was that he was being challenged, and almost rudely, right from the start. He looked at this intense little man who had suddenly dared to confront him. He did not know, until long after the dinner, that this man Riklis, son of a Palestinian orange exporter, had singlehandedly assembled one of the largest corporations in the world, that he was one of the highest paid executives in the world, and that he was not a man to back down easily.

"These men came from two different leagues," said one

of the guests. "Here was George McGovern—a very gentle Midwesterner—who was just not used to that kind of man. I don't think he'd ever met anybody like Riklis."

But McGovern would not back away either. The United Nations is the only hope, he insisted. The only way to forge any kind of lasting Middle Eastern peace, he insisted, would be through the United Nations, the only fair forum for resolving it equitably and to the satisfaction of all the parties involved, including Israel.

"I don't think you have your facts correct, Senator," Riklis is quoted as having said. Again McGovern continued to insist the United Nations was the only practical route. Finally, Riklis ended the exchange, his final words more accusatory than questioning: "Let me ask you a question, Senator. What did you expect this group would ask you? Why are you so poorly prepared on a question of this importance?"

With that, the near-freezing chill of Park Avenue outside seemed to permeate the room. "It cast a pall over the whole evening," said one guest.

The meeting continued. McGovern fielded the other questions with relative ease and, on America's involvement in Southeast Asia, was passionate, even eloquent. And about a third of those present at the Regency sent small checks to Kimelman a few days later (a considerable help at that point in McGovern's quest). Yet that meeting perhaps destroyed McGovern's entire effort to win the approval of traditional Jewish contributors in 1970, 1971, and 1972. Further, the fact is that, in general, Jews in America never felt at ease with McGovern, even though two of every three who voted in 1972 ended up casting their ballots for him.

Besides the meeting's having foreshadowed McGovern's

problem with some Democratic Jewish givers, analysis of it yields a more important glimpse into the unique role Jews now occupy in American politics: in most respects, they command influence far out of scale to their tiny proportion of the population. That McGovern's first pitch for big money came before an all-Jewish audience was tacit acknowledgment of a new reality in national politics: that members of this small ethnoreligious group are so active politically that they normally donate more than half the large gifts of national Democratic campaigns.

Politicians are becoming increasingly aware of Jews' extraordinary political activity. Pollsters, for instance, have discovered that a surprisingly high percentage of the people who ask to do their interviewing turn out to be Jewish. Strategists are learning not to base campaign planning on population statistics in states or cities where Jews live, because they vote far out of proportion to their percentage of the population. (This comes not only from the hyperactivity of Jews but from some other groups' tendency not to vote.) The stategists are particularly aware of this in the eight states where Jews tend to congregate— California, Maryland, Massachusetts, Pennsylvania, New Jersey, Connecticut, Florida, and, in particular, New York. In New York State, Jews compose an estimated 14 per cent of the population but cast between 16 and 20 per cent of the votes. Because of their political energy, their close association with the Democratic Party, and because of other groups' apathy, they cast at least one of every four votes in state-wide Democratic primaries and nearly half the votes in Democratic primaries in New York City, where one of every five residents is Jewish. Nationally, Jews make up just under 3 per cent of the population, yet cast 4 per cent or more of the votes in presidential elections. The extra

1 per cent may not seem like much at first glance, but it translates to about three-quarters of a million votes, certainly enough to be decisive in a close election, and even more influential considering that these votes tend to be cast as a bloc and are clustered in big electoral-vote states.

America's Jews are behaving as if heeding the admonition of their ancestor, Rabbi Hanina, deputy high priest in the first century after the birth of Jesus, who warned: "Pray for the welfare of the government, since but for the awe thereof men would swallow each other alive." While many of America's Jews have given up prayer altogether, much less praying for government, a large number have instead become involved in government, in power, in politicking, as never before in the thousands of years of Jewry. Milton Himmelfarb, regarded as the intellectual in residence at the American Jewish Committee, put it this way: "The zeal of untraditional Jews for politics is their *de facto* religion. With all they've gone through, those Jews are still messianic, and their religion is politics." Indeed, after interviewing hundreds of politicians—Jews and non-Jews—about the subject, this writer estimates that Jews now comprise between 10 and 20 per cent of all those actively involved on the Democratic side of American politics today—an astounding level of involvement considering the size of the Jewish group and the kinds of bars to participation that Jews have faced and, in some cases, still face. In any city where any substantial number of Jews live, they are likely to be far more active in the process of politics than are members of any other group.

Further, because Jews tend to strive for achievement, they stand out even beyond their actual numbers. It is no accident, for instance, that the most respected political reporter of the day, David S. Broder, is Jewish; or that the best-known political media expert, David Garth, is too; or that the top political filmmaker, Charles Guggenheim, is. Or that of the three principal national public opinion surveyors, two (Louis Harris and Daniel Yankelovich) are Jewish.

The most successful popular political historian, Theodore White, of *The Making of the President* books, is Jewish too. As is the leading authority on campaign financing, Herbert E. Alexander of the Citizens' Research Foundation; and the pre-eminent producer of political radio commercials, Tony Schwartz, and the best-known political satirist, Art Buchwald.

The most prominent activists of the radical left when it was at its peak—Jerry Rubin and Abbie Hoffman—were Jews. As are many of the most prominent political fund raisers, like the Republicans' Max Fisher and the Democrats' Arthur Krim. As are many who have been leading political speech writers, like the Republicans' William Safire and the Democrats' Richard Goodwin and Adam Walinsky. And so, too, is the chairman of the Democratic National Committee, Robert Strauss.

Of the five principal candidates for the 1972 Democratic nomination for the presidency, only one—George Wallace—had no Jew in his top managerial entourage. The onetime favorite Edmund S. Muskie was managed by Berl I. Bernhard; Henry S. Jackson had Ben J. Wattenberg; Hubert H. Humphrey had Max Kampelman; George McGovern had Frank Mankiewicz. In the general election campaign, of the three men who managed McGovern's national field operations, two—Harold Himmelman and Eli Segal—were Jewish. Perhaps even more revealing of Jewish involvement was the Republicans' view of "the opposition." Of the twenty people on the top priority list of "enemies" drawn up in the White House in 1971 and released by the Senate Watergate Committee, seven of the first eight were Jewish (and a total of twelve out of the twenty). The first four, all Jews, were Arnold Picker (identified in the document as "Top Muskie fund raiser"); Alexander E. Barkan of the AFL-CIO's Committee on Political Education ("Without a doubt the most powerful political force programmed against us in 1968"); Ed Guthman, a former Robert Kennedy aide who is national editor of the Los Angeles *Times*; Maxwell Dane, the advertising man.

The source of all this activity is an American Jewish community that has become overwhelmingly middle class, a community that has provided about 20 per cent of the nation's lawyers, a community whose sons and daughters flock to higher education like no other people in history (upward of 80 per cent of all Jewish youths of college age attend college).

Analyses of that college group, via huge surveys taken each year by the American Council on Education, provide invaluable insights into the Jewish community. These surveys encompass so many freshmen (160,547 of them in 1969) that the number of Jews in the total group questioned is large enough to yield statistically valid data for the Jewish group as a whole.* For the Council on Education's 1969 survey of the class that graduated in June 1973, the American Jewish Committee financed a "break-out" of the responses of the students who identified them-

* A national Gallup survey result typically lists only Protestant and Catholic data, with an "X" by Jewish; this is because the number of Jewish respondents—about fifty—in the survey's customary 1,500 or 1,600 interview sample is too small to be statistically valid for projections.

selves as being Jewish—10,609 of them. The answers of these students tend to yield a reasonably valid picture of young adult Jews in America and the differences between Jews and the rest of America that sends its children to college.

Interesting disparities show up in the columns of computer printouts between Jewish and non-Jewish students. One that is particularly striking is the far higher level of political activity and interest by Jews. In one series of questions, as to what the students had or had not done during the previous year, the responses were similar in most areas; for instance, no meaningful difference separated them on the percentage who had read poetry not required in a course, played chess, smoked cigarettes. But more than twice as many Jews as non-Jews had protested some racial policy. Nearly four times as many Jews as non-Jews had protested American military policy. About twice as many had participated in a real-life political campaign outside of high school (whereas the figures were equal for participating in high school politics). In another section of the survey, in which students were asked which objectives they "considered to be essential or very important," a significantly higher proportion of Jews felt it essential or very important to influence social values and to "keep up with political affairs." In sum, Jews are more active and more interested in politics than are their fellow Americans.

In America, Jews stand out in every political area save one: holding elective offices. Every one of the Jews mentioned earlier in this chapter, for instance, occupies a position of "secondary" political power; that is, few Jews—compared with the level of Jews' activity in politics—occupy "primary" positions of power, and they must depend

on the actual legislators and executives to act in their behalf for the causes in which they believe. In the history of
the United States, 108 Jews have been elected to high
office—governor, senator, or congressman. Six-tenths of 1
per cent of all congressmen have been Jewish; nine-tenths
of 1 per cent of all senators have been Jewish. Even today,
with the enormously high level of activity by Jews, they
are represented only proportionately—relatively speaking
—in high offices: two are governors, three are senators,
twelve are congressmen, or 2.9 per cent of all the high
elected officials in the nation.

Many "universalists" would claim that to separate Jews
from the rest of the polity constitutes racism and is un-
American. Yet when one examines the ethnic or religious
pattern of the nation's high officers, the pattern of numeri-
cal domination by the "Protestant elite" is unmistakable.
Half of the nation's thirty-six presidents have been members of two Protestant denominations: Presbyterians and
Episcopalians. That domination is present in the Ninety-
third Congress, which took office January 3, 1973. More
Jews live in America than either Episcopalians or Presbyterians, but both of those denominations can claim far
more "success" than the Jews in terms of adherents who
have been elected to high office. Here is the religious
breakdown of the Ninety-third Congress:

Roman Catholic	115
Methodist	84
Presbyterian	78
Episcopal	66
Baptist	55
United Church of Christ (includes Congregational)	27
"Protestant"	19

Lutheran   16
Jewish   15
Latter Day Saints   10
Unitarian-Universalist   9
Christian Church (Disciples)   9
Churches of Christ   7
Christian Science   5
Eastern Orthodox   4
Society of Friends   4
Others   10
None   4

While Presbyterians and Episcopalians combined make up about the same percentage of the population as Jews, 26.7 per cent of the American Congress are either Presbyterians or Episcopalians, compared with the Jews' 2.8 per cent. This disparity is particularly striking considering that the Jewish group exceeds all others in America—including Presbyterians and Episcopalians—in professional standing, in education, in income, and, most pertinent to this discussion, in political activity. The reason, simply, as surveys have shown, is that Jews still rank relatively low in social standing, that they still are not considered to be appropriate governmental representatives in the United States. Or—and this may be more important—they themselves may not consider themselves to be appropriate representatives of the people and in effect relegate themselves to the back rooms of politics.

America has been a country of slogans. But when one goes beyond the moralistic slogans about melting pots, pluralistic societies, and equality—as social scientists by the score have been urging Americans to do for the last two decades—one finds the position of America's politically active Jews to have striking parallels with their historic role in European politics: that of being court Jews. It may seem farfetched to apply the court Jew concept to the American experience, but the comparisons are too compelling to overlook. In Europe, the Jews served as moneylenders and brokers and tax collectors and performed chores so that the political and ecclesiastical rulers could hire armies to fight their wars. In America, the Jews act as though those same roles were compulsory, although the job descriptions have, of course, changed with the times. Here one calls them strategists, computer experts, media managers, fund raisers, but in the main they are still raising money and doing chores for the Protestants and Catholics who can then hire the manpower to fight their (political) wars. Thomas B. Morgan, a writer and a Jew who was a lance bearer (as press secretary) for former New York Mayor John V. Lindsay, summed it up well when he said, "I guess it's really still like it was in Vienna. You sent one guy out of the ghetto to negotiate with the prince, and he brought back some rights." In 1972, then, Frank Mankiewicz might have been that guy in the case of George McGovern. During an interview prior to the election, he said of his candidate, "Here's the best that American Christianity has to offer, with that whole tradition of the social gospel. These are our kind of people." But then perhaps Abraham A. Ribicoff, one of the two Jews then in the United States Senate, thought he was that guy, too, as he hurried through the Jewish communities of the Eastern seaboard assuring his people that his friend McGovern was educable and that he, Abe Ribicoff, would teach McGovern about the Jews.

II

Pursuing salvation
The basis of the activity

ANTI-SEMITISM has proved to be one of the most intractable melanomas in the history of the world. Some Jews are more apprehensive of it than others, and, when they perceive the slightest trace of it here or there, they fear its metastasis across America. One man named in the first chapter of this book reacted with alarm when he was shown a draft of the chapter. "Oh no!" he exclaimed. "You can't do that. *Please* don't do that." He explained that, while he felt flattered to be included, identifying him as being Jewish would cause him problems. "You just don't understand; it's getting bad out there," he said, pointing his forefinger back over his right shoulder. "I pick it up everywhere I go. It's increasing like you wouldn't believe. I really wish you wouldn't do this book at all."

This man's reaction was not unique. While several hundred Jews involved in politics consented to being interviewed, a number—once they learned the subject—refused even to pick up their telephone. The writer was not surprised when two of the principals of the 1970 Regency Hotel dinner, Meshulam Riklis and Laurence Tisch, refused to talk about it. Though well aware of the inbred dread of impending doom, this writer was startled by responses of noted public men on the subject of anti-Semitism. One question was repeated to most of those who gave longer interviews for this book: "Do you think it could happen here?" (Never was it necessary to define the "it.") In almost every case, the reply was approximately the same: "If you know history at all, you have to presume not that it could happen, but that it probably will," or "It's not a matter of if; it's a matter of when."

Fear undoubtedly is the greatest single factor accounting for Jews' high level of political activity. In one way or another, Jews in politics are, at the extreme, striving to avoid becoming lamp shades or, at least, striving for a "just" society—which may ultimately be the same thing. The Jews of America are, in the main, a product of the psychic ravages of the Western world's deeply entrenched pattern of Jew-hating. They are the progeny of thousands of years of man's brutality to man, culminating in the events of the 1940s. But while much of America perceives Jewish fright as emanating from Hitler's death camps, most of the Jews of America are the progeny of a different era of Jew-baiting and discrimination, that of Eastern Europe in the nineteenth century. Two million souls do not wrench themselves from their homes and journey, nearly penniless, across a great ocean to a foreign land without a compelling motivation. Most of the Jews of Russia were in straits that one today finds inconceivable, barred from most avenues of earning even a crumb of bread, their sons hauled off to slavery under the guise of military conscription (for *twenty-five*-year tours), their lives in constant jeopardy, if not from starvation, then from the vicious beatings and attacks from their non-Jewish neighbors and from the czar's agents. The memory of Russia is indelible, even in the grandchildren of those who endured the risks of the steerage-class journey nearly a hundred years ago.

The Jews of Russia never harbored the prospect, much less had a chance, of gossiping with a candidate for czar over a scotch and soda. As a whole, America has provided a miraculous home for the Jews and they have made the most of the opportunity and want to keep America the way they hoped it would be when they and their ancestors arrived. They work hard for the political system and for putting responsive people at the controls of that system, at making certain that the egalitarian idea is, in fact, carried out and perpetuated. The fear is pandemic among Jews and, whether that fear is at the surface of those Jews who involved themselves in politics, or buried deep within them, it *is* there and is the prevailing motive for a great part of their activity.

For this reason, many of the Jews in politics are exceedingly sensitive about being pointed out as Jews. They dread being identified as "different." Even more, they cannot escape the thought that not many years ago that kind of identification, by itself, could mean a yellow star, a tattooed number, or worse. The deprivations of Russia and of the murder of six million Jews is nearer than many like to think. Anne Frank, after all, would be but forty-five years old today. Thus while some Jews who made it onto the White House "enemies" list of 1971 good-humoredly pronounced it a reverse sort of honor, some others were aghast; Ed Guthman, for instance, reminded his friends that the last time such lists of political enemies were so carefully prepared in high places, they were compiled by the Gestapo. Such nervousness has resulted in millions of America's Jews trying to hide—or at least ignore—the fact that they were born Jewish. One prominent American frankly confessed in an interview that he has often been tempted and often been urged to run for office but has declined for fear that campaign conditions would somehow uncover the fact that he is a Jew.

In an ethnic era, as the early 1970s have been in America, many people have proudly proclaimed their ethnic origins. Many Irish-Americans, Italo-Americans, Chicanos, Puerto Ricans, and others parade their ethnic roots as if they were hard-won badges of honor; Representative Herman Badillo, for instance, insists that his aides always insert in his press statements the fact that he is the nation's first elected Puerto Rican congressman. But most Jews in public life would never consider making similar public proclamations.

The influences of a Jewish past can seem so subtle that some Jews have to ponder deeply to determine whether Jewishness has any role in what they are doing. For example, journalist-politician Frank Mankiewicz had such a response when asked about Jewish influences upon him. "I don't think Jewishness affects it," he said during the 1972 campaign. "But of course I can't tell. I have a whole set of values and I regard them all as immensely threatened by Richard Nixon. You can't tell how much those values are there because of the way in which I was brought up and the tradition and the historical impact of the way I acquired those views. How can a Jew who lived in the first half of the twentieth century say that doesn't affect everything that he does?"

Another Jewish politician, Alex Rose, leader of New York's Liberal Party since its founding in 1940, is far more certain of the impact: "When you have an accumulation, a historical background of persecution within your race, that becomes part of the legends among your people," he said. "When you are a very young kid and you hear your grandfather tell stories of how Jews were persecuted in this village where he was, you don't even know that it has sunk into your subconsciousness, but it's there. It goes from generation to generation, sometimes through books, sometimes through word of mouth. You absorb that. I remember as a young fellow in the city of Warsaw, when I heard of so many things going on in the treatment of Jews and the treatment of the poor, I had a feeling that, when I grow up, I'm going to fight for what is right, and that was a commitment I made to myself when I was 14 or 15 years of age." Rose, who is now seventy-five, says some Jews carry out their commitment "by going to an extreme, because for some reason or another their pulse is more rapid; others do it more moderately, but they're actually motivated by the same thing. That's why you can find a father who was a Socialist and the son was a Communist. You find sometimes that it's the other way around, or the grandson is a Reform Democrat, or a liberal activist, but it's all part of what I would call the Jewish heritage. You cannot deny that. . . ."

Rose's analysis is not far different from that of his old

friend, Jacob K. Javits, New York's senior senator, who says that "Jewish to me is, really basically, that fundamental ethic which preceded Christianity which said that, 'Give me a just society and I'll give you everything else.' The Christian ethic is different from that—very, very appealing, but different—and that is, 'Give me love between human beings and I'll give you everything else.' I still believe in the first . . . I'm struggling for a just society. That's the highest Jewish ethic that I know of and that's the major premise. I think the people of New York consider that my first priority—that I never fail to fight for justice. Maybe other people have bigger hearts—I don't think so but maybe they do—and greater solicitude for the child who's crying or the person in the hospital who's suffering and so on. I want a just society. I want a society where a man gets his due, where he pulls out a fair recompense for what he puts in, where he gets dignity and square shooting. Then the rest will fall into place, in my judgment."

That statement recalls a story involving the late Louis Dembitz Brandeis. Woodrow Wilson, who appointed Brandeis to the Supreme Court, used to call him Isaiah because of Brandeis' obsession with justice. A friend is reported to have asked Wilson, "Isn't it a pity that a man as great as Brandeis should be a Jew?" Wilson is said to have answered, "But he would not be Mr. Brandeis if he were not a Jew."

In essence, such words describe the same phenomenon that Himmelfarb has noted—a form of political messianism, a cry for justice from a people denied justice for thousands of years. Jewish theologian Seymour Siegel, who also is a political activist, points out that the "messianic drive is present in many great Jews. Having lost the faith that there is a God, but not wanting to give up messianism, they go into politics. . . ."

One finds that the overwhelming majority of the Jews in politics today harbor this essential outlook. It usually is mislabeled as "liberalism." Instead, the ethic is an almost religio-cultural obsession with the egalitarian ideal. Even those Jews whose life style is anything but egalitarian—who in fact live better than did the pharaohs of old—utter the "right" words of sympathy for those less fortunate. Former Supreme Court Justice Abe Fortas is certain that this is the Jewish heritage. "Science hasn't advanced far enough," he said, to know how it is transmitted. "Whether it's genetically induced or induced by some mysterious process that we don't understand, I believe it exists."

Yet one can encounter a man like Joseph L. Rauh, Jr., who denies that his being a Jew has anything to do with his passion for justice. His career, he said, has been shepherded by luck and not by any cultural or genetic heritage. Rauh, a national vice chairman of Americans for Democratic Action, is the man who defended more national security cases in the Joseph McCarthy era than any other lawyer, who in 1964 fought for the seating of the Mississippi Freedom Democratic Party at the national convention, who for years has been counsel to the Leadership Conference on Civil Rights, and who fought successfully to overturn the election of Tony Boyle as president of the United Mine Workers after Joseph A. Yablonski was murdered. "It's all accidental," Rauh insisted. "It really is. I honestly believe that luck and accident determine these things. I had no control over the fact that this man Yablonski walked into my office one day with Ralph Nader and, the next thing you know, the man is murdered, and then you take on a cause because somebody's got to vindicate it." Even after it is pointed out to Rauh that not just any lawyer would have taken on the cause, and that Nader had a reason and did not accidentally select him to bring Yablonski to—not to any other lawyer—Rauh persists in claiming that it's all an accident.

Fortas is sure it is not. "Joe Rauh is a wonderful, marvelous man," he said, "one of our greatest citizens and greatest lawyers, but to say the great things he's done have no cultural roots is nonsense." Fortas said he considers himelf "a Jew all the way through, from top to bottom—I can no more separate my Jewishness from anything that I do than I could unmake the rest of my education or separate out my emotional components."

The four thousand years of the Jews have produced the kind of person that writer Herbert Gold has described in this way:

There is a boiling of both righteous anger and dread, in varying balances, in most Jews, though some may not admit it, and in many the righteous anger has been converted into moral fervor for causes as far afield as Africa, the Cherokee Nation, and the Palestine refugees. Anxiety and dread are base metals which can be converted into moral coin.

Thus are the likes of an Abbie Hoffman and a Ben Wattenberg or a Daniel Ellsberg and a Meshulam Riklis united in peoplehood.

But there is more. Other groups have encountered discrimination too, although none share the dubious distinction of facing it for as long or in as many variations. Yet members of other "out" groups are not as politically active —proportionately—as the Jews. In the case of the Jews, unique factors inherent in the religion and culture have combined with the anti-Semitism to produce a particularly

Jewish outlook toward government and politics. Primary in the difference is the fact that Christianity stresses salvation in the afterlife, whereas Judaism stresses man's obligation to perform good on earth—to create utopia in this life. As Lawrence H. Fuchs has pointed out in *The Political Behavior of American Jews*, Judaism emphasizes that this world is man's to make what he will of, made for him, "that he is much more the creator of history than its creature."

An important difference, too, lies in the Jewish view of law—that it was made for man and changes with the growth of man. This view of law, as an ever-contemporary vehicle for the improvement of mankind, is in a sense the very historical essence of Jewish life. In Europe—from whence came the forebears of most American Jews—Jewish society was dominated by the rabbis, who were those who interpreted the law. The rabbis' readings of the law determined the day-to-day existences of every person, as prescribed by the religion. Although many of the Jews in America are no longer religious, this essential view of the law and of the world—that the world and the law are flexible to the changing reality—is hallowed still. A government of laws is thus looked at as the means to the utopian end, rather than as an end in itself.

By contrast, the Irish, another immigrant group that partook hugely in American politics, perceived government and the law quite differently: as ends in themselves. In Ireland, the Irish were certainly no strangers to discrimination but, Edward M. Levine wrote:

The Irish acquired an immutable contempt for and distrust of the law, as well as for those who made, administered, enforced, and interpreted it. The sum of their political experiences forced them to adopt the view that political power was to be sought by all conceivable means, that it was to be used only in the interests of those who possessed it. This was the dominant political component of their ethnic identity.

When the Irish flooded into America's cities, they took over, politically. In those early days they came to regard city politics as a life style, hobby, profession, career, and, indeed, as a religion. Fervid urban politics supplanted the rigid piety of the old country and the political pecking order replaced the hierarchical structure of the church. The Irish sought the law's protection by becoming its makers and enforcers. They yearned after power for the jobs that power could provide, for the prestige and security those jobs meant. But, as Levine pointed out, "issues were their anathema."

Jews, on the other hand, were compelled toward politics by issues, principally by those issues relating to human rights and civil liberties, those "rights of man" that were denied to them for so many centuries. The United States' secular government of laws coincided perfectly with the outlook of the soon-to-be-secularized Jews. And, in specifically legal terms, it meant that Jews would come to study secular law as they once had studied Talmudic law. It meant that, by the 1970s, one of every five lawyers in America was Jewish. Many of these lawyers, had they been born in another age, doubtless would have been scholars of the ever-evolving Jewish law; it is no coincidence that the five Jews who served on the Supreme Court—Brandeis, Cardozo, Frankfurter, Goldberg, and Fortas—all gained their initial prominence because they viewed the law as the ultimate vehicle for social change and social justice, for protecting the "rights of man."

Most Jews in politics today may not seem very "Jewish." But although they may not differ in dress or manner or

speech from other members of the well-brought-up and
well-educated middle class, in common with Jews the
world over, they retain that fear, fear that is always just
below the surface. The outer coating may be resplendent
with the rhetoric of universalism and equality, but inside,
most Jews maintain a sophisticated, subterranean scanning
system. This Jewish radar performs at peak efficiency
around non-Jews, ever alert to the slightest nuance, swiftly
sensing intimations of anti-Semites or, in larger political
contexts, conditions or circumstances that could lead to
outbursts of anti-Semitism. Michael Novak, the Catholic
intellectual, mentions the syndrome in his *The Rise of the
Unmeltable Ethnics:*

I've noticed it . . . in Jews, just around the corner of attention. Everything is going well; they've forgotten the familiar
feeling. Then something you say prompts uneasiness in their
eyes, the eyes of one hunted, almost found, in danger. . . .

The syndrome operates when most Jews read their morning newspaper: as their glance flits across the headlines,
they might overlook the word *Jewish* in one. Not so with
the word *Jew.* The eye rivets to that word, as if it has
goose-stepped off the page. To a non-Jew, the two words
might seem interchangeable. But the short noun form is
clipped and harsh and, when used by a non-Jew, is considered usually as almost pejorative in itself, as if in other
surroundings it might be followed by, say, bastard. Its use
by a non-Jew almost automatically makes him suspect of
being an anti-Semite, for anti-Semites often use *Jew* as a
verb, as in *to jew* someone down in price.*

* Webster's Third New International Dictionary defines the verb
form as "to cheat by sharp business practice—usually taken to be
offensive." In Britain last year, a similar definition in The Oxford
English Dictionary was challenged, unsuccessfully, in court.

Jewish radar, the knot of fear, is a characteristic of many of the Jews in politics. At least while they are there, they can work to keep the system free from the terrors that almost all other systems before have meant for the Jews. But along with this, the political Jews have, in the main, tried very hard to seem un-Jewish, as if to make themselves acceptable in the "other," White-Anglo-Saxon-Protestant world. This is part of the American urge to assimilate, to be as much as possible like the Anglo-Saxonish "Americans" and as little different. Many Jews, like many other new Americans who were "different," worked hard at what sociologist Milton Gordon called "Angloconformity." Thus, up until very recently, many Jews were pleased if someone told them they didn't look very Jewish. If they did look Jewish, they hastened to correct it with a "nose job" and/or hydrogen peroxide. Even in an industry as permeated by Jews as was (and is) the film industry, the Jewish movie stars enjoyed prominence not under their richly European Jewish names but as WASPS. So one got the celluloid version of Issur Danielovitch as Kirk Douglas and Bernie Schwartz as Tony Curtis and Emanuel Goldenberg as Edward G. Robinson and Daniel Kaminsky as Danny Kaye and so on. Out in the real world, Steins became Stones, Goldbergs became Golds, and Davidoviches became Davises.

Many of these assimilationist Jews are the very ones who tend to be active in politics. They often will deny that their Jewish roots play any part in the factors of the equation that makes them what they are. Some will say that calling attention to the fact that they are Jewish is totally irrelevant to their being. But this very urge to separate from their tribal roots is integral to their political identity. Only in this way could they stand out as the ultimate

universalists—always concerned about what is good for
mankind, never concerned about what is good for the
Jews (except, of course, as a part of mankind). They have,
for the most part, looked the other way—or even run the
other way—when "Jewish" issues have arisen, always
masking their moves behind the universalist position.
Their fear of Catholic anti-Semitism and of a state-
established religion in America leads to a vigorous insistence on separation of church and state even though that
means that Jewish day schools founder along with the
other parochial schools. They are the true democrats, the
true believers. Perhaps, after all, this is the salvation their
forefathers prayed for and risked their lives for, a place
where, at long last, a Jew could be judged as a man first,
before being condemned as a Jew. Said Norman Podhoretz, the acerbic editor of *Commentary* magazine: "The
pursuit of salvation through politics is a modern disease.
And a lot of Jews are infected with it."

III

Room near the top
The role as staffer

MANY JEWS have risen to the top of political "staffing" in recent years because of the changing nature of politics in America. As politics used to be practiced, successful careers often were the result of a man's relationship with a political organization or because he was a friend of the right political leaders. Certainly the most conspicuous illustration of that system was a onetime Missouri haberdasher by the name of Harry Truman, whose friendship with "Big Tom" Pendergast of the Kansas City Democratic machine fostered a career that culminated in the Presidency of the United States. Other current, if less celebrated, examples include Representative John J. Rooney, who rode the Brooklyn organization to twenty-nine years in the House until he was told he would be dumped in 1974, and Philadelphia's Bill Barrett, now in his twenty-fifth. Most of the political machines kept tight reins on Jewish participation, except in those rare circumstances—as in Chicago and Baltimore—where Jewish bosses like Jake Arvey and Jack Pollack helped control the organizations.

But things have not been going well for the machines. Few people have interest these days in becoming ward chairmen or block captains. The appeal of such jobs was based on the status that came with being able to deliver—whether it be a turkey on Thanksgiving, a load of much-needed coal in the depth of winter, or a job for Cousin Rosemary. But those functions have been usurped by the welfare state. At the same time, the working-class constituency of the organizations largely disappeared into the middle class. Since the machines have relatively little to deliver any more, they have suffered defeat after defeat at the polls, whether in Richard Daley's Chicago or Pete Camiel's Philadelphia. The machine cannot deliver when it is the mayor or county executive who controls all the levers of delivery. This happened not just in Philadelphia, but in every city across the country. In fact, the word *delivery* has become the new key word of city managers' bureaucratic argot.

No longer must a candidate put in the twenty-five years of loyal service to the party; what matters now is whether a candidate can be sold successfully to the voters. If any organization remains, it tags along for dear life and for what few scraps of favor it can grasp and what few claims of victory it can try to claim credit for. A few of the city organizations, like Joe Crangle's in Buffalo, have become relatively sophisticated. Crangle's, for instance, has put computers to work in calculating data on voters, keeping the data current, mailing materials out. His organization has come to understand that selling is now the name of the game. But even Crangle's organization went under to a mostly untrained cadre of enthusiastic young zealots in the 1972 Democratic presidential primary. Things are just not what they used to be. While most of the old-time leaders have looked the other way, politics has fallen into step with the rest of a merchandised society.

Therein lies a key to understanding the substantial presence of Jews in today's politicking: selling has become the most important aspect of politics and selling is what many Jews have had to do for centuries. Their major roles in merchandising and advertising, for instance, represent a natural extension of Jewish history and tradition. From their earliest days in America, Jews have exhibited many skills and talents, but most of those who immigrated to America tended to follow historic patterns. Some of the great mercantile fortunes of today were generated by men who once had traversed the American countryside with packs on their backs. As American business evolved, so did American politics, and the importance of a historic Jewish talent came to play a larger and larger role in both. Since promoting is a sophisticated concomitant of selling, it is unsurprising to see the descendants of Europe's mercantile class appearing now as political advertising consultants, media specialists, speech writers, campaign managers, mail order fund raisers.

In effect they are, as political analyst Ben J. Wattenberg says, *tummlers*—"the kind of guys in the Borscht Belt who make noise and beat the drum a little bit to get the guests down to the tennis court or calisthenics or what-ever." The road from the Borscht Belt of the Catskills to Washington's Vichyssoise Circuit is well traveled. Wat-tenberg himself went from waiting tables at Catskills re-sorts during college to sitting in on councils of power during the Lyndon Johnson era. Wattenberg is himself a kind of *tummler*.

A broad-shouldered, forty-year-old writer-strategist, Wat-tenberg wrote speeches for President Johnson during Johnson's last two years in the White House and for Hubert Humphrey in Humphrey's last race for the Sen-ate; co-authored the important book *The Real Majority*; helped manage the unsuccessful presidential campaign of Senator Henry M. Jackson of Washington in 1972; and, after the election, became chief spokesman for the new Coalition for a Democratic Majority. While Wattenberg has attained a greater prominence than many in politics, how he got there is not atypical of the Jewish "staffer," the man or woman whose career is largely devoted to the back rooms of politics and who rarely ends up in elected office, who tends to move from candidate to candidate and job to job rather easily, and who has a significant impact on public affairs.

Until 1966, Wattenberg's experience in politics was not very different from that of tens of thousands of other Americans. In college (Hobart, in Geneva, New York) he had been elected a member of the board of representa-tives, Hobart's student council. Later, while working as an editor of two trade magazines in Stamford, Connecticut, and writing two children's books, he ran (and lost) for the city's board of representatives and for the Democratic Town and City Committee. While there, he also was in-volved in a re-election campaign of then-Representative

Don Irwin, spending a month doing "general political handiwork." This was Wattenberg's political background until publication of his first serious book, *This U.S.A.*, which he wrote in collaboration with the then-director of the U. S. Bureau of the Census, Richard Scammon. The book was an outgrowth of Wattenberg's reading of Theodore H. White's *The Making of the President* 1960. "He had a long section on the results of the 1960 Census as to what they meant politically," said Wattenberg, who then set out to, as he said, "breathe humanity into those statistics." The book was published in 1965 and was a critical success. He soon agreed to take on a similar effort on world census data. While working on that project and still living in Stamford, he received a telephone call from Hayes Redmon, deputy to Bill Moyers, the presidential press secretary.

"It was the summer of 1966," said Wattenberg, in describing the leap from small-town Connecticut to big-time politics, "and Hayes said that the President had read some of the book, that he had quoted from it in one of his speeches. They were planning to deliver one hundred speeches in ten weeks—it was coming up on the '66 elections—and they wanted help writing speeches. Would I come on a temporary basis? Well, I went down and spoke with Moyers. I had never met him and I was kind of awed. I was in the White House mess and Humphrey was eating there. He came by and Bill introduced me to him and he said he had been reading my book, and that was kind of nice. Walt Rostow came by and Bill introduced me, and he said he had been reading my book, and so I was really kind of awed by all this. After lunch, Bill says, 'Come with me, I want you to meet somebody,' and we go through this long maze and I realized later, it was out past the Rose Garden and up through the mansion and up the elevator and then we go into Lyndon Johnson's bedroom and there's Lyndon Johnson in a pair of blue pajamas sitting there, finishing a meeting with Henry Ford. So the four of us guys stand around and talk for a while—Lyndon Johnson, Bill Moyers, Henry Ford, and Ben Wattenberg—you know, nice—and I was appropriately scared. Ford left after a while and then—Moyers had spoken to Johnson about putting me on staff—Johnson talked at me for a while. I didn't say much more than 'yessir' or 'nosir.' Well, I had some ideas about which directions the speeches ought to take—the stuff from the book I had just written—and I went on staff there."

At that point, says Wattenberg, "I had never written a speech in my life for anyone, including myself. The first real speech I ever wrote was for the President of the United States. How about that? It was a speech on the Alliance for Progress, which was not used, but I still think my draft was better than the one he did eventually use." From 1966 to 1968, he wrote speeches and was a middle-level political aide to Johnson. Wattenberg moved his family, by then with three children, from Stamford to Chevy Chase. Wattenberg's temporary job lasted the rest of Johnson's term.

"At bottom," said Wattenberg, "I don't like the idea of being a speech writer for somebody else. You know, I write books on my own, I write articles on my own, I'm a generally outspoken person. If I go to a college to make a speech tomorrow morning . . . great. If you write a speech for the President of the United States, it's on the front page of the *Times* the next morning and it's really very exciting for a while." But only for a while.

Working for somebody else as a speech writer, sublimating one's own entrepreneurial nature, seems to be difficult for many Jewish political professionals. Often, as well, speech writers have to function through a hierarchy, and bureaucracies are inherently Kafkaesque to Jews. Most believe bureaucracies to be especially susceptible to anti-Semitism, since any unfriendly official anywhere up the line can cause immense problems. When options are available, Jews usually opt for self-employment, where lineage is not as much of a factor as is the simple matter of whether one can get the job done—i.e., a merit system. Further, this facet of politics enables political professionals —Jews and non-Jews—to move between candidates and jobs in such a way that they are able to pick jobs that match their personal ideologies.

The relatively low level of Jewish participation in government is particularly obvious on Capitol Hill, where —despite prevailing conceptions—only a handful of Jews are employed. Of the more than eight hundred professionals employed on the staffs of Senate committees, about sixty are Jewish and, of the 2,700 employees in the Senate, fewer than two hundred are Jewish. The misimpression probably exists because, in government, as elsewhere, Jews tend to be achievers. "A lot of the more prominent [legislative and administrative assistants], who work for the very aggressive, energetic senators, are Jewish, but numerically it doesn't work out," said C. Wesley Barthelmes, a veteran Capitol staffer who is administrative assistant to Delaware Senator Joseph R. Biden, Jr. "It's the old case: whatever X per cent it is, it is more energetic and more forceful and more at the cutting edge of things than the goyim. . . . Their influence is beyond their number."

Several reasons underlie the relative sparsity of Jews in

congressional jobs. One is that new senators and congressmen tend to recruit staff from their home states, either as
payment for help or because people from their home states
will have a better knowledge of and sensitivity to legislators' constituencies. A new legislator usually will bring an
administrative assistant with him and hire a legislative assistant who knows the ropes of the Hill from the pool of
staffers made available by the turnover in Congress. Since
Jews tend to congregate in the Eastern states and since
Congress is apportioned partly geographically, Jews tend
to be rare among administrative assistants. More are legislative assistants, but still there are few, reflecting the ethnic
makeup of Congress itself. Second, those Jews who play
campaign roles often are at such a high professional level
that they would not consider taking a job as a staff assistant
to a freshman senator or congressman. If they do want a
government position, they are more likely to use their influence with a legislator to secure a job in an executive
department where they feel they can have more of an influence on government policy.

The strong entrepreneurial bent of Jewish political professionals is discernible in careers like those of Mankiewicz, William Safire, and Wattenberg, to select three of
the more prominent ones. Mankiewicz, who has a degree
in law, has moved from law to journalism to political staffing to journalism, back to direct politics, then to book
writing. Safire went from journalism to television produc-
ing to public relations to speech writing in the Nixon
White House and then again into journalism, as a colum-
nist for the New York *Times*. Wattenberg moved from
journalism to book writing to speech writing to book writing to political analysis and strategy and back to book writing.

In examining Wattenberg's career specifically, after he left the White House, he became an entrepreneur more seriously. He and Scammon undertook the writing of *The Real Majority*, completing it early in 1970, after which he did consulting jobs for various corporations—by then he had become recognized as an expert on demography. Soon came the 1970 elections and Wattenberg was back into direct politics. Humphrey, whose vice-presidential office had been four doors from Wattenberg's in the Executive Office Building, was running to reclaim his Minnesota Senate seat. "I had never really worked at length—full-time, full-scale—in a campaign, and I thought it would be a good idea to do that," said Wattenberg, "seeing as how I was about to become a political pundit." Through Humphrey aide Norman Sherman (he is Jewish too), Wattenberg became Humphrey's man in charge of speeches and issues. Many of Humphrey's speeches took on the tone of *The Real Majority*, which, when it was published later that year, quickly became one of the most-read and most-discussed new political books.

After Humphrey defeated Clark MacGregor, Wattenberg returned to Chevy Chase, where he spent the next five months writing a political novel that he was collaborating on with Ervin Duggan, a young former reporter who had also written speeches in the Johnson White House. Wattenberg had planned to stay out of direct politics in 1972 but said, "I got sucked into it." His intentions originally were to work for Humphrey again, but Humphrey couldn't seem to be able to make up his mind whether or not to run. Muskie offered Wattenberg a job, but Wattenberg disapproved of Muskie's apparent strategy of what he described as making "nice-nice to the new politics guys." Meantime, he had "started to read various things about Jackson. I tended to agree with everything that he said." He and Jackson had lunch in the Senate Dining Room one day and "I got to know him and started to give him some advice—a memo and a speech or two—and got to know Sterling Munro, who is his administrative assistant. . . . Then, gradually, as that fall became winter, I was working more and more full time on the campaign and worked on it until it collapsed in April in the Ohio primary." After April, Wattenberg was consulting for publishing firms, still working on the novel with Duggan, working on two new books with Scammon. Then, shortly after election day 1972, came announcements of the formation of something called the Coalition for a Democratic Majority. Its principal spokesman: Wattenberg.

"The Coalition," said Wattenberg, "is what the Americans for Democratic Action used to be before it went bananas." It is an attempt to pull the Democratic Party back to its coalition bases—intellectuals, workers, ethnics, and away from the new politics and its emphasis on the poor, black and unwashed. In a sense, the Coalition is an attempt to yank the Democratic Party back to where Wattenberg has been making his reputation, where the demographics are. (Jews were disproportionately involved in the forming of the Coalition, incidentally, as had been the case with the A.D.A. when it was formed in 1947. Of the ten originators of the Coalition, five are Jews.) The Coalition set up offices down the hall from Wattenberg's on I Street in downtown Washington where he could keep an eye on things as an unpaid overseer while continuing with his writing projects.

Where is any specifically Jewish input in the political doings of Ben J. Wattenberg? It turns out that when one dips below the surface, one finds that many Jews have a far more important Jewish component than meets the eye. In Wattenberg's case, the Jewish influence is perhaps greater than in most. In fact, Ben J. is not his given name. His birth certificate reads Joseph Ben-Zion Wattenberg. Both of his parents are from Israel. His father, Judah, came to America to recover from malaria he contracted while building roads in Palestine. His mother, Rachel, came to Columbia University from Palestine to study "large-scale cooking procedures so she could go back to be a cook on the kibbutz," according to Wattenberg. Rachel and Judah met in New York, fell in love: "They married and he finished law school and she finished dietetic school and they had a baby, my sister, and it was during the Depression and they were out of money and then came another baby, me, and then came a war and, well, here we are."

"As a kid," said Ben Wattenberg, "I was basically interested in two things: stick ball and the Brooklyn Dodgers. And my parents, they wanted me to study Hebrew. . . . When I was a kid in school, the kids used to call me 'Benzine,' driving me crazy. I was never called Joseph. . . . I've always felt an interest and a kinship with the Israeli situation but not to a point that I ever felt I was anything but born and bred and grown up as an American. I was an American-type kid and not a Jewish kid. Jewish interests were not my primary interests then nor are they now."

Pressed, however, Wattenberg acknowledged that his emotional ties to Israel played a part in his politics in 1972. "One of the reasons, but by no means the dominant reason, that I went to work for Jackson was his strong position on Israel," said Wattenberg. "The way I see that situation, the only real threat that faces Israel's existence, if you talk cataclysmically, is if America turns off. McGovern essentially was saying we ought to have two foreign policies: one for the rest of the world, and one for Israel, because they're 'good people' and they're a democracy and they're all those wonderful things. I disapprove of that. I believe America should provide a shield for Western Europe and for some of the Asian nations. I view that very much as a whole. But obviously, emotionally, I would be more interested in the survival of Israel than in the survival of Holland, but I cannot believe for a moment that a foreign policy keyed to being internationalist in Israel and isolationist around the rest of the world and militarist in terms of our willingness to defend brave, little, democratic Israel and our unwillingness to defend anybody else for anything would ever mean anything, if it ever came to a crunch. . . . McGovern went around saying international disputes shouldn't be settled by force anymore. Fine. Who would disagree with that? But you find out how valuable that sort of a view is when you don't have the force . . . and the Jews, of all people, have learned that. The difference between what happened to the Jews in Europe in the 1940s and what happened to Jews in Israel, in Palestine, after the 1940s is attributable only to strength. . . . What matters is when you're the strongest power in an area. It's like that great story about where does an eight-hundred pound gorilla sleep? The answer is, anywhere he wants to sleep is where he sleeps."

Wattenberg's outlook parallels that of some Jews who could not abide the Democrats' presidential nominee in 1972. But "strong America" ideology is, of course, not unique to Jews. If anything, that variety of nationalism is a main stem of American political thinking. The important

Benjamin V. Cohen *(left)* was the intellectual genius behind many of the New Deal's legislative thrusts. In this 1935 photo, he is shown with Thomas G. Corcoran, a fellow Roosevelt aide. Jews did not serve in the federal government in any significant numbers until Roosevelt's presidency. *(Photo by Harris & Ewing)*

Another young New Dealer was lawyer Abe Fortas, shown here years later, in 1965, when President Johnson announced the appointment of his old friend Fortas to the United States Supreme Court. The five Jews who served on the Supreme Court— Brandeis, Cardozo, Frankfurter, Goldberg, and Fortas—all gained initial prominence because they viewed the law as the ultimate vehicle for social change and justice. (*Photo by United Press International*)

Presidential candidates have traditionally paid their respects to Jewish labor leaders in New York. In this photo, taken just after the 1960 campaign, President-elect John Kennedy dons a hat (unusual for him) in deference to Alex Rose's United Hatters, Cap and Millinery Union. FROM LEFT: David Dubinsky of the Ladies' Garment Workers; Rose; Kennedy; and Jacob Potofsky, head of the Amalgamated Clothing Workers.

Myer Feldman served as a White House aide in the Kennedy administration. He is also an expert at fund raising and acted as an intermediary between McGovern and large Jewish contributors in the early stages of the McGovern presidential campaign. (*Photo by City News Bureau*)

ABOVE: Presidential candidate George McGovern courts leaders of the ultra-Jewish Hasidim in Brooklyn. McGovern had much trouble attracting Jews' votes, but in November two of every three Jews who voted did vote against their perennial enemy, Richard Nixon, and for McGovern. (*Photo by United Press International*) BELOW: As his national political director, McGovern chose a Jew, Frank Mankiewicz. (*Photo by Wide World Photos*)

fact here is that Ben Wattenberg's politics may seem from afar to be non-Jewish, but in fact Jewishness does play an important role in his thinking. The same is true of many of the Jews in politics who appear to have made a new "ethnic" home in the world-unto-itself of those on the periphery of politics.

Another example is media expert David Garth, an intense, gregarious, crew-cut New Yorker who has handled media for Republicans and Democrats all across the country, men like John Lindsay, John Gilligan, Dan Walker, Brendan Byrne, Adlai Stevenson III, Arlen Specter, John Heinz, Ogden Reid, John Tunney, and Thomas Bradley. Dave Garth has said that the principal, overriding concern of his youth was baseball. But, after a while, Garth acknowledged another concern. He was bedridden through much of his childhood due to illness. He used to listen to the radio, his only link to the outside world, hour after hour. But things other than baseball were broadcast. His strongest memory: listening to the speeches of Adolf Hitler, his mother translating the horrifying words from German into English. The impact on Garth's current politics is obvious: all the candidates he chooses to purvey—whichever party they are of—are "liberals," in the sense that all are anti-Right.

Garth and Wattenberg are two examples of a relatively common syndrome among Jewish political staffers. That syndrome might be labeled as "modified priorization." Sociologists use "priorization" to summarize the process of reordering priorities, of gradually coming to value Americanization, say, over Jewishness in one's scale of values. It means that a lawyer might have come to the conclusion—knowingly or not—that the legal profession has become more valuable and more meaningful to him than his family or his religion or ethnic group or nationality or whatever. This has been particularly noted among academics, many of whom are Jews. In *America's Jews,* Marshall Sklare noted that:

The problem of maintaining a Jewish identity among academicians comes not so much from the possibility of a sudden rejection of that identity but rather from a diminished involvement in and commitment to the Jewish community. Gradually, such commitment becomes less meaningful than commitment to one's profession and to the academic community, and to the value that the academic community places on universalism over particularism.

Sklare adds that the process of priorization sets in gradually and

Because cultural patterns are generally substituted in bits and pieces rather than as a total set of values, he is unaware of how fast and how far he is moving.

This suggests that the switch in values occurs more or less accidentally. Sometimes, perhaps, that is true. But certainly an equally strong factor is a fervent desire not to be Jewish, to assimilate and, while doing so, gain a status befitting true upward-strivers. James Yaffe writes that the intellectual

doesn't need the Jewish community, he has another world in which he can live. He is one of the few Americans lucky enough to be able to escape from the pluralistic system. With his enthusiasm for certain books, pictures, pieces of music, his closest bond, his deepest sense of solidarity, is with others whose lives revolve around the same things . . . No six o'clock shadow separates the Jewish professional from the rest of the academic community, the Jewish artist from other artists, the Jewish scientist from his fellow scientists. They are all intellectuals first, Jews second—if at all.

While one can, and should, add political professionals to that list, there is a slight difference. Many Jewish intellectuals feel so little Jewish that they sometimes go to great ends to avoid being perceived as Jews. They bury themselves in logarithms and cosines, in the relative plasticity of acrylics, or the import of Mycenaean culture. The political professionals, too, thrive on organizational trappings similar to those of doctors or psychologists. They speak in their own argot, share their own inside humor. They have their own trade conventions, although the conventions fall every four years instead of annually, and get far more attention from the media than conventions of the American Medical Association or the American Psychological Association. They feel a new group belongingness, a new ethnicity, a new closeness. But their commitments are of a wholly different magnitude than Yaffe's intellectuals.

While political professionals may also be secularized and priorized, they can never quite forget—or are never quite allowed to forget—where they are coming from. Their daily dealings are never far from the reality of life and the relevance of how governance relates to Jews as Jews. While they may not be constantly aware of their Jewishness, it is nonetheless present. The levels of consciousness vary, but in common these political Jews have been profoundly affected by a "Jewish influence." So one encounters Ben Wattenberg with his close relationship to Israel; Dave Garth, whose childhood memories vibrate with the echo of Hitler's vitriol; Frank Mankiewicz, who once worked for the Anti-Defamation League of B'nai

B'rith; Lawrence Goldberg, who ran the Jewish section of the 1972 GOP campaign, got his job via a former role in Providence's Jewish charities; Maxwell M. Rabb, at the same time he served as secretary of Dwight Eisenhower's Cabinet, was chairman of the government division of the United Jewish Appeal; Myer Feldman is a director of the Jewish Publication Society of America; Isador Lubin, one of Franklin D. Roosevelt's key economists, has spent his later years supervising the spending of United Israel Appeal funds; Benjamin V. Cohen, one of the giants of New Deal legislation, had been so affected by what he heard of the pogroms in Russia that he ended up as counsel to the American Zionists at the London and Paris Peace Conferences from 1919 to 1921. Political professionals, yes. But Jews, too.

IV

Modern scribes

Intellectuals and the media

JUST AS THE *tummlers* of politics are descendants of the mercantile class of Jewry, the Jewish intellectuals and journalists involved in politics also are derived from a significant strain of Jewish history. From the first days of Judaism, intellectualism was the most hallowed endeavor, and the most respected individuals were those of The Book—the rabbis, the scribes. From the religious base came a people who are among the most literate of all the peoples of the earth, who had a system of compulsory education in the first century after the birth of Jesus. It is said that, during the Middle Ages, the only group even remotely comparable with the Jews in literacy was the Christian clergy. While the brightest and ablest of the sons of Jewry studied Torah, those sons who were less scholarly were forced to go into trade, and, even there, literacy was fostered. Jewish tradesmen, after all, had to be literate not only in Hebrew but had to speak and write the languages of the people they dealt with.

One finds the descendants of history's scholarly Jews reporting on and commenting on public affairs much as their ancestor, Jospehus, did in the first century of the Christian era. Today's Josephuses—the political reporters, commentators, book writers, academics, intellectuals —wield a significant influence in the political system.

The political journalists and intellectuals have, like the political professionals, secularized and priorized, but in a wholly different form. They have not as much priorized as they have deliberately suppressed—in the spirit of "objectivity" and unbiased inquiry—whatever it is that is apparently Jewish in them, somewhat like the Marranos of fifteenth-century Spain who were forced into being secretly Jewish.

The characteristic of suppressed enthnicity is probably most evident among political journalists, who are divorced from direct participation in political manipulation and whose role is that of dispassionate observer and commentator who serves the public, not any single group. Perceiving "Jewishness" in most of these journalists is difficult, indeed. Some choose to ignore their roots, never mentioning their being Jewish, perhaps never even thinking of it, as seemed to be the case with Herbert Bayard Swope, editor of the old New York *World* two generations ago. Walter Lippmann, the greatest of all modern political journalists, always became very unsettled and nervous when his being a Jew came up. One certainly could never conclude from his writings that he was Jewish. The same was true of Arthur Krock and David Lawrence. It is true of Joseph Kraft's columns and Theodore H. White's books. That they are Jewish is almost totally irrelevant to the journalistic product of Herb Block (Herblock), David Broder, Elizabeth Drew, David Halberstam, Seymour Hersh, Sander Vanocur, Daniel Schorr, Max Lerner, and others like them who are prominent in political reporting and commentary.

One reason is that journalism, like all forms of mass education, prizes the nonethnicity of universalism. Journalism offers a haven to the secular Jew who wants to assimilate and yet has a typically Jewish passion for involvement in public affairs. American journalism's oft-proclaimed goal of "objectivity" places the serious practitioner above the fray, stripping away attachments that can be construed as conflicts of interest, material or ideological. Thus the Jew in journalism finds that he cannot be "Jewish" and at the same time be a good journalist in terms of the value system that the mass media in the United States have built over the years.

Another key reason is the nature of Washington, D.C., which is a far different city in terms of ethnicity than is, say, New York. Washington's tenor is, in general, white, Anglo-Saxon, and Protestant, an attitude established and maintained by the civil service bureaucracy and by the legislators who take up temporary or permanent residence, usually outside the heavily black city of Washington in suburbs like Arlington or Chevy Chase. Jews are not immune from the yearning for acceptance by Washington's WASP "establishment," which in turn has not been renowned for making Jews—or other ethnics—feel comfortable about being what they are. Basically an overgrown Southern town, Washington begets nonethnicity, much as academic communities do. The result is that, the longer a Jew associates with Washington politicians and society, the more he learns to suppress his Jewishness.

The tendency to reward nonethnicity is not confined to Washington, however. Until recently, the nonethnic façade of communications has nowhere been more evident than in network television. The ethnic line has now been broken by the introduction of a few, token blacks. But until the recent appearance of those blacks, the façade of television news was consistently WASPish. In terms of Jews, television news is still a-Semitic, even though—or perhaps because—the networks are owned and managed largely by Jews. This has meant that, despite the abilities of individuals like Mike Wallace, Sander Vanocur, Elie Abel, David Shoenbrun, Herbert Kaplow, and many others, no Jew has been a network "anchor man." The outfront faces have been those of Walter Cronkite, John Chancellor, David Brinkley, Harry Reasoner, Eric Sevareid, Howard K. Smith, Frank Reynolds, and others. Jews could be the "back room" presidents of the networks' news divisions, as in the cases of Louis Cowan, Fred W. Friendly, and Richard Wald. But that no Jew could be an "anchor man" raises the suspicion that the networks have bent backwards to avoid any suggestion of being "Jewish," as well as to purvey a comforting WASP image to the overwhelmingly WASP audience. Able as they are, the Cronkites, Chancellors, and Smiths have served as a de-emphasis for the historical accident that all three commercial networks grew up under brilliant Jews—the National Broadcasting Company as part of General David Sarnoff's Radio Corporation of America, the Columbia

Broadcasting System under William S. Paley, and the American Broadcasting Company under Leonard Goldenson after its split from NBC's old "Blue Network."

The same overcompensation for Jewish ownership was a factor at the New York *Times* for many years. It was widely believed that no Jew could hope to become managing editor because the owning Ochs-Sulzberger family was acutely sensitive about the *Times'* reputation for "objectivity." Gay Talese touched on some of these aspects in his book *The Kingdom and the Power* about the *Times*. Editors around the country long felt that the real managing editor of the *Times* for years was Theodore M. Bernstein and not the men who consecutively held the title, Turner Catledge and, later, Clifton Daniel. Talese mentions that Bernstein recognized that he had no chance to become managing editor for a number of reasons, "to say nothing of his being a Jew." Ivan Veit, who happens to be Jewish, an employee of the *Times* since 1928 and its executive vice-president until late in 1973, insisted that the *Times* had no Jewish managing editor early on because no Jews were then qualified for the job. "In the '20s, I'm not sure what year—I think it was around 1923 to 1925—Mr. Ochs hired Lester Markel as the Sunday editor, and he came over from the *Herald Tribune,* so there was no inhibition about having a Jew in a key editorial spot," said Veit. "I wasn't aware of any policy. There might have been a sensitivity. They were anxious to be known as an objective and a universal newspaper. I know they didn't want to be labeled as a Jewish newspaper. But it never, in my observation, functioned in the assignment of people to jobs."

The *Times'* present publisher, Arthur Ochs ("Punch") Sulzberger, spoke slightly differently: "I can remember my father discussing it. I can remember even Orvil Dryfoos [the late Mr. Sulzberger's late son-in-law and "Punch" Sulzberger's predecessor as publisher of the *Times*] discussing it—a question of sensitivity in that they were always deeply concerned lest the newspaper have a Jewish look to it—in other words, all the reporters and the managing editor and the Sunday editor and everything like that—but I never heard of it as a specific bar in any way, shape or form." That the *Times* is still aware of who is and isn't Jewish became obvious when Sulzberger, off the top of his head, noted that whatever the case may have been it was mooted by the appointment of Abraham M. Rosenthal as managing editor in 1968, and then ticked off who was and wasn't Jewish among his current editors and managers.

Reluctance to put Jews out front has been clearly evident in newspaper journalism nationwide. Many Jews are attracted to journalism and they hold many key newspaper positions. Yet of the approximately eight hundred members enrolled in the American Society of Newspaper Editors, which limits membership to "directing editors," fewer than twenty are Jewish. It happens that these few include ranking editors of four newspapers that are especially influential in terms of national politics, those being Rosenthal and John Oakes of the *Times*, Howard Simons and Meg Greenfield of the Washington *Post*, Warren Phillips of *The Wall Street Journal*, and Dorothy Schiff of the New York *Post*. And, although Lippmann and David Lawrence were members of the Society for years, the organization did not elect a president who happened to be Jewish until 1969.

The phenomenon of selecting non-Jews to be directing editors seems to be a constant, whether or not a newspaper is owned by a Jew. As it happens, few American newspapers are owned by Jews: 3.1 per cent of the 1,748 newspapers in the United States, comprising about 8 per cent of total daily newspaper circulation. The Newhouse chain of newspapers, which represents more than half of that 8 per cent circulation, employs only non-Jews as editors or publishers except for members of the immediate Newhouse family. In fact, in 1951, when Philip Hochstein was a directing editor for Newhouse, he conducted a search for a new editor for the chain's newspaper in Harrisburg, Pennsylvania, stipulating that the editor could be neither a Jew nor a Catholic. Apparently unable to locate a suitable Protestant, Newhouse chose a Catholic.

The syndrome of a-Semitism, Jewlessness, occurs as well in the two major American news agencies, the Associated Press and United Press International. No Jew has ever served in a top capacity in either agency.

Although the subject of Jewish involvement and ownership in the media may seem tangential to this book, it once was a political issue and recently became one again. In 1941, as anti-Semitism in America was building, aviation hero Charles Lindbergh told an audience in Des Moines, Iowa, that Jews' "greatest danger to this country lies in their large ownership and influence in our motion pictures, our press, our radio and our government." An internal communication of the American Jewish Committee in the early 1970s noted that

The theme of America's press being controlled and dominated by a small group of eastern Jews has been a dominant one in the anti-Semitic lunatic fringe type press at least since the halcyon days of the German-American Bund, the Christian Front and the numerous native American fascist groups.

Intentionally or not, the issue was refreshed in 1969 in, of all places, Des Moines, the same city where Lind-

bergh's assault had come. The attacker this time was Spiro
T. Agnew, Vice President of the United States, who as-
sailed the (Eastern-based) television networks and certain commentators as being elitist news and thought managers who withheld truth from the public. Soon thereafter,
Agnew went before the Chamber of Commerce in Mont-
gomery, Alabama, to say that:

When *The Washington Times-Herald* died in the nation's
capital, that was a political tragedy; and when *The New
York Journal-American, The New York World Telegram and
Sun, The New York Mirror* and *The New York Herald-
Tribune* all collapsed within this decade, that was a great,
great political tragedy for the people of New York. *The New
York Times* was a better newspaper when they were all alive
than it is now that they are gone.

One can argue the advantages and disadvantages of more
or fewer newspapers forever, but that is beside the point
of how Agnew's remarks were received: many Jews and
many Jew haters interpreted his remarks as anti-Semitic.
The Washington *Times-Herald,* owned by the McCor-
mick-Patterson family, had been purchased by the Washington *Post's* Eugene Meyer, a Jew. The defunct New
York newspapers all were owned by gentiles; the lone sur-
vivor mentioned by Agnew, the *Times,* is owned by a
Jewish family. He did not for some reason mention the
New York *Daily News,* which is read each day by far
more people than read the *Times* and which is not owned
by Jews.

   After those two speeches, the issue was fueled further
when *U.S. News & World Report* published a question-
and-answer interview with Agnew, in which Agnew said
he never intended to castigate all the media. Instead, he
said he had in mind certain "Eastern," "big city," "liberal"

newspapers and commentators. The words Agnew used have long been code words to many Americans: each of them means Jew, or under Jewish influence. Thus what Agnew was understood to be saying was that he and the administration were upset with Jewish newspapers and commentators. Despite the disclaimers of Herbert G. Klein, a non-Jew who was then assistant to President Nixon for communications, the *Times'* Veit thought otherwise: "The pros who are doing those speeches don't blunder into that kind of thing," he said. "They know what they are doing."

The head of the American Society of Newspaper Editors was then Norman E. Isaacs of *The Courier-Journal & Louisville Times,* the Society's first Jewish president. He attacked Agnew's statements in speeches and via network television, holding that a Vice President's openly attacking the press constituted a distinct threat to freedom of the press. Isaacs did not mention the anti-Semitic undercurrent in Agnew's words. But the response Isaacs received in his mail was not about the First Amendment rights of the press. As he told his old friend Klein at the time, "I've never seen such a flow of hate mail in my life—just plain, vicious anti-Semitic stuff." Reflecting on that response recently, Isaacs said that "I spent a lifetime being what one might call a eunuch in the religious sense. It never occurred to me that there were 'Jewish judgments.' One treated news and commentary in the clinical sense—antiseptically professional. This experience shocked me. It proved that there is a button one touches in America and an expectable response ensues." Hate mail similar to that Isaacs received was sent to newspapers and columnists all across the country, whether or not the owners and journalists were Jewish. The American Jew-

ish Committee, which is organized to defend against out-
breaks of anti-Semitism, immediately mobilized to assess
the impact of Agnew's remarks and found that "anti-
Semites are using Vice President Agnew's recent speeches
. . . to justify their hate programs" and "in some instances they are urging their followers to rally to the
Vice President's support."

Media representatives and the Vice President had an
opportunity to work out the issue when Agnew set up an
informal meeting with a group of New Yorkers at the "21"
restaurant. Because Sulzberger was in Europe, Veit went
as the *Times'* representative. "There were a lot of Jewish
leaders there," Veit said, "uncomfortably taking drinks
and standing on one foot and then the other. And then
Agnew came in and he made a plea to these so-called Jewish leaders of finance and business and publishing that he
was not anti-Semitic, that he was being smeared, that he
was a good friend of the Jews, and that he'd already been
smeared as anti-Negro and he didn't want this to happen
when it wasn't justified. It was sort of an uncomfortable
occasion, so we ate the smoked salmon and drank the
drinks and went home." Agnew's protestations of innocence, he said, did not go over.

(The Nixon administration's attacks on the networks,
the *Times* and the Washington *Post* not only fizzled, it
happened to have been the *Post*—which may not even have
been aware of the anti-Semitic undercurrent in Agnew's
assault—that overcame steady abuse from the White House
to uncover what became known as the Watergate scandal.)

The suppression of ethnicity that is so much a pattern
at the *Times* and among political journalists generally also
occurs among Jewish political intellectuals, those who are
one step up the line from the daily reporters and com-

mentators as being heirs to the ancient scribes. Jews play a markedly disproportionate role in political intellectualism in the United States. Jewish intellectuals tend to stand out because many of them have been heavily advertised and, having a touch of the tummler, they themselves often are experts at self-promotion. They thrive not on mass awareness of their concepts but on the quality of their audience. The Jewish intellectuals predominate among the editors of the small but influential intellectual journals, such as *Commentary* (published by the American Jewish Committee), *The Public Interest, Dissent, The New York Review of Books.*

Until recently, suppression of ethnicity has perhaps been the leading characteristic of the trend of thought of these Jewish intellectuals. Some, like Noam Chomsky and I. F. Stone, have been considered by some Jews to be so suppressed—or at least so overcompensating for their being Jewish—as to be regarded as anti-Semitic on some issues. Such men flaunt their universalism like Excaliburs of truth and objectivity. But although the Jewish intellectuals have sought "objectivity" and have as a result tended to be ultrauniversalists, there is anything but monolithic agreement among them politically. As the old joke goes, put two Jews in a room and you'll get five opinions and three political parties.

These political intellectuals include a number of people who have known one another well for many years and who have been tagged the "College of Irvings" after Irving Kristol (a professor at New York University and co-editor of *The Public Interest*) and Irving Howe (a professor at the City University of New York and editor of *Dissent*). Included in this small group, many of whom were acquaintances when they were students at the Col-

lege of the City of New York, are Harvard sociologists
Daniel Bell, co-editor of *The Public Interest*, Seymour
Martin Lipset, and Nathan Glazer; and Milton Himmelfarb, a contributing editor of *Commentary*, co-editor of
the *American Jewish Year Book* and, incidentally, Kristol's
brother-in-law. And then there are Norman Podhoretz,
editor of *Commentary*; Podhoretz's wife, Midge Decter,
of *Saturday Review/World* magazine; Sidney Hook, professor at New York University, and Rabbi Arthur Hertzberg, a frequent contributor to *Commentary* in its early
days, who presided at the wedding of the Podhoretzes and
who headed the American Jewish Congress from 1972
through 1974.

Outside this group are many more Jewish political intellectuals, such as Chomsky and Stone, Hannah Arendt,
Herman Kahn, Hans Morgenthau, Sidney Hertzberg,
David T. Bazelon, Nat Hentoff, Oscar Handlin, Ronald
Steel, David Riesman, Daniel Boorstin, to name a few.
That a disproportionate number of today's intellectuals
are Jews is consistent historically, since many of the
world's great modern thinkers have been Jews. In a class
by themselves, certainly, have been Sigmund Freud, Karl
Marx (who was born to Jewish parents but baptized as a
youngster), and Albert Einstein. Sociologists' best answer
to the phenomenon seems to lie in a combination of history and the theory of "marginality." Historically, of
course, one has the traditional Jewish respect for learning,
education, and intellectualism. According to the theory
of marginality, Jews are marginal to the societies in
which they have lived, outside of dominant cultures, and
thus less encumbered intellectually by the prevailing patterns of thought that have tended to proscribe the thinking

of members of the dominant culture. According to this proposition, Jews' minds are supposed to be freer to create original thought. The brilliant Isaiah Berlin has extended the marginality theory one step further. According to Berlin, Jews as the minority, outsider members of societies have in effect been forced to study the majority with great care so as to survive within the majority. They have had to know more about the "host" group than members of the majority themselves, he has written, since the survival of individuals within the majority does not depend on such intimate knowledge; they can take their society for granted. Thus are the intellectuals, sociologists, journalists all of a piece. Wrote Berlin:

. . . The Jews, like the strangers seeking to lose themselves in the strange tribe, find themselves compelled to devote all their energies and talents to the task of understanding and adaptation upon which their lives depend at every step. Hence the fantastic over-development of their faculties for detecting trends, and discriminating the shades and hues of changing individual and social situations, often before they have been noticed anywhere else. Hence too, their celebrated critical acumen, their astonishingly sharp eye for the analysis of the past, the present and sometimes the future also—in short, their well-known genius for observation and classification, and explanation—above all for *reportage* in its sharpest and finest forms.

Jewish academics-educators-intellectuals do not usually sit idly by and muse on arcane theories. Traditionally, the Jewish intellectual has been deeply involved in the political affairs of his community. The premiere intellectuals, the rabbis, were in fact the rulers of the community. Today's Jewish political intellectuals are within that tradition, and follow the teachings of one of the rabbis quoted in the Talmud as saying:

If a man of learning participates in public affairs, he gives stability to the land. But if he sits at home and says to himself: "What have the affairs of society to do with me? . . . Let my soul dwell in peace," he brings about the destruction of the world.

Some of the intellectuals take that advice literally. Theologian Seymour Siegel was deeply involved in the 1968 campaign of Humphrey and deeply involved again in the campaign of 1972, working in the Washington headquarters of the Committee for the Re-Election of the President. The Podhoretzes were actively involved in the founding of the Coalition for a Democratic Majority, as were Glazer and Lipset.

More often, however, intellectuals who take part in direct political action are window-dressing. Since the days of Franklin Roosevelt, politicians have felt it wise to surround themselves with intellectuals, as if to refute any notion that they might be unthinking political hacks. The politicians' intent, of course, is to hope that the aura of intellectualism will rub off on them and make them appear to be philosopher kings. So John Kennedy had his Arthur Schlesinger, Jr., (who is not Jewish) to help create the image he wanted for his "New Frontier" and for himself; many in America came to believe that Kennedy the politician was himself actually an intellectual. Then Lyndon Johnson, with his awe of Eastern intellectuals, had his own, like Eric Goldman, John Roche, and Daniel Patrick Moynihan. Richard Nixon kept Moynihan on and in the 1972 campaign specifically wooed Jewish intellectuals: Kristol, for example, was a frequent invitee to White House dinners.

Intellectuals have debated for generations whether ideas do in fact have political influence. Whether they do or not, the very Jewish eminence in intellectualism in America has caused anti-Semites to fear some sort of plot by Jewish intellectuals to control thought in America. A frequent claim is that Jews are scheming to pollute the nation's morals. Among the most vocal proponents of that general thesis is the long-time anti-Semitic propagandist Gerald L. K. Smith, who recently was warning about "the mindwashing establishment."

Smith and his fellow professional anti-Semites express particular concern over what they claim is Jewish dominance of book publishing in America. Even many Jews believe that Jews control the book industry, having heard the claim repeated for so many years. One Jew, Peter Schrag, in *The Decline of the Wasp*, wrote that "half the major book publishers are Jewish." In fact, most book publishing firms are not owned by Jews and many even have the reputation among Jews in the business of being anti-Semitic. In terms of volume, most books published in the United States are reference and textbooks; the firms and editors who publish those books employ few Jews. Jews do stand out disproportionately, but do not dominate in the so-called "trade" book field, that third of the industry that encompasses creative writing. Doubleday, Macmillan, McGraw-Hill, Harcourt Brace Jovanovich, and Harper & Row can in no way be considered Jewish, and they publish more trade books than most of America's other publishing houses. The impression of Schrag and some others was doubtless created by the strong creative role established by Jews like Bennett Cerf, who built Random House, Richard Simon, Max Schuster, and Alfred A. Knopf. And nearly 20 per cent of the National Book Awards over the last two decades have gone to Jewish writers, who have received much publicity on the late-night television talk shows and in other media. But the fact is that the large mass of trade books are not written by Jews and most of the companies that produce most of the trade books are not owned by Jews. Perhaps more to the point of the Gerald Smiths and those of his ilk, however, a large share of the editors in the trade book houses are Jewish. The trade book industry centers in heavily Jewish New York and has drawn its editors from the highly educated, highly intellectual Jewish community there. They have been, as sociologist Irving Levine observed, "just the talented working slobs." But these Jewish editors and most of the Jewish writers have suppressed their Jewishness, just as have the journalists and intellectuals, again on the grounds that mass culture in America required objectivity and non-ethnicity.

It is important to note the difference between the historic process of assimilation and the suppression characteristic so prevalent in the mass media. In general, assimilation comes from an internalized reaction to external pressure and internal pressure, the desire to seem to melt into the dominant culture. And, accordingly, the environment rewards the assimilationist. Suppression, on the other hand, is more the result of an externalized pressure to submerge one's "prejudices." This does not mean that one melts; rather, it means that one downplays. This process is very different from the one that involved Herbert Bayard Swope, who attempted to "pass" as a non-Jew in a non-Jewish world, or Joseph Pulitzer's attempt, which involved not telling his bride-to-be, Kate Davis, or her parents that his father, Philip, was a Jew. Most of the Jews who appear non-Jewish in their media roles today will readily acknowledge that, to be professionals, they intentionally submerge and repress that facet of their being. As Norman Isaacs said, "I have been guilty of suppression all my working life. I deliberately suppressed it [Jewishness]. It was part of my business. That was the way life was."

In time, whether the process is suppression or acculturation (that step that comes before assimilation, involved with adopting the life style, manners, language of the new society but not the intimacy of close personal relationships) or assimilation, one would think that Jewry would disappear into the dominant culture. Statistics on Jewish intermarriage—one of every three Jews now marries someone not Jewish—would seem to support that thought. One could then logically assume that the interest of Jews as more Jews in political affairs, in intellectual life, would subside and more vanish into the peoplescape. A non-Jew, psychoanalyst Ernest van den Haag, however, insists that is not happening. He wrote:

To be Jewish—religious or not—is too much part of one's identity to be shed lightly or fully. . . . Most Jews would feel guilty, as though traitors, were they to deny their Jewishness—however doubtful its meaning has become to them.

The American Council on Education's survey of the 1969 freshman class tends to show that Van den Haag is right. One of every three of the Jews was planning his or her academic career in areas connected with the social-political process, compared with fewer than one in every five of the non-Jews.

V

Avoiding bureaucracy
The non-government role

AN ESSENTIAL INGREDIENT of the political profile of
America's Jews is their relatively low representation in
government itself. To many of the persons involved in
politics, winning an election means winning the nonelec-
tive jobs that accompany victory, ranging from that of
sanitation worker or stenographer on the local level to a
Cabinet position on the highest federal level. But Jews
have not flocked to government. This is particularly true
on the highest federal level, where only seven Jews have
served as Cabinet members. Correspondingly, the number
of Jews who serve and have served in executive depart-

ments is few compared with the high level of political interest and activity of the Jewish community as a whole.

In no area are myth and reality more divergent than in that of law and justice. As described earlier, about a fifth of this nation's lawyers are Jews. And if one thinks of American jurisprudence, one is apt to think of at least a few Jews among the principal names in American legal history—perhaps of Cardozo and Frankfurter and Brandeis along with those, say, of Marshall, Holmes, Hughes, Stone, and Warren. But just five of the 104 Supreme Court justices have been Jews, and not one of the seventy attorneys general has been Jewish.

Further, those Jews who do hold government jobs are of relatively recent vintage. Jews did not serve in the federal establishment in any significant numbers until the presidency of Franklin D. Roosevelt. This highborn Episcopalian was a superb New York politician, which among other things meant that Roosevelt had come to know many Jews well. Jewish labor leaders, in particular, adored Governor Roosevelt. David Dubinsky of the International Ladies Garment Workers Union recalled how Roosevelt would yank industry executives into his office in Albany and knock heads to force agreements out of them. As governor, Roosevelt often called on one old friend in particular for help with tricky legal parts of the pioneering social legislation he was planning for the state. The old friend was Harvard law professor Felix Frankfurter.

After March 1933, the bright young lawyers, many of them Jews, who Frankfurter had been sending to Albany were diverted instead to Washington. The new immigrants were called "Frankfurter's happy hot dogs." Among the first was Benjamin V. Cohen, who was called in for assistance in drafting emergency legislation to deal with the

Wall Street crisis. Cohen, James McCauley Landis, and
Thomas G. Corcoran—with regular telephone calls to
Frankfurter in Cambridge—wrote the Securities Act of
1933 based on the idea that corporations were in fact public and therefore ought to be publicly regulated. The idea
may have seemed somewhat radical in America, but it was
not so radical according to precepts of Jewish communality
and to the Talmudic recognition that "property is funda-
mentally a social object . . . subject to social control." The
team of Corcoran and Cohen that traipsed in and out of
the White House became famous; tagged the "gold dust
twins," they lived in a much-publicized "little red house"
on R Street in Georgetown. Corcoran was the suave and
articulate front man, Cohen the withdrawn, bespectacled
genius who would ponder late into the night considering
how to fit what it was they were doing into the framework
of the Constitution. They took on one project after another; after drafting the Securities and Exchange Act of
1934, they worked on the Public Utility Holding Act of
1935, the Federal Communications Act, the bill establishing the Tennessee Valley Authority, the Wagner Act, the
Minimum Wage Act. While Frankfurter set the tone and
while the glib Corcoran did the talking at the White
House and on Capitol Hill, Cohen did the work. While
Cohen would never admit that he wrote much of the most
important New Deal legislation, in fact, said Joe Rauh,
"Ben was the intellectual leader of this thing. Even Felix
would call him for advice." Cohen, a remarkably self-effac-
ing man, insisted otherwise, saying, "Corcoran was no
slouch, you know."

More prestigious advice came from another Jew, Louis
Dembitz Brandeis, who had been sitting on the Supreme
Court since 1916. He transmitted counsel on how to make

this or that constitutional, pressing his long-held philosophy that, the larger corporations became, the more dangerous their bigness was to the public weal.

Cohen, Frankfurter, and Brandeis were but the top echelon. Other Jews joined the New Deal apparatus. Abe Fortas was assigned to the new SEC; Mordecai Ezekiel was sent in as the Agriculture Department's economist; Henry Morgenthau, Jr., ("Henry the Morgue," to the ebullient F.D.R.) became Secretary of the Treasury; Charles Wyzanski went to the Labor Department; Isador Lubin took over the Bureau of Labor Statistics, in effect becoming F.D.R.'s economist; David Niles became the first of what is by now a line of special White House "point men" for handling minorities' affairs; the young Joe Rauh became part of it, after serving as a law clerk first to Justice Cardozo, then to Frankfurter after his appointment to the court; and there were Bernard Baruch, David Lilienthal, and Sam Rosenman (the man who coined the words for it all, "New Deal"), to name a few others.

Although today some Jews are displeased by Roosevelt's inaction concerning European Jewish refugees, Roosevelt still is given great credit for displaying courage for appointing Jews to prominent posts. He was operating in a full-blown depression and, as the scapegoats of history, Jews usually have been blamed for economic depressions. Roosevelt was attacked repeatedly as a Jew-lover. Some articles in the anti-Semitic, anti-New Deal press claimed to trace Jewish ancestry for his wife and for him ("Take note that the spelling of the name at that time was Rosen-velt, not Roose-velt," concluded one such document). Each member of Congress received a spurious, sloppily researched pamphlet that listed some four hundred men in government who, it said, were Jews (many on the list were not) and claimed that Jews were beginning to execute a plan to seize the government. The New York *Daily News* reprinted the pamphlet in 1938. In the 1930s, 121 different organizations in America devoted themselves to attacking Jews; one survey, in April of 1939, found that 42.3 per cent of the population believed that hostility toward Jews stemmed from unfavorable Jewish characteristics. The attitude of most of the non-Jews around Roosevelt, said economist Lubin, was to shrug off the attacks as the product of crackpots. But the administration was not unaware of the growing anti-Semitism. Although Cohen said that F.D.R. never brought the subject up with him, Lubin recalled one occasion when Roosevelt spoke with him about it. In 1937, the economy seemed to be taking a new turn for the worse and Lubin, Harry Hopkins, and others had spent an afternoon in Roosevelt's office "dicussing what we ought to do. We adjourned around 5 and while everyone was leaving, the President said, 'Lub, I want to talk to you for a minute.'" Lubin sat down in the chair always at the side of the crippled F.D.R.'s desk and the President said, "'Lub, we've got to do something about this and we've got to do it quick and we've got to do it right. Because if anything happens and we get any sort of recession, the first people who are going to suffer will be the Jews.'"

Roosevelt gave the impression of being blind to criticism of his appointees, and this was also evident in many of the people around him. Once, before appointing a new man to head the Wage and Hour Division of his Bureau of Labor Statistics, Lubin went to Frances Perkins, Roosevelt's close friend and his Secretary of Labor, to forewarn her. "I told her I was going to appoint this guy to the head of this division, that this was an important job. She said,

'It looks perfectly okay' and I said, 'You know that he is Jewish, and I'm Jewish and there are three or four other people in the department who are Jews?' She said, 'What has that got to do with it?' In other words, she in a sense chided me for even raising the question."

When Roosevelt again ignored the anti-Semites and appointed Frankfurter to the Court in 1939, a storm erupted. Rauh said that "in my opinion, McCarran [the late Senator Pat McCarran] went after Felix as a Jew, but there's nothing in the record to prove that." Many Jews felt that one more controversial appointment of a Jew was more than they needed at that point, and Rauh recalled that a delegation of Jews went to Frankfurter to ask him to refuse the nomination. Rauh remembered Frankfurter's asking them, "So you would create your own ghetto?" in rejecting their fear mentality.

The influx of Jews into government was in general limited quite sharply to traditional Jewish career areas— law, economics, and social work. Thus the kinds of areas where Jews are represented in relatively large numbers in government are in fact small islands. Indeed, much of government consists of vast bureaucracy, Jews' old anathema. It was one thing to be a professional who could affect national policy, quite another to become a a lower level civil servant locked into a hierarchical box. Nathan Glazer has observed that even in the depression when Jews, as everybody, so needed work the number of Jews in government remained small because of the fear of bureaucracies.

Another important factor in the relatively low number of Jews in government is the "making it" syndrome. Some Jews have doubtless felt that they could do better in private practice or business than they could in government, especially if they were that kind of person that government sought—a professional. And those Jews who have chosen to accept or seek out posts as lawyers or economists in government have tended to use those jobs as steppingstones rather than as the beginning of a long government career —as means rather than as ends. Usually they work in the Justice Department or Treasury Department for five years or so, then they parlay their knowledge of the government into a job with a Washington or New York firm that specializes in threading its way through the Washington bureaucratic tangle. As Ben Wattenberg explained, those who are lawyers often end up not just as lawyers but as "able lawyers-who-get-to-the-top kind of lawyers. . . . These are not the people who tend to be called in as Cabinet members and then go back to Peoria. These are the men who are permanent-based Washington lawyers or Washington personages—guys like Kampelman, Berl Bernhard, Dave Ginsburg, or Mike Feldman."

Because of the career propensities of Jews, five of the Executive departments/agencies in 1974 had a high proportion of Jewish employees—i.e., considerably more than the 3 per cent share-of-population ratio. These are the Department of Labor, the Department of Health, Education and Welfare (in particular, its National Institutes of Health), the Department of Justice, the Federal Reserve Board, and the National Aeronautics and Space Administration. The first, Labor, reflected that department's large number of lawyers and the significant role of Jews in the American labor movement. HEW attracted Jews who were social work-oriented, as well as socially motivated lawyers, and the Institutes of Health employed many Jewish scientists and doctors (about 9 per cent of the doctors in America are Jewish). The Department of Justice, of course, is charged with seeing that justice is done, coinciding with the oldest of Jewish ethics, and a large proportion of its employees are, of course, lawyers. The Federal Reserve Board, small and less bureaucratic than the Commerce and Treasury Departments, hired many economists, accounting for the heavy Jewish complement there. The large role of Jews in NASA was the only deceptive area, since none of the NASA's out-front people (none of the astronauts, for instance) have been Jews. The space program, it seems, is similar to the insurance industry; historically, the back-room technicians were Jewish and the executives and salesmen tended to be non-Jews. At NASA, most of the back-roomers—the scientists—were Jews, and here one is speaking in absolute rather than relative terms: at one time, 60 per cent of NASA's scientists were Jews.

Four of the seven Jews who have headed Executive departments have served in these "traditionally Jewish" areas. Two Jews served as Secretaries of Labor: Oscar S. Straus (the first Jew to serve in a Cabinet role, as what was then called Secretary of Commerce and Labor) from 1906 to 1909 and Arthur J. Goldberg from 1961 until his appointment to the Supreme Court in 1962. Two have served as Secretaries of HEW: Abraham A. Ribicoff in 1961 and 1962 and Wilbur J. Cohen in 1968 and 1969.

Two other Jewish Cabinet members have headed departments that have a somewhat disproportionate but not an overly heavy percentage of Jewish employees, since both tend to have large areas of bureaucracy. Henry Morgenthau, Jr., was Roosevelt's Secretary of the Treasury, serving from 1934 to 1945, and Lewis L. Strauss served without Senate confirmation as Eisenhower's Secretary of Commerce in 1958 and 1959. The seventh Jew named to a Cabinet post was Henry A. Kissinger, President Nixon's second Secretary of State, who was appointed in 1973.

Other departments or agencies whose number of Jewish employees is more or less proportional to the Jewish ratio of the general population are the Interior Department, the General Services Administration and the Civil Service, Federal Communications, Power, Trade, Interstate Commerce and Securities and Exchange Commissions—all of which employ a fair number of lawyers—and the National Science Foundation.

The largest of all federal bureaucracies, however, has the smallest proportion of Jewish employees. The more than one million employees of the Department of Defense exceed a third of the total federal work force. Not only is Defense's massive bureaucracy a deterrent to Jews' seeking employment there, Jews have a historic antipathy to military careers. For centuries in Europe, the military was perceived by the Jews as the ultimate of Christian exclusivity. While Jews in some countries were conscripted for military service—often really extended periods of servitude—Jews were prohibited from advancing into the career officer ranks.

A similar factor is responsible for the relatively low number of Jews who work in the Department of State. Many Jews regard the State Department as being staffed by a white, Anglo-Saxon, Protestant elite that is all but openly anti-Semitic. Some Jews felt that that element in the department would present Kissinger his first serious obstacles in getting control of the agency. Those few Jews who are or have been in the department came to expect anti-Semitism along the bureaucratic line, especially in the Foreign Service. For many years, Jews were considered somehow to be too foreign, not American enough, somehow not well enough immersed in the niceties of proper diplomatic manners and graces, to be proper representatives abroad of the United States. In 1946, the department began a strong effort to attract Jews to the Foreign Service, and, since, ten Jews have advanced through the service to attain ambassadorial rank. Nonetheless, the WASPish control of the middle levels of the service has continued to hold sway, and the number of Jews has correspondingly remained relatively small. Just how uneasy some Americans feel about Jews in the State Department became apparent after Kissinger's appointment, when the White House and the Senate Foreign Relations Committee received mail questioning Kissinger's loyalty. Kissinger, in fact, caught it from both directions because of his Jewish birth. The right-wing New Hampshire Sunday *News*, published by William Loeb, headlined an editorial about Kissinger's appointment, "Kissinger The Kike?" and referred to him as "the Jew, Kissinger." And some Jews were notably unhappy with him, too. Marvin Schick, in his weekly column in the Jewish *Press*, noted that'

The circumstances of Henry Kissinger's swearing in as Secretary of State did little to allay Jewish fears that his appointment does not augur well for our people. The ceremony took place on a Shabbos morning, a somewhat gratuitous bit of insensitivity since it could easily have been held on another day. Mr. Kissinger took the oath of office with his hand resting on the King James Bible. The offensiveness of this act is both patent and inexcusable. . . .

Kissinger himself had to respond to reporters' questions as to whether his being Jewish might impede his functioning, especially with regard to America's policies in the Middle

East, even though Kissinger had been responsible for America's foreign policy as Assistant to the President for National Security Affairs for the preceding four years.

Two other agencies that have relatively few Jewish employees, despite historic concern with the subjects, are the Department of Housing and Urban Development and the Equal Employment Opportunity Commission. Both have in recent years become largely black. Some Jews who had been working there felt out of place. At HUD, in fact, some black employees are openly hostile to Jews, partly because of resentment over Jews' supposedly being authorities in a field that now primarily involves blacks and not Jews, and partly over some Jews' remaining as landlords and businessmen in city slums.

A strong Jewish role is ebbing in another area—that at the top of the various departmental bureaucracies, in the so-called "supergrade" positions. A source in the Civil Service Commission estimated that, as of January 1974, Jews filled about 6 to 7 per cent to the supergrade positions in departments within "Jewish" areas of interest. These men and women have been career civil servants rather than career bureaucrats, sharing the traditional Jewish unease with low-level bureaucracy. But high-level bureaucracy was another sphere altogether. Hyman Bookbinder, a government watcher in Washington for the last two decades, said that "in the 1930s and early '40s, Jewish professionals, who were coming out of college in great numbers but who could not [because of discrimination] go into other types of activity, really made the federal civil service an important objective. It's getting to be a little bit less so today because a lot of that '30s generation is now starting to retire, but this town has been populated with a very significant number of the nation's best, top bureaucrats, bureaucrats who have run very, very important operations, and who were Jews, and who have made a very, very important contribution to this government and to this country."

VI

Progeny of the pogroms
The influence on modern America

AT FOUR IN THE AFTERNOON, all of the shades were drawn in the apartment on New York's Upper West Side. Daughter Anna turned on lamps so the visitor could find his way in and, in the process, admire her paintings and her late mother's sculptures. She helped her father into the room and into a chair, then turned off all but one lamp; light bothered his rapidly failing eyes. He started to talk, then stopped. Anna reached over to adjust his hearing aid; it never had worked quite right. Then this beautiful, talking history book, born Joseph Melechinsky, barely able to walk by then, to see or to hear, told about the day—was it seventy years ago or seventy-one?—when the Cossacks rode down out of the hills to arrest him and his fellow Jewish revolutionaries: "I heard the screaming of a woman: 'The Cossacks are coming! The Cossacks are coming!' We were in the valley and the Cossacks were on top of a hill coming down on their horses with their large picks, which of course in the olden days were used by the cavalry as weapons. They were coming down. We fell on the ground. They forced us to get up and run. Run for what?" Several hundred of the Jews were herded "like cattle" into the armory in Grodno—a city in Western Russia near the Polish border—and "the moment I was in the armory with all my friends, I began to think of escape. That thought of escape began to grow in my mind, but every exit was covered by the Cossacks. And yet, again, youth is reckless, even in the face of danger. I must have been very reckless . . ." Jews in Europe in those days were very resourceful. Joseph did escape. He bribed his way out, giving a ruble to one of the Cossacks guarding an exit.

Not long ago in America, many Jews wanted to forget they had ancestors like Joseph Melechinsky, viewing them as vestiges of a radical and foreign past and as an unremitting reminder of how genuinely humble their origins were. One can still find some of them, eking out an existence south of Lincoln Road in Miami Beach. A few others cling to the Lower East Side in New York or to "Bagel Alley" in Los Angeles, while their grandchildren zoom off in their four-on-the-floor Mustangs to private high schools in manicured suburbs or practice specialty medicine in grand offices along New York's Park Avenue or tax law in handsomely paneled suites along Chicago's La Salle Street. But the Joseph Melechinskys exerted inestimable influence in making America into something it had not

been before their migration via Ellis Island toward the
Lower East Side. Nelson A. Rockefeller, in one of his
last speeches as governor of New York, mentioned that:

Square foot for square foot, it's hard to imagine any place
that offered so little in material advantages—yet produced so
much in human achievement as the Lower East Side of New
York City.

Some of their actions were direct—political action, the
forming of unions, writing contracts that insured rights
for blacks (who weren't called blacks then) as well as
Jews, demanding health insurance rights—and some were
indirect. For part of Joseph Melechinsky's progeny is a son
who was a New Deal economist and who later became
head of the Washington chapter of the Americans for
Democratic Action, and a grandson who was Robert F.
Kennedy's idea man and who, a few months after the
Senator was assassinated, was making pronouncements as
New York State co-ordinator for the Vietnam Moratorium
Committee.

Many Americans are descendants of those millions of
Polish, Russian, Lithuanian, Rumanian, and Latvian Jews
who flooded America in the four decades after 1881. In
1924, an increasingly nativist American Congress sealed
the valve on this torrent of the poor, the unwashed, and
the un-American with passage of legislation that imposed
strict national-origin quotas on immigration. The Jews who
risked all to come to America were not alone, of course,
but they had been spurred all the more by restrictions on
their lives and by a series of vicious pogroms that began in
April of 1881. Pogrom is a Russian word that originally
meant riot. After 1881, its meaning changed to an attack
on Jews specifically. The czars themselves became in-

volved in instigating the riots, and their eager pogrom-fo-
menters were known as *pogromchiks.*

Joseph Melechinsky was brought up in Russia during
these pogroms. The province of Grodno was not a pleasant
place for a bright Jewish boy to grow up in; constantly
stifled and, from time to time, terrorized. In today's America it is difficult to visualize the life of the European Jew
of those days, described in the remarkable *Life Is with
People,* an anthropological study of small Jewish enclaves
of the time, as:

. . . There were also periods, for some, in which a child
would become used to the shrieks from outside, the banging
of doors being broken in, the wails for nonexistent help . . .
Such a child the next day might peer out into the streets and
see the Gentiles' pigs snuffing and eating the corpses of the
people who until yesterday had lived next door.

In Grodno, Melechinsky said in his still booming voice,
"The Jew could not be a peasant. He could not possess any
land. The Jew had no means of working in a larger factory
because the Gentiles would hate them because the Jews
would become more adapted to the various kinds of operations, and they were afraid of competition—the Jews had
more intelligence."

Joseph's grandfathers had been rabbis and his parents
had sent him to Yeshiva (a Jewish religious school);
they wanted him to be a rabbi, too. To the despair of his
mother and father, he became a revolutionary instead. At
the age of sixteen, Joseph joined the Bund, the General
Jewish Workers' Union, which had been established five
years earlier to try to organize Jewish workers in the Pale
of Settlement, the provinces along Russia's western borders to which Jews were confined. Almost immediately,

Joseph was orating before hundreds of fellow revolutionaries: "Perhaps I was a little too self-asserting and perhaps
I exaggerated everything but myself," he said, "but there
is one sure thing I knew: that I was different, that I was
born for the platform, and perhaps I was born for the pen,
for writing, perhaps for poetry. What is more important, I
began to think about myself as a leader." Joseph Russified
his name to Ossip, which became his revolutionary name.

Soon, Ossip was in custody, for participating in a quiet
form of rebellion, but revolt nevertheless: walking down
lovers' lane on May Day, wearing a red tie to symbolize his
solidarity with the revolution. His parents managed to get
him paroled through a policeman his mother sewed clothes
for. He quickly broke parole, however, leaving Grodno to
proselytize elsewhere in behalf of the revolution. He settled in Bialystok. He was beginning to spread the word,
which he described as "a trade union idea, an idea of organizing the workers along trade lines instead of party
lines, the basic philosophy being that we are all proletarians
regardless of our ideologies. The Zionists, the Bundists,
the anarchists, the Social Democratic party members are
all, first, last and all the time, workers in the shops and
should fight together to improve their conditions today,
not to wait for the millennium or for the promised land."
After three months in Bialystok, Ossip returned to Grodno
to work in hiding. He was instructed by higher-ups in the
Bund to prepare a manifesto to distribute among the workers.

"We used at that time a plain, simple contraption called
the mimeograph. We ran off copies, ink copies, from the
written manuscript. I did not know about any typewriting
machines. I can't even remember whether any typewriters
were in existence. Again, I am talking about the year of

1902 or 1903. . . . One didn't have to be a genius to figure out the writer when you wrote in your own handwriting and ran it off on a mimeograph machine. Should such a manifesto or such a proclamation or such a pamphlet fall into the hands of the secret service . . ." The secret service did find the manifesto, learned that Ossip was back in town and that he had written it, searched him out and arrested him. Ossip was beaten and thrown into a cell. "I didn't know anything about courts in Russia. . . . The only thing I knew about the courts of the secret service men covering revolutionaries was from what I was told. They were kangaroo courts with the judges sitting in judgment. No defense. No lawyers. Who could afford a lawyer? Even if one had money, was there any defense for a revolutionary against the czar and czardom?"

For days alone in his cell, the only word Ossip had about his fate was from his mother's customer, the policeman, who said "that I was good for about three to five years of exile to Siberia. He said he was very sorry for me because he knew me as a child, he saw me grow up, and he knew my parents—what nice people they were, what religious people they were. He knew my sisters, and he knew my brother. Why was I so stupid and reckless as to get mixed up in the bad company of revolutionaries? . . . He told me probably Siberia, in the frosty, wintry faraway deserted places, would be a good cure for a youngster who still has mother's milk on his lips." Ossip, a veteran revolutionary at the age of sixteen, slept on the stone floor. Finally, a week or ten days later, "my father came to see me. . . . He was very depressed and dejected, it goes without saying. But he looked me straight in the face and said in Yiddish, 'Son, not only are you in big trouble, but the entire family is. Mother doesn't know that you are in

prison. . . . All I can say to you is that, if you can re-
peat your performance of escaping while you are taken to
court, I believe that I can arrange for you to leave the
country.' All I told my father was, 'I will make every effort
to escape.' We didn't carry on further conversation. The
few words that we exchanged were in whispers. Father
left after seeing me, and I was waiting for the call to appear in court. I believe it took several weeks. . . . Five of
us—and I only knew one of the five—were taken from the
prison to the court where the hearing was to be held.
Seemingly Valodia [his higher-up in the Bund] must have
found out through his own connections the time, the hour,
the route. As we walked about a block and a half or two,
I saw a few people coming not very far from where we
were on the other side of the street. I don't remember now
just exactly what happened: there was an exchange of
shots. Who did the shooting, what the shooting was about,
all I remember now is that I walked away very nicely
and very quietly."

Ossip went back into hiding. His father meanwhile
pawned most of the family's possessions to raise the 275
rubles it cost to smuggle his son out of Russia. "It is so
strange to think now of those days," said the eighty-six-year-
old Ossip. "A man comes to see you and tells you that everything is ready, hands you over a few rubles, and tells
you, 'Now you are under my guidance and my orders. No
luggage, no bags—just as you are.' . . . Empty-handed as
I was, not a toothbrush or toothpaste or a razor, I walked
out in the darkness of night with my escort, with a few
rubles in my pocket." First a ride in a carriage, then on a
train, then into a barn with some other escapees, then
"walking in the darkness of night. I don't think we walked
for longer than fifteen or twenty minutes when we heard

some whistles. The uniformed guards guarding the borders against illegal crossings stopped us. But I was soon relieved when I was told by one in charge . . . that all they want is a ruble apiece from everyone and they would let us go and cross the border. . . . It didn't take very long, and we were across the border into Germany." On the boat to England, "uppermost in my mind was the city of London, the city universal where I knew all the revolutionaries find a place, find safety and liberty, and are permitted to carry on their work, all the revolutionary activities, print 'illegal' papers, arrange 'illegal' meetings. Everything was legal. While in Russia I lived with one word—illegal, illegality. Here I was sailing to the shores of a country of a people where everything that was illegal in Russia was legal in England. . . . I was very happy."

Ossip Melechinsky arrived in London November 12, 1904: "As we got off the planks I saw . . . an exceptional old policeman, a strange figure, not like the policemen in Russia with their swords and guns or revolver on the side. Here I saw a man dressed differently, no sword, no revolver. I can't remember whether the policeman even had a club in his hands. I think he had nothing. He stood there just like a statue, saw the people coming off the planks of the boat, looking them over as if used to it, because so many people came to England. I don't even remember now whether anybody recorded my coming or the coming of anybody else." Ossip spoke no English. "I inquired in Yiddish of the first person that looked to me Jewish." His guess was right. The man told Ossip how to get to the address of his aunt, which was written on a slip of paper, and paid his bus fare.

Free at last, Ossip determined that he was going to learn English as fast as possible and learn a trade. He did both.

He worked as an underpresser (he ironed the seams, the presser put in the creases), as a latherer in a barber shop (he lathered, the barber shaved), in a chocolate factory, in a cabinetmaker's shop, and weaving canes, bamboo, and reeds into toy baby carriages. He worked by day and studied English by night and, as a revolutionary to begin with, helped organize unions. He formed a small federation of unions, became editor of a trade union newspaper. Impressed with what he heard of the Workmen's Circle in America, a secular, socialist, Yiddish-speaking fraternal organization, he helped organize one in London.

And he changed his name. "'What kind of name is Melechinsky?'" asked a cousin. "'Who will be able to spell it?' and he suggested the name of the second greatest poet in England after Shakespeare—Milton. 'Call yourself Milton,' and I said, 'My grandparents weren't Miltons, my father wasn't Milton, nobody will ever know Ossip Milton, I want to retain something of my family.' Finally, we compromised from Melechinsky to Walinsky."

At about the same time, Ossip met and courted a worker he met in one of the millinery sweatshops. Ossip and Rosa Newman were married in August 1905. Rosa Newman Walinsky died twenty-three years ago, forty-eight years after her marriage to the young revolutionary in London.

By 1907, Ossip had become known as an orator. He shared speaking platforms with other revolutionaries like Prince Piotr Kropotkin, Nikolai Cherkessov, and Nicolai Tchaikowsky. In 1907, Cherkessov introduced him to Lenin, Trotsky, and Stalin. Ossip particularly disliked Stalin. After eight years of Ossip's working in London's sweatshops by day, volunteering in labor causes, and speaking to Jewish unionists and revolutionists by night, Rosa wanted to migrate to America so they could be with members of her family who had already gone there. As Walinsky's grandson, Adam, put it, "He hit the docks running. He was a hardened revolutionary by the time he arrived." Ossip Walinsky was twenty-six when he landed in New York in 1912. Those twenty-six years had molded an American Jewish labor leader. His union, the International Leather Goods, Plastics and Novelty Workers Union, was and is no giant organization with a multimillion-dollar pension fund and a feared political action arm. But his little Jewish union, together with others like it, directed by men molded by much the same forces that had shaped Walinsky, helped reform the lives of America's workingman then and today, through setting a moral and humanistic tone that, before them, was unknown in the American labor movement. Whether it was housing or welfare or culture, the little Jewish unions were the innovators. They "played a major role in the evolution of the American labor movement," said Arthur J. Goldberg, who as the AFL's lawyer helped engineer the merger of the American Federation of Labor and Congress of Industrial Organizations many years later. Goldberg, of course, later became Secretary of Labor and, then, an associate justice of the Supreme Court. "The Jewish labor movement has been imbued with humanitarian ideals and, in a very real sense, has given a moral tone to our labor movement," he said.

Men like Walinsky became ardent reformers because of the kinds of repression they had undergone. Although they were bright, Russia refused to let them use their brains, and their frustration evolved into anger, and then into revolution. This, Werner Cohn has written, explains the prominence of Jews in the 1917 Bolshevik revolution. Cohn says the marginality of the Jew in Russia also brought on a kind of reality-divorced political theorizing, and an "abundance of extreme and utopian ideas . . . were developed and debated in illegal organizations. Such ideas do not change overnight.

When the Jewish intellectual came to the United States, he was suddenly given an opportunity to theorize openly and to his heart's content. He took full advantage of it: for many years, the Lower East Side was one big radical debating society.

This explains why labor leaders like Ossip Walinsky, Alex Rose, David Dubinsky "hit the docks running."

Not all new immigrants were reformers, however. Most, says Rose, "just wanted to survive." Rose became vice president of the United Hatters, Cap and Millinery Workers International in 1927 and its president in 1950. He also has been the chief strategist of the Liberal Party since he and Dubinsky founded it in 1940. "The average Jew," he said, "came over here with a pack on his back, with traditions of enslavement, of fear, of persecution. They felt they were close to God when they prayed for moral objectives." In the old country, these were the souls "who worried all week long how to make for shabbas [sabbath]. Most of the Jews were merchants, tradesmen. They only had a few crafts they were working at. They didn't have time to worry about changing the world." Henry L. Feingold has written:

For most, the act of immigration proved to be revolution enough for one lifetime. . . . They wanted nothing so much as to become Americanized. It was a small fraction of the eastern immigration who were imbued with radical political idealism and, of these, an even more minute fraction held fast to their revolutionary radicalism in the new country.

Alex Rose, whose family had been well off, nonetheless empathized with Jews who had to struggle for survival.

He was one of the minority who, he says, "felt they had a mission to perform. They were the enlightened Jews. They were probably those Jews who created the image of Jews. It takes a small percentage to do it." These men were bright, and they were hardened. David Dubinsky, for example, was mugged on his eightieth birthday; five feet six inches and 130 pounds of him swung at his attacker. Asked about it, Dubinsky smiled and said, "I went through everything. Don't forget that when I was arrested the first time, I was 15 years old. When I was 16, I was sent to jail for eighteen months, and I went to Siberia and from Siberia I escaped." If Walinsky's escape was interesting, Dubinsky's was harrowing: hiking for days across Siberia, sneaking aboard railroad trains and, because of his small size, curling into a ball and hiding underneath the benches on the trains, behind passengers' legs.

"In 1911," said Dubinsky, "I was only one week in this country, and I was at the time 18 years old. Within that one week I was out stumping in political campaigns. I was a Socialist in the old country and here was a Socialist movement and I became immediately active. I happened to be some kind of speaker, originally on the corners, later on at meetings." A year later, Dubinsky and nine of his friends organized a co-operative restaurant in a basement on Tenth Street. "Then we moved to 61 Second Avenue and we grew into a big, big undertaking at that time." As the immigrants arrived, they would quickly avail themselves of the co-op's cooking and prices: a complete dinner cost twenty-five cents. A frequent co-op diner after his arrival was Ossip Walinsky. Dubinsky recalls hearing Walinsky speak back then and being impressed by Walinsky's oratorical skills; Walinsky had already spent eight years studying the English language and the labor organizing business in London.

Dubinsky went to work in the garment trade. He had been a baker in Brest-Litovsk, learning the trade almost in his sleep: the master bakers in his father's bakery would stack the cooked loaves on his bed in the cellar. By 1932, Dubinsky was president of the 400,000-member International Ladies Garment Workers Union.

Walinsky, meanwhile, was asked by men he had known in London to come to Canada and help organize unions there, and he went to Toronto in 1913 to become manager of the Cloak, Suit, Skirt and Dressmakers Union there. By 1915 he was back in New York. In 1918, he had become leader of the Leather Goods Workers' Union and had negotiated their first collective bargaining agreement. In 1918, as well, Walinsky began working in behalf of Palestinian Jews, and presided at the first Jewish Labor Congress for Palestine in New York. Over the years he devoted increasing amounts of his energies to Israeli labor problems and, in effect, diluted his own influence on the American labor scene.

Walinsky and Dubinsky were but two of the dozens of Jewish intellectual reformers working to change the face of the American labor movement, which at that time was a far different kind of movement than it is today. Rose said that "the other unions confined themselves originally only to one simple formula and that is, how to get more money for their members. They looked upon their union as an instrument for bread and butter, whereas the Jewish unions looked upon their unions as an instrument for social advancement, not only for their members but for society. . . . We participated on all questions, on all issues, and we always gave the progressive point of view. When they were exposed to it, many of them saw the logic of it— many of them wanted to become progressive themselves."

Rose said that the Jewish leaders "began to organize the unions in a certain way. They organized social institutions —banks and camps—and generally said the union movement not only has to be for bread and butter, but has to be for more than that." Dubinsky, the first Jew since Samuel Gompers named to serve on the executive council of the American Federation of Labor (in 1934), says, "the American labor movement was conservative, not political minded. It was a pure and simple trade union matter, not concerned in social problems, in international problems, maybe to a limited extent on national problems. . . ."

What changed the labor movement, Dubinsky said, was the passage of time, liberal leadership from William Green (late president of the AFL) and from George Meany (who, said Dubinsky, "is a New Yorker: he lived with the Jews, he worked with the Jews"), and the influence of the Jewish unions: "While I was sitting on the council, it never gave a nickel to any cause or institution. Now they're giving out hundreds of thousands of dollars. They are more community minded than they were in those days. I won't take the entire credit. I will to a degree. It was Jewish influence and, I would say, time, too. . . . They had a lot of respect for the accomplishment of the Jews in the field of trade unionism, in the field of social welfare, in the field of politics. It rubbed off a little bit."

Dubinsky said he did not argue with other members of the executive council. "You don't have to talk," he said. "They know what's going on. And I was getting along very well with them and them with me. I would say with 90 per cent of them. Ten per cent were different. But I became one of them. . . . I didn't bring up the Jewish issue, I didn't advocate support for Israel—Israel wasn't in

existence then. . . . It was friendship and sometimes pro-
posing action of this sort, support this cause, this situation.
Gradually, they went along."

These men are describing a crucial difference between
the Jewish unions and the others, which had been mod-
eled after British unions. British unions had been organized from the bottom up, from the needs of workers
for some kind of collective action with which to bargain
with managements. The Jewish unions, on the other hand,
were sociopolitical vehicles for their leaders, who were not
trade unionists as much as they were reformers. Their attitudes toward life had been conditioned by the repression
of the czars. Not accidentally were the leaders men like
Dubinsky, who had escaped from Siberia, or Sidney Hill-
man, who had spent six months of his life in one of the
czar's prisons and who, after coming to America, became
president of the Amalgamated Clothing Workers. The
American Federation of Labor had been molded by a Jew
as well, but a different kind of a Jew. Samuel Gompers
was the son of Dutch Jewish parents. He was born in London and migrated to America in 1863, long before the
pogroms struck Eastern Europe. Gompers, who headed the
A.F. of L. from 1886 until his death in 1924, felt unions
should be just unions and was openly hostile to socialism.

If the Russian Jewish Socialist leaders influenced the
nature of the American labor movement in general, their
impact on the workers in their unions was massive. Because of the high economic position of Jews in America
today, one tends to forget just how many of the immigrant
Jews were in the needle trades. In 1900, 34 per cent of the
former East Europeans were operating machines in the
thousands of small firms that made up the garment industry, and another 23 per cent were blue-collar workers in

other industries. The immigrant workers were very new
to such conditions. Will Herberg has written that the
Jewish workers were unaccustomed to working together;
their lives in Europe had been so desperate that they had
grown intensely competitive, and they arrived in America
with "little of the social spirit, of the solidarity so essential
to unionism." The socialism of the Jews' leaders was so
intense that they converted this mass of unco-ordinated
humanity into a spirit of true trade unionism.

With this, the new union force became virtually in-
distinguishable from Jewish politics, and was intertwined
with Socialist drives to elect representatives to public office. New York Jewish Socialists tried five times to get
Riga-born Morris Hillquit, founder of the Socialist Party
of America and organizer of the United Hebrew Trades,
elected to Congress. Each time, however, Tammany stole
and bought votes, and pointed out that his universalism
was, in effect, anti-Jewish. The Hillquit Jewish Socialists
scorned the particularism of Polish-born Meyer London, a
different kind of Socialist, but London did win election to
the House in 1914, 1916, and again in 1920. A number of
Socialists were elected state legislators. Such political experience was used later: George Meany called on his old
associate Alex Rose for political advice, since Rose had already travailed for years in such politics, as the A.F. of L.
became increasingly political. In 1948, Rose was one of
the two men Meany asked to draft some kind of political
program for the A.F. of L. This led to Labor's League for
Political Education, forerunner of C.O.P.E., the AFL-
CIO's potent Committee on Political Education, now
headed by Alexander E. Barkan, who also happens to be
Jewish.

In discussing the aims of these Jewish "revolutionaries,"

it is important to understand that their presumed radicalism was not what it appeared; in terms of Jewish tradition,
and in hindsight, they were anything but radical. Said
Rose, "There was nothing radical in what we stood for.
But in [the other unions'] eyes, we were radical." Beneath
their romantic labels and rhetoric, these "revolutionaries"
were in fact reformers and most of their objectives were
also the objectives of the New Deal. This became very
clear when Rose and Dubinsky organized the American
Labor Party in 1936. The purpose: giving Socialists a
way to pull the lever for the New Deal (Roosevelt) without having to pull the Democratic lever, which included
hated Tammany politicians. When the Labor Party was
taken over by Communists, Dubinsky and Rose turned
around and established yet another party for Socialists to
vote for Roosevelt, calling it the Liberal Party.

Despite this, many non-Jews in America then perceived
Jews as dangerous radicals, and that perception lingers to
this day. Charles Glock, in his studies of anti-Semitism,
has noted that "the stereotype of the Jew as a political un-
reliable has had a long career and received considerable
reinforcement from the visibility of Jews in radical left
movements."

This Jewish "radicalism" was forced on the Jews of
Europe centuries ago by the reality of life. Because they
were so isolated by the dominant society, and because of
their extreme poverty, a sense of communality developed
that presaged much of the modern welfare state, from
public works projects to food stamps to rent controls.
Richard G. Hirsch has written that, in the Middle Ages,
the Jewish communities were forced to join together to
fulfill community obligations that individuals could not
possibly meet. This included taking care of the communi-

ties' poorer people. To do this, prices were regulated so that the poor could buy food and other necessities at low prices; rents were kept low so that the poor could afford decent housing. Helping the poor became such a complex undertaking, Hirsch wrote, that "the Jewish community supplemented the obligations of private charity with an elaborate system of public welfare—the first in history." Helping the poor was not considered a burden, but an opportunity, for Talmud pointed out that the poor give the righteous the chance to perform good deeds, that "the poor man does more for the rich man than the rich man for the poor man." Moreover, the Bible declared that poverty should be eliminated, and the prophets bewailed "economic inequalities that resulted in loss of freedom, injustice and oppression." When certain men became too rich for the good of the community, Milton R. Konvitz has written, they were "declared enemies of the people and the chief sinners against God." It should not be surprising that Jews yearning to become Americanized were attracted to the ideas of these "revolutionary" labor leaders who preached at them at every opportunity; the union leaders were telling them things no more radical than the traditions of their forefathers in Europe.

As the progressiveness expounded by the Jewish intellectuals/unionists spread throughout much of the American labor movement, in effect setting up a susceptibility to the innovations of the New Deal, progressiveness also became a daily fact of life in the homes of the labor leaders and of many of the Jewish workers. But while the social ideas may have been passed to the next generation, the children were destined not to follow their parents into the grueling work of garment making. "No sacrifice was too great," Herberg wrote, to keep the children out of the

shops. More than four of every five men's garment workers in 1913 were Jewish; sixty years later, said Dubinsky,
it was fewer than one of every five.

The children of the garment workers disdained more
than just the sewing machines and cutting tables. Herberg noted that they regarded the Jewish labor movement
itself as "something alien, even offensive" that intruded
in their becoming Americanized and became "part of
the immigrant background that had to be sloughed off as
fast as possible. A chasm, spiritual and cultural, developed
between the generations, one that all the Yiddish-labor
schools in the world could not hope to overcome." However, if reaction was strong to the foreign-sounding flavor
of the United Hebrew Trades, the political dogma that
had been part of the tradition was not so readily cast aside.
The theory that man is a product of his environment is
bolstered by the fact that, in general, the children were
progressives too.

Ossip Walinsky's son, Louis, an economist, consultant
to the World Bank, asked how one could be otherwise.
Progressive thinking, he says, was part of "the atmosphere
in which I grew up. We lived in the Bronx when I was
small and the circle of my parents' friends was a Jewish,
intellectual and, I guess, radical group, many of whom
had known one another in England. I remember one of
my early memories is going to a Socialist Sunday school
in the Bronx. My father was in politics—he ran for the
state assembly—and of course the trade union group was
a part of my youthful background. And my mother was a
kind of suffragette and activist in the Women's Consumers League and in the Peace Society and a parader and
all that. It was part of the atmosphere, it was the ambience,
it was natural."

It was perhaps natural, too, that Louis J. Walinsky would teach economics and work for the economic organization in Washington of Robert R. Nathan Associates (Nathan was a national vice chairman of Americans for Democratic Action) and, in 1951–52, served as president of the Washington chapter of A.D.A. Years earlier, he had been drawn to A.D.A.'s predecessor, the Union for Democratic Action, "because it was the only thing around that came anywhere close to being a positive statement that a guy could go for."

Just as Louis's career had evolved, so did that of Louis's son, Adam, who joined the Department of Justice under Robert F. Kennedy and who, after Kennedy became New York's senator, became the house radical of Kennedy's staff. It was Adam Walinsky, the wild-eyed "revolutionary," who was yelling at Kennedy in 1966 to oppose America's involvement in the war in Vietnam. And it was Adam Walinsky who, after Kennedy was murdered, became a leader in the antiwar movement.

When Walinsky became Democratic candidate for attorney general of New York in 1970, he failed to win the nomination of the Liberal Party of New York. Walinsky, of course, had written Kennedy's most evocative speeches about poverty and the underprivileged, had ramrodded Kennedy's plan to uplift the disintegrated areas of Brooklyn, had been the principal force in the state's progressive New Democratic Coalition. But progressives, of course, have been renowned for arguing over who is or isn't progressive enough. This was no salve to Ossip Walinsky, who almost three decades earlier had helped form the Liberal Party. No matter. Soon, a rump group of anti-Rose members of the Liberal Party, calling themselves the Liberals for New Politics, criticized Rose for failing to endorse Walinsky, endorsed him themselves, and announced that they planned to "democratize" the Liberal Party.

Adam Walinsky, thirty-six years old, asked his grandfather, Ossip, at the age of eighty-six, to talk for hours into a tape recorder so that Adam's son, Peter, now ten, would have a living record of his progressive heritage when he is grown and his great-grandfather had passed on. Tape recordings, of course, are not the means by which cultural values are transmitted from one generation to the next. As Ossip influenced Louis, Louis influenced Adam, and Adam is influencing Peter.

Ossip Walinsky's heart finally gave out. He came out of a coma on the afternoon of March 4, 1973, in his room at Beth Israel Hospital, to regale his great-grandchildren with stories of "the olden days," as he called them. Then, several hours later, he died quietly.

VII

Opposing the powerful
Jews as radicals

FOR RELIGIOUS JEWS, Passover is among the holiest of observances, commemorating the flight of the Jews from slavery in Egypt more than three thousand years ago. The *seder*, read on the first night or nights of Passover, celebrates the deliverance. Arthur Irving Waskow, son of an immigrant Socialist tailor, was reared on the traditional seder in his childhood in Baltimore. Thirty years later, after earning his doctorate, after serving as an aide to a congressman, and after having become a key ideological resource of the "New Left" in America, Waskow found Judaism anew through the seder and wrote his own—a seder that shocked, and still shocks, most traditional Jews. A segment of it reads like this:

Our people have been frightened into allowing themselves to be purchased at such affluent prices that they have forgotten to be angry. . . . They must stop collaborating. Jewish businessmen must stop buying grapes from farmers who exploit their hired laborers; Jewish organizations must not lend money to banks that oppress Black people; Jewish political leaders must not serve the military-industrial complex.

The seder, says Waskow, barefoot and bearded, "was the one serious identification of Jewishness all through the years. Through the seder, really, in the beginning of 1968 and '69, I rediscovered being Jewish, I mean thinking seriously about it and working on *The Freedom Seder*." Waskow's rediscovery and his passage from "straight" American-Jewish "liberalism" personifies the important role Jews currently play in the radical left of American politics.

Waskow, in his living room, paused to cuddle his young son and daughter; he was looking after them in his house, in the midst of Washington's black ghetto, while his psychologist wife was away at a convention. The house was furnished sparely—functional, unlike the places one identifies with modern Jewry in Beverly Hills or Great Neck or Skokie.

"For a while," Waskow said, "I was an accidentally Jewish radical, then I was a Jewish radical in the sense of being a radical who more and more felt something coming out of Jewishness which affected radicalism. And now I'd say I am a radical Jew, in the sense that I want to pierce to the root of the Jewish tradition to learn how to live . . ."

"I just about saved Arthur Waskow's life once, and he probably doesn't even know me," said a very different kind of Jew in politics, Ben Wattenberg. "It was back in '68 or '69," he said, smiling. "Lee White [the onetime head of the Federal Power Commission] had talked me into joining his temple, Tifereth Israel. It's right up there on 16th Street, right across the street from Lew Alcindor's house—the one where all the people were murdered. Anyway, I was a member of this temple maybe two weeks when the high holidays [Rosh Hashanah and Yom Kippur] came along, and they had too many reservations, so they decided to hold two high holiday services—one upstairs, and one downstairs for the overflow. The rabbi would lead the services upstairs and downstairs, for the so-called cheap seats, they decided to invite four sermonizers. Waskow was one of them. And I was an usher. His sermon was Kol Nidre night, the eve of Yom Kippur, the most solemn day in the Jewish calendar. Now this is a pretty liberal synagogue, but it's pretty far from an Arthur Waskow. So here he was, reading this big sermon about Vietnam and Jewish racism and how Jewish landlords were screwing black people and people in the audience were really getting up tight and, you know, this was the time of the urban fever zone and here was Waskow, Mister Fever Zone himself. To tradition-minded people in the audience, it wasn't going over. But Waskow keeps going. He gives the Jewish prayer for the dead and starts reading off the Vietnam dead.

"There was very close to a riot. He was talking about how America was genocidal, barbaric and the people were yelling, 'Stop it! Enough of it!' and then he was going to say some sort of a Vietnam prayer before the open ark. In a sense, it was almost anti-Jewish. When he turned and headed for the ark, the people weren't about to let him open that thing up and they started coming up on the stage. It was very close to a mob scene. Here I was, two weeks a member and an usher—well, I interposed my body between the surging masses, so to speak, and the radical Arthur Waskow, my ideological non-soulmate. And when it was all over, he went away and I went away and that was it."

Four years later, in the calmer setting of his living room, Waskow said that, "I think in a way I went through the process that lots of younger liberals—or younger people who would have been liberals, who grew up in liberal homes—went through in the '60s, of finding that the liberal answers didn't work, that's all. That the liberal correctives for American society just kept failing at every point. I came to Washington thinking that *The Power Elite* stuff and C. Wright Mills was bullshit, and then I worked on the Hill and discovered the overwhelming power that the military had in manipulating American politics. I knew that Congressmen were afraid that the military would go into their districts and defeat them if they spoke out on questions of the budget. I talked to guys who said that and I talked to assistants who said, 'Well, my guy just can't move on that question. I'm sorry.' Kastenmeier [Robert W. Kastenmeier, the "liberal" congressman from Robert La Follette's old district in Wisconsin, and Waskow's boss from 1959 to 1961] fought against gas and germ warfare and I've got a very vivid memory of the day three full generals from the Chemical Corps came marching down the office in uniform to try to straighten him out on this question and the sense of the power relationship in that office was that they were powerful and he wasn't."

Approximately until that time, said Waskow, "I was sort of a peacenik—I mean a more peace-oriented liberal than most—but I was a standard American liberal in the sense that I thought there were things wrong with the society which could be corrected and then kept finding that they couldn't be corrected and that the institutions which were supposed to correct them didn't. . . ."

In 1961, Waskow left Capitol Hill to become a member of the staff of the Peace Research Institute in Washington. He had opposed John Kennedy's sending advisers to Vietnam in 1961.

"In 1963, I took part for the first time in an illegal demonstration, a sit-in in Baltimore," Waskow recalled. "That was the first time I got arrested and I did it with the people who were the first generation of S.D.S. [Students for a Democratic Society], the golden age of S.D.S., and the reason I did it with them was that my secretary was an S.D.S. member and she got arrested on July 4th and I felt really upset. She wasn't from Baltimore and I'd been to Gwynn Oak [an amusement park] dozens of times when I was a kid, when it was segregated. I grew up in Baltimore's segregated schools and I sort of felt that ought to be my job to integrate Gwynn Oak, not hers."

From 20 to 50 per cent or more of New Leftists have been Jews, according to varied estimates. One source (Jack Nusan Porter) said that "a third of the S.D.S. Weathermen arrested in the confrontation with police were Jewish." Another (James Yaffe) said, "50 per cent of the members of leftist groups are Jews." The 1972 *American Jewish Year Book*, in assessing the proportion of Jews among "young American war protesters" who had fled America for Canada reported that a "likely and reasonable estimate" would "put the maximum number of American

Jews at 8,000, out of a total of some 30,000 draft protesters."

Any way one appraises a group that is less than 3 per cent of the American population, one would have to agree that a disproportionate number of New Leftists are Jewish. But to take a quantum leap and therefore assume that all or most Jews are New Leftists (or other radicals) is arrant distortion. The New Left is quite small, in absolute numbers; its importance lies more in the way America at large has reacted to its assaults—seeming to regard it as a momentous threat to the very foundations of society—than in the small number of its adherents. The size of the reaction compared with the small size of the action is reminiscent of reaction to the Communist Party three decades ago; when the party was at its peak, membership was only about fifty thousand. While Jews were disproportionately involved in the party in the '30s, "at the most, a small fraction of 1 per cent of Jews were party members," according to George Eaton Simpson and J. Milton Yinger. That such incorrect stereotypy still exists was evident in the remarks of Attorney General William B. Saxbe, when he told a group of reporters on April 3, 1974, that he was considering elimination of the Attorney General's list of subversive organizations partly because Jewish intellectuals were no longer "enamored of the Communist Party," as they once were. The same kind of stereotypy is often true today in the case of the New Left. While Jews are disproportionately involved, few Jews are New Leftists. Thus the Abbie Hoffmans are far outnumbered by the Ben Wattenbergs and Herbert Alexanders; the Max Palevskys (the New Left has been financed principally by Jewish contributors like Palevsky) are far outnumbered by Jewish financial men like Abe Feinberg and Gustave Levy.

Just as plainly, some of the most vigorous opposition to
the New Left comes from Jews. *Commentary's* Norman
Podhoretz, for instance, has called the Left "a threat to
the Jewish position." "Whatever the case may have been
yesterday, and whatever the case may be tomorrow," he
has written, "the case today is that the most active enemies
of the Jews are located not in the precincts of the ideological Right but in the ideological precincts of the Radical
Left." Myron M. Fenster has written, "Let me admit to
feeling sad and cheated when some marvelously idealistic
college kid is ready to lay down his young life to inch along
the Negro struggle but would not lift a pinky to save the
whole Jewish enterprise from oblivion."

The special propensity of Jews for the left of center
shows vividly in the American Council on Education-
American Jewish Committee survey. Nearly two of every
three Jewish freshmen expected that, by the time they
graduated, they would be "liberal" or "left," compared
with slightly more than one of every three non-Jews:

CURRENT POLITICAL PREFERENCE	Jewish students	Non-Jewish students
Left	8.8	2.7
Liberal	46.0	28.6
Middle of the road	33.5	45.1
Moderately conservative	10.7	21.2
Strongly conservative	1.0	2.4
EXPECTED PREFERENCE IN 4 YEARS		
Left	10.1	3.0
Liberal	51.4	34.7
Middle of the road	24.7	29.7
Moderately conservative	12.5	27.6
Strongly conservative	1.3	5.0

That more than three times as many Jews as non-Jews said they expected to be "left"—at least at that age level and at that particular time—raises the question of why? The traditional suggestion is that the Jewish tendency to leftism is abetted by "self-hatred," that some Jews are so embarrassed that they are Jewish that they will go to extremes to identify with the ultimate in non-Jewishness. The traditional theory suggests, too, that these left inclinations are a direct outgrowth of the old socialism, that these sons and daughters and grandsons and granddaughters of the Lower East Side are merely carrying forward a tradition. Undoubtedly, some of both elements are there. But Jewish radicalism of the 1964–74 decade is not quite that simple.

In considering self-hatred, Henry L. Feingold argues that "there is precious little to be embarrassed or confined by," and maintains that "few radicals have had the kind of emotional relationship with Judaism to warrant generating a feeling of hate at its rejection." "Their anti-Zionism," he says, "grows out of the ideology rather than from what preceded it."

As to their bearing the standards of the old socialism, one has to question how that is quite possible when Jews have become the most affluent in an affluent society. Roger Kahn has made the point in *The Passionate People* that the old socialism was bred from the Jews' being have-nots. He quotes an acquaintance as saying, "'My father was a Socialist, but for only one reason. He never saw a thousand dollars in his life. Give any Socialist a thousand —make it ten thousand these days—and right away he becomes a capitalist.'"

Why, then, does one find a result like the one below as long ago as 1967 in a survey of ethnic groups' feelings about the Vietnam War—with Jews far and away the most opposed to America's military involvement in Vietnam?

GROUP	PERCENTAGE
Jewish	48
Western European Catholic	29
Southern European Catholic	26
Western European Protestant	17
Long-time American Protestant-Catholic	15
Eastern European Catholic	7

The reason certainly has very much to do with World War II. The survey cited above was conducted during the height of America's involvement in Vietnam. Since Moshe Dayan and Yitzhak Rabin are Jews too, it is not accurate to assume that Jews are peaceful *per se*. But American Jews are not Israeli Jews. The last war that was at all close to American Jews was the "necessary" World War II, which saw the slaughter of half the world's Jews before it was over. The remnant here has not shaken that memory.

When one talks about opposition to the involvement in Vietnam and starts seeing young Jews bewailing "fascist Amerika," the connection becomes clear. These Jews are evidencing personal fear that, if they remain silent, they will dishonor the six million who died in German concentration camps. Obviously they cannot bear the thought of their being like the "good Germans" who went along. The alienated young members of society coalesced as the New Left in response to America's foray into Southeast Asia. As Waskow wrote in his *The Bush Is Burning:*

The Vietnam war shaped the consciousness of a whole generation of American youth—and often shaped it into not wanting to be "American." To young Jews, especially, the war was an earthquake. Brought up on memories of the Holocaust and genocide, they were horrified to discover that the United States government—which they had been taught defended the world against Hitler—was behaving in Vietnam like Hitler. "Genocide," "Holocaust," began to ring with new meaning around these young Jews. They linked the Nazis to the present by naming their Government "Amerika." They whose parents had proudly embraced the American Promise, the quasi-Methodist suburban synogogue, and the quasi-Rotarian B'nai B'rith Lodge, fiercely rejected being Americans at all.

Their grandfathers' targets had been the czars. Theirs became Dow and the CIA. One of the characteristics of the New Leftist, as Kenneth Keniston has shown, is that he is not certain about what he wants. As Keniston wrote, the estranged young "are rarely able to define alternatives to the conventional life of well-adjusted Americans." So in heaving a brick through the front window of a "capitalist" bank, waving a flag exalting Ho Chi Minh, refusing to pay his telephone tax, or turning in his draft card, the New Leftist may not have been accomplishing any affirmative act, but at least he was not acquiescing in the annihilation of a people.

"I was involved in draft resistance support in '67–8," said Waskow. "I was one of the unindicted co-conspirators in the Spock trial and so on." Through a foulup, his friend Marcus Raskin ended up being charged with the "crime" that Waskow committed. "We handed over a thousand draft cards to an assistant attorney general," said Waskow, and the official refused to accept them. He recalled saying to the man, "But you say these are evidence of a crime, because you say it's a crime. Now you—you, a sworn officer of the United States Government—you say you're not going to take evidence of what you say is a crime?" "Mark didn't do that," said Waskow. "*I* did that, not Mark. They had a guy testify it was Marcus. . . ."

Feingold analyzed the symbols of the New Left and found that, indeed, traces of Holocaust-fear prevailed. For radicals, he wrote:

. . . The Holocaust is proof that racialism, tribalism, in a capitalist setting, is a murderous force. It leads to "aryan" Germans killing Jewish "bacillus." This idea is incorporated into their rhetoric even while the Holocaust itself is separated from the people who underwent its agonies. It applies to Biafra, to the Communist Indonesians, to Bengla-Desh and, of course, to the powerless minorities within our own country. A cut in the poverty program is viewed as another step in the planned genocide of American Blacks and Angela Davis is magically transformed into a Jewish housewife en route to Dachau.

"Judaism at its best is a synthesis between particularism and universalism, but the power of the two things, the tension between them, is very great," said Waskow, "and it's very easy to spin off into either direction. It's very easy to spin off into a totally particularist, ultra "Jewish" trip in which people care only about the Jewish people and don't even view it as the Jewish people in relation with the universal god, of just the Jewish people, that that's especially easy in the aftermath of a Holocaust, but on the other hand, it's very easy to take a totally universalist trip out of Judaism and so does Marxism, I think, and it's not surprising to me that modern liberalism and radicalism would have a heavy infusion of Jews who have been very strongly affected by the universalist trajectory out of Judaism. . . ."

Harvard professor Seymour Martin Lipset, a sociologist, has spent much time analyzing Jewish participation in the New Left. He emphasizes that many of the new radicals are repelled by the hypocrisy of their parents, who espouse liberal causes, then turn around and exploit those less well off in their business or on vacation; they imbue their children with the message of mankind's equality, then complain about uppityness when the maid asks a five-dollar raise to sixty-five dollars a week. "Many Jewish parents," Lipset has written, "unlike gentile parents of equivalent high economic class background, live a schizophrenic existence. They sustain a high degree of tension between their ideology and their life style." What kind of models are these, who started out wanting to change the world and then, when they accumulated a few dollars, suddenly lost their reformist zeal? Further, anything that threatened their new life style was to be resisted.

Rabbi Arthur Hertzberg, president of the American Jewish Congress, preferred an economic explanation of Jewish prominence in the New Left. "These kids are not merely the children of left-wing parents," he said. "These kids are now the new *rentiers*. They don't need economic careers, therefore they can really stay out of society and hang around at Berkeley. The key to Mark Rudd [leader of the S.D.S. disruption of Columbia University in the late 1960s] is not left-wing politics but an unlimited expense account." Indeed, young Jewish radicals do generally come from well-off families. As Feingold noted, ". . . we can see youngsters who seem poverty stricken but carry around their necks the most expensive cameras or who spend small fortunes on other 'arty' hobbies such as film making."

"What the media have missed," said Morris B. Abram, speaking in the scenic office once occupied by Arthur J. Goldberg at Paul Weiss, Rifkind, Wharton & Garrison, "is that these are the children of affluent families. The movement is drawing from a heavily Jewish base. Ninety per cent of Jewish children of college age are attending college but only 45 per cent of the population as a whole who are of college age attend college. And the colleges they're attending are not just any colleges—they're the good schools in the East. The revolt, you know, occurred in the best institutions, not the average ones. You'll never have a revolt at a military school, or a religious school. You would never have one at a place like Oral Roberts College. The revolts are at places like Columbia, Harvard, Brandeis." Abram was president of Brandeis during its most turbulent days and he sees economics, of both the student protesters and of the faculty members of the colleges, as a key factor:

"Much of the student protest movement was the direct result of faculty participation. You had a case of grown people trying to get student adulation and, without that, I don't think the protest movement would have amounted to a hill of beans. Remember, in 1968 and '69, the universities were struggling to retain good faculty people. The Ph.D. market wasn't flooded then, as it is now. The professors felt secure, and they acted irresponsibly. It's interesting to note that, when the Ph.D. market dried up, the protest movement dried up. In the good schools in the East, up to 30 per cent of the faculty members are Jewish and, very frequently, these are the younger faculty. The older [predominantly gentile] faculty members were hired when there was discrimination in academia. By 1968, a large proportion of the younger faculty was Jewish and this younger faculty felt an affinity for the students who were Jews—the Jews, after all, had the higher board scores, and the brightest students are always the most yeasty." Along with this, Abram said, the Jewish students were ripe for the anticapitalist tone of the movement because "their parents talked very liberal at home, as Jews always have. The parents' liberalism, of course, was largely as a reaction against fascism, which colored the thinking of almost any Jew who could read and write. The parents talked liberal and then, in the 1960s, the thrust of the civil rights movement was no longer for civil and political rights. In the middle of the Johnson years, the civil rights movement began to switch into an economic and social movement. Suddenly, the civil rights movement had a price tag. I suspect that Jews, like everybody else, started to look at the civil rights movement differently. They began to get up tight and their children tended to look askance at their parents' sense of values." The children Abram was describing were not particularly the children of onetime Communists or onetime Socialists. They are the downward-striving offspring of the most upward-striving parents. "They are repelled," as Feingold wrote, "by the strident cult of success hammered on incessantly by their ambitious parents. For some, it is clear that Judaism means simply 'making it,' becoming a doctor or a lawyer." Further, he says, the kids "have not read Marx; all they really know is that, for them, the 'system' doesn't work."

In his youth in Baltimore, Waskow said, ". . . shabbas [the sabbath day] was Mr. Shapiro up the street yelling at me because I was carrying books to the library. I've

never dug that and I still don't, the notion that shabbas
was prohibitions, that it was unfree. . . . Beginning
about two years ago, I began to get a sense of shabbas as a
liberation, not as unfreedom, not as restrictions. All right,
you're not supposed to work. But the whole point in what
we're reaching for is a society in which people don't have
to work, in which work and play get intermixed. My
dream for a society of the messianic age is a place where
you get what you need when you need it because you
need it. . . . I discovered a few years ago that there's a
strand in tradition, a very long strand, which says shabbas
is a moment in the messianic age, it's the nearest we can
get. Every week, we try to create a little piece, just to remind ourselves what it's like. And there's even a strand
in the tradition that says the messianic age will come
. . . when the whole Jewish people celebrates two shab-
bases in a row. The way to get there is to do it. I guess the
theory in my head and my gut sense of what the world
should be like is that there should be a community, a
neighborhood. . . . I put the best things about the neighborhood together with my best dreams and I began to see
how they relate and I also see the ways in which the neighborhood is messed up and begin to see what it would mean
to create a really good neighborhood, a really good community. . . ."

Waskow and his fellow radicals represent an enormous
threat to most older Jews, especially the intellectual elite
that has set the agenda for discussion of Jewish issues over
the past several decades. When this writer evinced ad-
miration for Waskow's gentle nature and humanism, one
Jewish intellectual blurted out:
"The amazing thing about Waskow is that he doesn't
know anything; he's an am ho'orets [Hebrew for ignora-

mus]. He acts like he's the first one to discover all this stuff—like he thinks he discovered the wheel."

Eventually, Waskow went beyond the New Left, into the nether world of Jewish mysticism, grappling with what life is all about in specifically Jewish terms, even organizing an experimental kibbutz in the Pennsylvania countryside. Waskow is not the society wrecker that some believe him to be. If anything, Waskow is directly within the rabbinic tradition, searching and wrestling as rabbis always did for some meaning to the past that will guide the present and future. Waskow, beyond the rhetoric and bombast of 1970s radicalism, is a loving soul and deeply emotional in his fortieth year of life: "One of the crucial moments for me was in the spring of '70," he said. "There was a Freedom Seder at Cornell. The Berrigans [the brothers Philip and Daniel Berrigan, Jesuit priests who became the living saints of the New Left] had just gone underground and, before they had gone underground, when everybody thought they'd be in jail, the people at Cornell—Dan Berrigan was chaplain there—had decided to get together a weekend, sort of honoring the Berrigans and a rededication of the resistance, and so on. They decided to begin the weekend with a seder and asked me to come up and help lead the *Freedom Seder.* I went up and we began the seder in this incredible Cornell fieldhouse with several thousand people in it, and at the moment in which we say, 'Let all who are hungry come and eat, et cetera, et cetera,' Dan Berrigan came up and joined us on a kind of head table that we had going. It was his first surfacing from underground and the place went out of its mind. People were crying and laughing, and we went through the rest of the seder with Berrigan there and it was just an incredibly poignant, high moment, and then we snuck him out—you know, got him away from the F.B.I., which was there—and he stayed underground for the next several months. . . .

"The next night I was still up there and the same field-house and I went back there to get a sense of what was going on and it felt very good at first. The music was good and people were smoking and I walked around. I was feeling good. And then I started getting angry and I couldn't figure out why I was. I kept walking around and talking to people. Everybody was kind of giddy, and I got angrier and angrier and finally realized that, what had been really good about the seder and what *is* really good about the seder is that the bitter herb is there as well as the wine, and that the bitter herb is very clear, that you have got to absorb the bitterness of slavery even while you're celebrating liberation, and that Berrigan had been kind of—I mean as well as we had the bitter herb, Berrigan also was kind of a living bitter herb—and it was true he was free but it was also clear that he wasn't really free and the fact of his presence meant the fact that the war was still going on, and so on. But that was all gone that night, and the Woodstock Nation was having its celebration and that's all. It was really a one-dimensional celebration, it had no depth to it and no tragedy underneath it or anything, the second night. And that was really crucial for me in becoming a radical Jew and in discovering that I was enormously more greatly strengthened by the Jewish tradition than by modern radicalism, including the New Left, counter-culture, Woodstock, et cetera, kinds of things and that those things are really comparatively shallow."

If one has spoken with a number of members of the New Left, one comes away disturbed. The words from their mouths have flowed rapidly and urgently. They have conveyed sincerity in what they say about love and feeling and caring for other people and mankind, about kindness and consideration. Their earnestness is believable when they have chanted about oppression, about racism, about imperialism, about the evils of the government, about the evils of big business, the tax system, the inequitable distribution of wealth, the big brainwash of the society. But something in this torrent of words has not rung quite true, appealing as some of it may first have seemed. The clues pile up as one has asked questions. The questions never are answered. What has come back is programmed rhetoric that disdains details and specifics, the basics of what living in a mass society is all about. They put down the prevailing values but put forward no alternatives, which is, of course, not easy to do. Perhaps more important, as Keniston has written, "Theirs is an ideology of opposition, and the world offers so many targets for their repudiation that they have little energy left for the development of affirmative values."

In sum, these nice but alienated Jewish boys and girls from nice, upper-middle-class Jewish homes are well meaning and honest and sincere and utterly naïve. They have lived the good life, from receiving a plethora of expensive toys on Christmas morning—and it probably was Christmas that was celebrated and not Channukah—to their own phones almost as soon as they could dial, to their own television and stereo sets, to trips to the South of France not on five dollars a day. David Dubinsky said he had been through "everything" by the time he was eighteen. These Jewish children have been through a great deal too, but a different kind: the kind that has so much of

ABOVE: Nelson Rockefeller campaigning in 1966 for re-election as governor, wearing a yarmulke to please Jewish voters. In 1970 he claimed he was "one of the staunchest supporters of the state of Israel" even though his opponent, Arthur Goldberg, was a lifelong Zionist. *(Photo by United Press International)* BELOW: Herbert Lehman *(center)* served nine years (1933–42) as governor of New York. At left is Alex Rose, at right, David Dubinsky.

One of the more enthusiastic Jewish politician-campaigners has been New York Senator Jacob Javits. Javits said that "in the cause in which I fight, I can be very aggressive." Running for office is anathema to many Jews because they think it epitomizes "pushiness," a stereotype they dread. Javits is shown in this picture in Manhattan campaigning to keep his seat in 1962. *(Photo by United Press International)*

RIGHT: Arthur Goldberg campaigning in 1970 for governor of New York. Goldberg is regarded as symbolic of many of the myths about Jewish politicians — stiff, awkward, unaffable. In an interview, Goldberg acknowledged that "I personally take a dim view of ethnic campaigning, which probably proves that I am not a good politician since all politicians engage in this type of campaign. I personally found it demeaning to engage in ethnic appeals." Goldberg was trounced.

Governor Marvin Mandel of Maryland is the antithesis of many of the stereotypes about Jewish politicians. He is a strong "male bonder," comes across to voters as a nonidealogue, and is far from "stiff" as a candidate. Here, in his 1970 campaign, he is shown playing checkers with a voter. *(Photo by United Press International)*

Abraham Ribicoff, here with Harry Truman, was elected governor of Connecticut after a last-minute speech in which he summoned up voters' patriotic sentiment by talking about how he, the son of impoverished immigrants, could believe the American Dream and aspire to his state's highest office. Ribicoff, now a senator, probably still benefits from reverse discrimination by Connecticut voters.

everything—at least materially—that one cannot find a gift for them. Their parents were part of a culture that was intent on "making it" and "making it" often meant spending increasingly less time at home. Even though the Jewish family has retained some of the closeness traditionally ascribed to it, more and more sons and daughters have grown up seeing only a glimpse of their parents' attentions and emotions. Consumer goods are no substitute for love.

At the same time, they have been protected from the world, as good Jewish parents are inclined to do with their children. Despite the interest and activity of so many of the parents in politics, the children have often remained ignorant of the realities of power. The situation is wholly different with the Jews of Israel, as Feingold has written, since they are "accustomed to exercising power and assuming responsibility for their own interest and security. They cannot afford to hold . . . universalistic assumptions because the experience of governing has taught them that in the real world, civilization, whether it calls itself 'open society' or 'socialist humanism,' is not nearly so generous or so rational as ideologists assume." These new Jewish radicals of America are ignorant about power.

Jews, until the birth of Israel in 1948, held little if any power. For thousands of years, the Jews as a people have existed as a relatively powerless minority wherever they have lived. As new middle-class Americans, they still have exercised little group power. The offspring that have emanated from the bosoms of such homes often harbor a vague sense of distrust of power, whether it was held by the Borgias or Tsar Nicholas II or the Chase Manhattan Bank. Power to these young prophets is evil per se. All of their liturgy concerns power: they talk about the

power of the oil lobby, about power brokers. They talk
about money as power, ergo money is evil. They want all
"power to the people." "If they are honest and intelligent,"
wrote Feingold, "and many Jewish radicals are:

they are ultimately forced to confront the fact that they have
been presented with an idealized image of the world. Then,
frequently, there begins a search for sham and hypocrisy
which takes them to the cultural surrogates—parents, teachers, spiritual leaders—who, they learn, usually possess the security of wealth, the greatest source of power in the society.
It is after this discovery is made that the Jewish radicals de-
nounce the protective suburban cocoon in which they first
learned the humanitarian principles which they espouse with
such fervor, and they sense their own hypocrisy in denounc-
ing poverty from the vantage of Larchmont and Shaker
Heights.

These fervent youths want something different, even if
they do not know what they do want. Some worship Che
Guevara, some think they are Marxists, some believe in
anarchy. Whatever it is, they're only sure that "this" isn't
it. In a sense, they have traveled a perfect circle—from the
marginality of the Jew of feudal Europe to assimilation
into the middle class and now, back again, to marginality,
displaying many of the same characteristics that have been
perceived in marginal men. Kurt Lewin described those
traits long before there was an S.D.S. or Yippees:

Marginal men and women are in somewhat the same position
as an adolescent who is no longer a child and certainly does
not want to be a child any longer, but who knows at the
same time that he is not really accepted as a grown-up. The
uncertainty about the ground on which he stands and the
group to which he belongs often makes the adolescent loud,

restless, at once timid and aggressive, over-sensitive and tending to go to extremes, over-critical of others and himself.

The marginal Jew, Lewin wrote, feels insufficiently rooted in any group and thus cannot be sure about his views and/or his relations with any group:

He is therefore compelled to remain in a rather vague and uncertain but permanent inner conflict. He is the "eternal adolescent." He shows the same unhappiness and lack of adjustment.

As a novice in power relationships, the Jewish New Leftist distrusts power from whichever source it comes—money, universities, parents, governments, the military, unions, even religious or ethnic blocs. When sociologists say that these Jews have embraced radicalism because it relieves them of their Jewishness, perhaps they are missing the point: it is not Jewishness they dislike. They would (and do) feel the same about any ethnic or religious power groups, Irish or Catholic or Italian or whatever—unless the groups are powerless, i.e., blacks or Chicanos or Puerto Ricans or Indians or the Ibos and, indeed, the Israelis before they displayed power. One suspects that if Zionists were now powerless, they too would be accepted on the New Left's list of preferred causes.

The naïveté about power means, too, that the New Left was really never the threat so many in America thought it was. It is one thing to have perceptions about Nigeria or Pakistan but quite another to evolve a system of "delivery" equal to that of the mayor of Chicago, whom they are so willing to berate. They speak of "trashing" but they have been unable to conceive of what real power is made of—organizing the sanitation men, for instance. Keniston has written that such goals are beside the point to the New

Left. "Its political goals," he wrote, "are not to win the next election or the one after, but to increase the social and political consciousness of the American people." These youths, caught in the nether world between adolescence and adulthood, are the ultimate universalists of society, so universal that they disdain loyalty to family, religion, ethnic group, race, nation. As the truly classless and casteless citizens, they feel they are noble. In a sense they are. But they are also depressingly frustrated, and disintegrating for having gone powerless for so long.

"I keep finding that, in the simplest sense," said Arthur Waskow, "a kind of very simplistic sense, the notion that the Jewish people survived the Pharaoh and Babylon and the Assyrian-Greek empire and Rome and the Inquisition and Hitler makes me feel that the Jewish people can survive the United States, the Soviet Union, and that feels very important to me. One of the reasons for the difficulties in the movement in the last two years has been the sense of weakness and hopelessness, that nobody knows how we're going to make it past what's a much stronger system than people had thought."

VIII

"Paying a little back..."
The contributors

"THERE IS NO COUNTRY that has given more people opportunities in the history of mankind than this country. And sure, there are abuses and sure, there are things that are wrong. And they are not going to be corrected by the S.D.S. type of people or the radicals. These things are going to be corrected by making goddamned certain that we have the right people in the political places. . . ."

WALTER SHORENSTEIN
Real estate developer, San Francisco
Democratic fund raiser

Jews take enormous pride in their prominence in financing campaigns, feeling they have done good for their country by helping good candidates attain office. At the same time, however, they are afraid that non-Jews misinterpret their motivations.

Typical of this fear is the reaction of some Jews to the words "Jewish money," political shorthand for contributions from Jews. "That term has an awful sound," said Lawrence Goldberg, who ran the Jewish section of President Nixon's 1972 campaign. "From there, it isn't much of a step to calling it 'Jew money' and from there to 'Jew conspiracy' and all the other connotations, like Jews' controlling this or that. Is Martin Peretz's money 'Jewish?' Is Max Palevsky's?" What Goldberg was contending is that no "hidden hand" directs giving by Jews. Some, like Peretz and Palevsky, contribute large sums to left causes; others, like Shorenstein and most large Jewish contributors, give heavily to progressive middle-of-the-road causes; yet others (though considerably fewer) give to Right causes, and to all shades in between. Goldberg also was saying that the term "Jewish money" might be construed to connote something conspiratorially un-American—as if the Jewish contributors were trying to seize control of government, as the spurious *Protocols of the Learned Elders of Zion* tried to convey. Despite the protests of Goldberg and many others, however, the term "Jewish money" is valid, even if the Jews are not monolithic, even if different Jews contribute across the entire spectrum of political America. The term is valid because giving by Jews is distinctive in America, by its very readiness, as was the pattern before Jews settled in America.

Giving is and ever has been an integral part of being

Jewish. In feudal Europe, communal efforts met obligations. Charity became a basic element of Judaism. Lawrence H. Fuchs has written that

Jewish charity has been more than just alms-giving by individual benefactors. It has been considered part of the governance of the community itself. In some countries in the
Middle Ages Jews "were obliged by law to provide for their
poor, or were made jointly responsible for taxes or fines imposed on members of the community. . . . Thus, in the
course of centuries, the support of the poor by the rich became a custom, a duty of the rich, and a right of the poor."

Charity was so basic to being a Jew that the Hebrew
language did not even include a specific word for it; instead, the word *Zedakah*, which means righteousness and
social justice, includes the concept of charity. *Life Is with
People*, an anthropological study of the *shtetl*, the small,
all-Jewish town in Europe, stresses that "Life in the shtetl
begins and ends with Zedakah. . . . At every turn during
one's life, the reminder to give is present." Giving, says
the study, is "basic to the functioning of the shtetl and
also to being a good Jew. . . .

Giving is both a duty and a joy; it is a source of heavenly approval and also a source of earthly prestige. The fortunate
man is the one who is in a position to give. The unfortunate
is the one who is under pressure to accept. Granted the correct situation, accepting is not necessarily painful—but under
any circumstances, giving is counted among the great grati-
fications of life.

The tradition of the *pushke* developed in the shtetl. A
pushke was a small box kept in every Jewish home in the
Pale of Settlement. Every family, no matter how economi-
cally pressed (and most were), would put a penny or two
into the pushke to be given to those who were even poorer.

Isaiah Minkoff, executive vice chairman of the National Jewish Community Relations Advisory Council, remembered it well from his youth in Russia: "There were beggars who used to come every Friday morning. The woman of the house would give them a penny. . . . In some houses, there were several pushkes for different causes, and every woman knew that part of her household expenses was to put a few pennies for charity in the pushke. The menfolk felt it was part of their obligation to take care of the needs of poor Jews."

The pushke tradition continued in the promised land, as the Jews from Eastern Europe migrated to places like Brownsville and the Lower East Side, or to New Britain, Connecticut, in the home of a young Abe Ribicoff. The tradition of helping one's fellow Jews, of community charity, extended to all forms of Jewish life in America, from the generosity of the earlier settlers from Germany toward the newer settlers from Eastern Europe to the organization of community centers to the building of Jewish hospitals (Jewish doctors often could not obtain privileges in hospitals run by non-Jews). In every city of any size, a federation of Jewish charities was established so that the raising of money could be co-ordinated. As philanthropy had been regarded "as the very badge of Jewishness in the shtetl," philanthropy came to be regarded as the key to acceptance within the American Jewish community. While some Jews strove for acceptance outside the Jewish world, often by generosity toward symphony societies and art museums, others strove for acceptance within the community by generosity toward the local federation or to the United Jewish Appeal. Today, the upward-striver who wants to crack the higher levels of Jewish society learns that an essential element is evidence of his level of charity.

In most communities, if a Jew fails to make a name professionally or politically, being a big giver to federation is usually the principal route to his becoming a member of a Jewish country club; membership committees of these clubs almost always include at least one member of the federation, somebody who knows who's given what.

The system of charity and inducing contributions is unique and has in fact developed into an American art form. The state of its development was perhaps indicated when four schools announced plans to develop a joint program to turn fund raising into a profession and "train people in fund raising for Jewish communal agencies."

The result of all this is that Jews give like no other group in society. The giving makes even the fund raisers' eyes bulge with amazement at the sums they raise. In 1972, the combined outlay by this relatively tiny group in Israel bonds, the United Jewish Appeal, and the federations across the country totaled more than half a billion dollars. To take one comparison, the American National Red Cross raised $132 million in 1972, from all Americans. Perhaps the most spectacular Jewish giving of all came during and after the Yom Kippur War of 1973, when more than $100 million was raised for Israel in several days. The war pushed the 1974 fund-raising goals to the vicinity of one billion dollars.

To illustrate the built-in giving impulse of Jews, Sam Freedman of the American Jewish Committee told a story about a naïve Jewish businessman he knew in an Ohio city. The man had worked his way up to the presidency of the Jewish federation. Customarily, the new president donated $5,000 to set the tone of the annual drive. This man continued the custom. Several years later, the same man worked his way up the ladder of the local Community Chest. When he became president, he assumed the same customs applied, and turned in a check for $5,000. His action shocked the members of the board and the new president became aware of what had happened. Each of the other officers, all non-Jews, was accustomed to contributing $100 to $200. His gift had made them look cheap. "He took his contribution back," said Freedman, and "made another, in line with their custom." "This business of learning to give, being educated to give, is something that most people don't really perceive," said Charles Zibbell of the Council of Jewish Federations and Welfare Funds.

What has all this to do with political campaigns? Everything. The big contributors to the political campaigns have been the same men who contribute most generously to U.J.A. and to federation. And the people who get the money from those contributors for politics are, generally, the same ones who have headed the U.J.A. and federation fund drives. For instance, the single most prominent Jewish political fund raiser in the United States has been Detroit's Max Fisher. Fisher is also president of the Council of Jewish Federations and Welfare Funds, has been president of the U.J.A. and almost every other philanthropic agency Jews maintain. Fisher believes it is obvious that political contributors would come from the ranks of the charity contributors. Only rarely, he said, have big political givers been nongivers to charities. Eugene Wyman was another example of the combined fund raiser for charities and politics. Wyman was the top Democratic fund raiser in California until his death at forty-seven early in 1973. But he was perhaps even prouder of having set a sales record for Israel Bonds in

Southern California when he headed that drive in 1971
than of having raised millions of dollars over the years for
his friend Hubert Humphrey.

The first Jewish fund raiser for national politics (and
one makes the distinction here between those who give
and those who go out and raise money) was banker Abe
Feinberg, according to veteran politician Alex Rose. "In
1948, when Truman was regarded as a losing candidate,
Abe Feinberg stood up for him and raised money for
him," said Rose. "When Truman won, Truman's triumph
to some extent was also Abe Feinberg's. Everybody knew
that Feinberg raised money for Truman's campaign. As
far as I know, that was the first time a Jew did that, promi-
nently." Feinberg's activities started a process of systematic fund raising for politics that has made Jews the
most conspicuous fund raisers and contributors to the
Democratic Party. As one non-Jewish strategist told this
writer, "You can't hope to go anywhere in national politics,
if you're a Democrat, without Jewish money."

Because of the way campaigns have been financed in
the United States, one has been unable to ascertain exactly who has given how much to whom. No matter how
stringent the campaign reporting laws that have been en-
acted, some money inevitably has been delivered in canvas
satchels or toted around in cash in money belts, all unre-
ported. But, of reported gifts, the pattern of Jewish pre-
dominance in Democratic national campaigns has been
clear. The lists of lenders to the campaigns are perhaps
the best indicators. In 1968, of the twenty-one persons
who loaned $100,000 or more to Humphrey's campaign,
fifteen were Jewish, ranging from the $100,000 loans of
Edwin L. Weisl and Arnold M. Picker to the $240,000
loans of John Factor and Lew Wasserman. In 1972, Jews'
financial support—or at least support from Jewish business-

men who customarily had supported the Democratic ticket —waned. But still, Jews were the main source of large gifts to the Democratic campaign. Two thirds of the lenders of $100,000 and more were Jews, from Howard Weiss and Philip Stern at that figure to Henry Kimelman's $390,000.

One reason that Jews give more freely than their non-Jewish brethren lies in the different nature of their ways of earning a living. The non-Jew is more likely than the Jew to work in an institutional or bureaucratic setting, where he may be a bank executive, utility company official, insurance company president, corporate officer, college chancellor. These jobs have traditionally been closed to Jews. Men who occupy such jobs may control vast amounts of power and deal with huge sums of money, but the money is not actually theirs—it belongs to the institutions they work for. Jews are driven to more entrepreneurial livelihoods. As their own bosses, they can use the money in the businesses any way they want, including contributing heavily to political candidates or causes. "You take a college president," said Joseph Willen, who said he raised *billions* of dollars from Jews in more than fifty years with the New York federation of Jewish charities. "Every month, he gets a check. But he doesn't actually handle the college's budget, whether it's $10 million or $50 million or whatever. But you take a businessman—say, someone in the dress business. To make $100,000 at the end of the year, he turns over $2 million. And it's *his* money. He's handling it. During the year he has a lot of money to play with."

Further, said Adam Walinsky, Jews tend to regard their money differently because it is not as institutionalized. Walinsky learned about New York money first as an aide

to the late Senator Kennedy, then as a candidate himself in
the state. Jews, said Walinsky, regard their new riches
differently than do gentiles whose money has been around
for generations. "There was a very large group of guys
who really started out without any money," said Walinsky, "who just ended up making tens of millions. Palevsky
is one, Milton Gilbert is another, Meshulam Riklis is another. Larry Tisch of Loews and his brother, they started
out with some little hotel in New Jersey. Now they give a
million dollars a year to the U.J.A. It gets like Monopoly
money to some of these guys." The newness of some Jews'
prosperity means that they may be more ready to part with
it—to show everybody else that they've "made it." Further,
Jews seem especially willing to show their gratitude at
their good fortune, which is why Jews who are newly rich
become prime political targets. One of the smartest ideas
that emerged early in Muskie's presidential campaign, according to Morris Abram, a veteran fund raiser, was a
young campaigner's suggestion to check new filings with
the Securities and Exchange Commission for names of
potential contributors.

The gratitude, the "paying a little back," cannot be
overstressed. "Every Jew admits the debt, a debt to society
for breathing," said Willen. "He'll never tell you 'No'
when you ask him for money. He'll tell you his uncle
gave, or his wife gave, or 'See me next week, I just bought
a house.' But he'll seldom tell you 'No.' He's just debating
the terms. I have found that the average Jew accepts the
debt, and he gets this from his religion, his Bible, his
home. He feels this tremendous sense of indebtedness—
'I'm lucky, I didn't have the inalienable right of the king.'
They feel they've got to explain why they have money."
Roger Kahn, in *The Passionate People*, echoed this when

he wrote that "most Jews have an urgent, touching need to explain and justify themselves. It is a response conditioned by centuries of persecution." That is true, and often it is not true of non-Jews. Jews often can be asked the most intimate questions about their finances yet will not seem to be offended, and will try to explain, as if to justify. Perhaps the readiness to bare one's finances is related to trying to explain how one has done well when so many others of his people have perished.

The economic rise of the Jew after World War II (Jews are now the most affluent group in America) and his growing political consciousness coincided with a great change in the Democratic Party. "The city machines, like those in Brooklyn, Philadelphia, Chicago, used to provide an awful lot of money," said Adam Walinsky. "There was never any suggestion of a national campaign putting any money into places like that. Most big cities used to be like Indiana is today, with everybody paying two per cent of their salaries back to the party. That was dying at the same time as these guys were coming on. This was really the money that was available, and people really started to 'work' it. And the money raising techniques had already been perfected; and it's the same pitch: one gift for the U.J.A. and it was tax deductible and one for the Democratic Party and it wasn't."

Irving M. Levine, the sociologist who organized the National Project on Ethnic America, said the social process pushed the contributors into the Democratic Party, as well: "These guys are largely first and second generation. Their social lives evolved around people involved in the Democratic Party—they saw them at the club, at home, in business—it was all around them. The Party maintained a coincidental relationship with Jewish philanthropy and enterprise. And, in the Democratic Party, the Jew's money spoke as loudly as anybody else's money."

Herbert Alexander, head of the campaign-finance monitoring organization called the Citizens' Research Foundation, who happens to be Jewish, pointed out that "There's a social register, and you have to be born into it. Very few people can get into it. There is also a political register. You can buy your way into it with contributions. For minority groups, the Jews and the *nouveaux riches*—and often the two are synonymous—you can buy your way into prominence, into rubbing shoulders with the great, into invitations to the White House or the governor's mansion or what have you, a lot quicker in the Democratic Party than you can in the Republican Party. You come in with $25,000 or $50,000 in the Democratic Party and, right away, you're a big star. It's much more difficult in the Republican Party. If that is what motivates you, and I think that motivates a lot of people—to show that they are good, to show that they are accepted, to show that they can do more than make money, to give them the kind of prominence that they want, to give them the ego satisfaction of being on the inside, to give them the feeling that they can have influence and maybe some modicum of power—all of these things they can do faster in the Democratic Party than in the Republican Party. The Republican Party has many more stable sources and many more habitual contributors, and it's a lot harder to break into the circle. You still don't get into the Union League Club just because you have a lot of money. The Democrats are always poor, they're always scrounging for dough, and this makes them much more vulnerable if a guy is interested in that kind of access. . . .

"Also, you have to look at it from the point of view of

fund raising. The Republicans as a party can approach almost any major industry in this country, systematically.
They get a guy who's big in the automobile industry, or a
guy in each of the firms, and they can almost go down the
line and approach the key wealthy men or people or the
top managers of the various companies. They can do that
in almost any industry—the rubber industry, the steel industry. The Democrats, meanwhile, have some very
wealthy supporters and, among them, some non-Jews, but
the point is that they can't do this fund raising as systematically in any industry except maybe a couple. Traditionally,
textiles was a good industry because it was a combination
of the Jews in New York and the Southerners, who were
Democrats. Secondly, the entertainment industry, where
a lot of Jews made money in movies or are performers. In
a couple of industries like that, they could almost go down
the line the way the Republicans can. But apart from that,
they don't have the resources of strength; it's much more
hit and miss. . . . It's just not as structured and as systematic as the Republicans are able to do. Therefore, all
that is a prelude to saying that you could typify the Jews as
an industry, as a Democratic supportive group that could
almost be systematically mined for money."

Most of the political money from Jews comes from New
York. California has been assumed to be the source of
much new political money, but the late Gene Wyman
used to insist that was simply untrue. "It was just fantastic," he said after the 1972 primaries. "Hubert sent me
to New York and I spent several weeks there. Was it
different! There's so much more money in New York. My
God, there's a lot of money there as compared to California."

"What people have to put in perspective—and fail to—"
said Texan Robert Strauss, chairman of the Democratic

National Committee after 1972's debacle, "is that the source of major Jewish giving is two cities: New York, Los Angeles. Other than that, there are no major areas of Jewish money for national politics. People talk about rich Texans. The truth of the matter is, there's no money in Texas compared to New York. There are a few outstanding examples of great wealth, and new wealth, but there are dozens, *hundreds* of people that rich in New York you never hear about—Jew and gentile, they don't just have to be Jewish. There's tremendous wealth there, and when people in Texas or California have multi-million-dollar deals, they come to New York to get their money to take it back to California or Texas."

All of this begs a question: why are the Jews so ready to part with their money for politics? Is a *quid pro quo* expected? The answer is yes, but on two levels. On the level of local politics, the *quid pro quo* is likely to be more tangible than on the national scale. In localities across the country, Jews like non-Jews have been known to invest in candidates in return for government contracts, favorable rezonings on potentially valuable plots of real estate. For two reasons, Jews have tended to be active in such instances of bribery. One has been that their types of livelihoods—real estate, for instance—have been like those of the Mafia, entrepreneurial and speculative.* Such businesses

---

* Mere mention of such activity tends to throw "establishment" Jewish agencies into a tizzy. As David Singer has written, they prefer "to project a 'nice Jewish boy' image of the Jew." But the fact is, as Singer has pointed out, Jews' pre-eminence as mobsters is very much within the syndrome of Jewish striving for achievement. Thus America has had such "achieving" Jews as Grodno-born Maier Suchowljansky (better known these days as Meyer Lansky), "Bugsy" Siegel, Mickey Cohen, and so many others that Singer has referred to their number as "comparable to that contributed by any other ethnic group." United States District Judge Herbert J. Stern, who won a national reputation as a corruption-busting United States

can be aided considerably by special help from city hall or
the county supervisor's office. The second is that bribery
has been an essential part of Jewish history. Veteran fund
raiser Willen pointed out that, historically, the Jews of
Europe "had to get favors to survive, through little gifts—
what you'd call today a bribe. They survived by their relationship with the police. So the tradition was that kind
of giving, too." The language of European Jewry, Yiddish,
had a word for the bribe: *shmeer*, a word that has somewhat come into the American English idiom. It is perhaps
natural that the "shmeer ethic" is more prevalent in New
York City, where more Jews live than any other city, than
elsewhere in the United States. In New York it is relatively common to have to shmeer a headwaiter (i.e., slip
him a five-dollar or ten-dollar bill to get a table) or to have
to shmeer building inspectors to get a construction job
completed on schedule or to shmeer the highway department to win a contract.

Some of the same Jews who have bribed local politicians—who usually have been non-Jews—however, have
approached national politics with a totally different outlook. In fact, Jews appear to have been the least demanding of all the political givers, nationally.

Myer Feldman, President Kennedy's liaison with Jewish organizations and contributors, said that "not once did
a Jewish contributor ever demand a *quid pro quo.* Nobody ever came to me and said, 'I've given this' or 'I've
done that.' All I ever got was requests for messages to
Jewish groups when they met."

Attorney in New Jersey, put it succinctly in an interview with this
writer: "When it comes to graft, there's no racial or religious in-
tolerance."

Richard Stewart, a hardened Boston newsman who had always suspected skulduggery in national political giving, related that he was surprised by his experience in national politics from the inside. Stewart served fifteen months as candidate Muskie's press secretary. "From the outside, everybody has this view that all these contributions have strings attached," he said, "but it's a myth. It really is. We got one hell of a lot of Jewish money, I'll tell you, and not once, never, was there a single string attached. And I can't say the same for some of what you call *goy* money. The Jews are the most altruistic givers in the country, the most patriotic. They give because they believe in the candidate, not to get something back."

Berl I. Bernhard, who managed Muskie's effort, said that "after what I'd been led to believe, I found it was one of the very peculiar myths that no one really focuses on—what is it that people want, how do they ask for it if they want something, what is your capacity to promise with any believability, what is going to happen, how're you going to handle all of that? I found out it was no problem at all and I was shocked by it. No one was asking for anything. I must have dealt with two thousand to three thousand financial people. Directly, some one of those people asked me for something [an ambassadorship], one asked me for something indirectly [a federal appointment], and that was it. . . . And there was not a major contributor I didn't deal with."

But that is not to say that the contributions from Jews to national campaigns have been purely eleemosynary. The Jews have still been *shmeering*, though the payoffs have been of a different nature; most Jews are paying to put in power the kind of men who will neither confiscate Jews' assets, wall them into ghettos, nor annihilate them. Most donations from Jewish contributors have been, at bottom, motivated by fear—fear that what happened in England, France, Spain, Germany could and may, indeed, happen in the United States, too, unless America's Jews are vigilant and insure that the "right" men get into office. And, since "right" has many meanings, the money has gone to a wide variety of candidates and causes. Some Jews have contributed to left candidates and causes. The left, after all, is still universalistic, within the tradition of the Declaration of the Rights of Man; if ultimately successful, the left would obliterate the boundaries that create conflicts between men, including the majority of the world and Jews. Other Jews have contributed to progressive middle-of-the-road candidates, who have appreciated and understood their fears, candidates whose conceptions of justice have embodied protecting minority rights (including those of Jews), who have pledged support for Israel (the final refuge, if/when it happens here), who have appeared philo-Semitic. These contributors, by far the largest number of Jewish political givers, have tended to talk in code: they say they invest in "good government" when they are in fact paying tribute for survival.

Jewish fund raisers know this implicitly, and some have been true artists in playing on Jews' insecurities.

"When I sit down with a person," said Walter Shorenstein, the developer who has been changing the face of San Francisco's skyline with his high-rise office buildings and who has been one of the principal Democratic fund raisers in California, "particularly those that came over during the Hitler Germany period . . . I very honestly say to them, 'Now look, if you had to do it over again—I'm sure that you lost a lot of your family in the Hitler era in Germany—now if you had the opportunity to help someone get into office, or to have helped defeat what Hitler represented—if you had to do this over again, you would have taken your last dollar to do it, and you have the same opportunity here, because unless you are willing to help preserve this system—you're not buying anything—but all you're saying is that you want decent people in government that you can relate to and relate to your thinking and your causes, you damned sure better support this, because if you don't, it very well could happen, the same thing could happen that happened in Germany.'"

Shorenstein, whose uncle was for many years the Tammany boss of Brooklyn, raised half a million dollars for Humphrey in Northern California in 1968 but sat out the presidential election in 1972 because he did not agree with some of McGovern's views, especially those involving America's defense structure.

Israel has played a part in his thinking, in terms of its needing a strong, supportive America to continue: "The mere fact that a candidate or a particular individual is favorable to Israel obviously makes the task a lot easier; this is a kind of frosting on the cake. They want to know whether he's a good man, one that they can relate to, and the fact that he's been good to Israel, has a strong record on Israel, is indicative to the person that he is one that they should really support and be considerate of. . . . But there's too much of an inference that it's Israel first and the United States second as far as the Jew is concerned. . . . When Hitler Germany came along, this was the only haven. Most all other countries were closed to the Jews and the Jews who were brought up in the period of F.D.R. and all that kind of situation were eternally grateful that they were in the United States and no place other than that. So they have a sense of saying to themselves, here's Israel and that should be preserved but, goddamn it, the place to really preserve is the United States. We won't have any money to give to Israel and Israel can't be taken care of unless there is the United States to look after it. So the great desire and feeling is to feel kindly toward the United States, and their way of expressing their gratitude is their ability to give money to the political candidate that they feel will perpetuate what they have and what their family has, because they're always conscious of a threat."

Shorenstein maintained that whatever success he has had in raising money was based on confidence his contributors had in him. He personally has maintained a "good list" of about twenty-five persons he has gone to and, "after that list of twenty-five, then you've got to start scratching." His pitch always has been open, and one-to-one. Never has he used the mass meeting, U.J.A.-type of suasion: "I never throw curves at anybody. I've got to be credible. You call a man and say, 'I'd like to go to lunch with you. We can make it a social lunch but, actually, I'm going to ask you to make a contribution to so-and-so's campaign, so if you say No, we're still going to be friends and it's going to be a social lunch.'"

Gene Wyman operated the same way: "I've raised money, really, without a great deal of effort," he said. "It's been basically a simple appeal to social consciousness, and I haven't used the U.J.A. technique at all. I use to a great extent the one-on-one technique, just talking to people, and I don't do it unless I feel I have a chance. There's no sense in me going to them—and I'm talking about them as a body—there's no sense in me trying to raise money for Adolf Hitler. No way. But if I feel there are causes and reasons that would appeal to the Jewish conscience and, generally, those are very high motivating things, I can get money. I think that most of the people I've gotten money from have such a feeling of gratefulness that they've got it, that they've been successful, and such an awareness that maybe their relatives were killed in a concentration camp, as mine were, heavily, on both sides of the family: my mother's brothers and sisters and my father lost six sisters in concentration camps, and grandparents on both sides—there's a lot of that. And so I think their general feeling is a duty to pay a little back, and we've been fortunate, and these are important things. . . ."

The method that Wyman disdained, that used at United Jewish Appeal campaign dinners, is much misunderstood. To outsiders, the method seems gauche and gross—blatant and ostentatious manifestation of all that is unsightly about the newly rich. To the unknowing, the U.J.A.-type affair appears to be a large gathering at which the names of all the guests are announced in turn, publicly, and each guest is expected to pledge a donation. They appear to be embarrassed by the public nature of it all and pressured into offering huge gifts. What the eye sees, however, is not what actually is happening. The scenario has in fact been carefully rehearsed and the actors know their roles. The real fund raising has come beforehand, at a meeting at which the organizers boldly dictate what each of those present at the preliminary meeting will give to the cause or, more to the point, to a candidate. While the method was designed originally for raising money for the U.J.A., like most things related to Jewish philanthropy, it has been adopted for, and adapted to, political use.

At this preparatory meeting—and the word "preparatory" may be misleading because the real hard pressure comes here—each person who will attend the dinner is discussed.

The person in charge will usually be able—via his knowledge of people, businesses, relationships—to dictate the size of each attendee's gift. The process is called "rating." He might tell one businessman that he won't have to give more than, say, five thousand dollars to Humphrey right now because the man has suffered a bad business year (the man, of course, might have thought no one knew business was bad) while telling another attendee that twenty-thousand dollars isn't enough this time. It hardly does any good for any of the men there to protest. For one, they have not come innocently. Two, they enjoy the scenario. Three, they cannot resist the community pressure invoked at such a meeting. Later on, at the larger dinner, the prearranged contributors' names are arranged so that they are "called" just before that of another man who was not at the organizing meeting, but whose ability to pay has been "rated" as equal to the man before him.

"What's seen on the outside world as vulgar fund raising isn't at all," said Irving Levine, the sociologist. "It's a way for fellow Jews to force the wealthy to help, invoking a community force to put pressure on the affluent. It's very much a Jewish tradition for wealthy people to be upbraided for being cheapskates, and this is very much a Jewish communal function. From the point of view of a dirty mind, this is viewed as cheap and vulgar."

"What is crass and vulgar, anyway?" asked Willen, who helped develop the method for the New York federation. "A man owns a Rolls-Royce car, which means 'I'm rich.' He has a fourteen-room apartment, which means 'I'm rich.' He has a hundred-acre estate with twenty servants, which means 'I'm rich.' They're all public expressions of money, and you invite all your friends to look at your money. Nobody has a hundred-acre estate and doesn't show it off. So how come it's not crass to spend a lot of money on your fourteen-room apartment and your estate, and it is to give away money? Somehow, something's been reversed. The fact is, synagogues and churches, cardinals' homes, bishops' homes, the whole thing is a manifestation of money. Have you ever seen anything more crass than a coronation? Some lady being pulled in a carriage by fourteen horses, all these people decked out in diamonds and jewelry. It's the crassest, vulgarest, most exhibitionistic thing in the world. I've always maintained that, for me to give $1,000, that's one thing. But then if I go and buy a painting for $10,000, and then not give the $1,000, that's a whole different thing. That's vulgar."

The key to Jewish giving, besides the historic and psychological reasons, is the "chit"—the obligation, be it social or business or whatever. If a man—for example, Gustave L. Levy, managing partner of the Goldman Sachs investment banking firm—contributed generously to a friend's charity or candidate (and Levy has been one of the more generous givers) he had every right to invite that friend to contribute to a cause or candidate that Levy was supporting. That request might have come by telephone, or in a private meeting, or in "public," at the preparatory session before a U.J.A.-type of affair.

Good fund raisers match up debts, pairing people who have helped one another. Such chits are the currency of fund raising. "You use the various leverages that men have on men," said Willen. "People give to people, not to causes." Thus the U.J.A.-type of meeting involves the tossing back and forth of chits. Usually a guest of honor will be involved, the best guest of honor being that person with the most uncollected chits. "The best guest of honor I can imagine," said occasional guest of honor

Abram, former president of the American Jewish Committee, "is Conrad Hilton. He buys more sheets, more pillowcases, more lamb carcasses, more ketchup, more electricity, steam, power, cigarettes, you name it, than anybody in the world." Willen agreed that Hilton would be good but said that another non-Jew, the President, would be better—"he can make people, he can make ambassadors, he can name this and that." "In Wall Street," said Willen, "the greatest guest of honor could be the head of J. P. Morgan, or somebody who gives out more business than anybody. In the dress business, it might be the head of J. C. Penney, who buys more dresses than anybody in the United States."

Business chits are those that are held most suspect by observers of politics. They are used routinely. If a firm is a supplier to a giant retail chain and is earning a good profit from its arrangement, it would be expected for an executive of the chain to call one day and ask the supplier to buy ten tables to a dinner honoring candidate X at one thousand dollars per table. The supplier can hardly refuse, lest he lose the business or, at the least, risk ill will. Although this practice happens to be blackmail, one such supplier told the writer: "There's really nothing wrong with it. It's part of the cost of doing business. Besides, I have suppliers, too, and I do the same thing to them and, I imagine, they do it to theirs."

In 1968, according to the lore of fund raising, Howard Stein of the Dreyfus Fund put extremely strong pressure on men who dealt with the fund to contribute to the presidential campaign of Eugene McCarthy, a claim that Stein has denied just as strongly. "That didn't happen," said Stein. "First of all, there was no threatening. Second, I personally leaned over backwards not to take any money from people in the financial community." Of those in the financial community who did give to McCarthy, he said, there were very few "and I think a good part of them were people we didn't do business with then and probably haven't since. There is always a tendency for people to assume things and say things."

Assumptions, in fact, are what much of fund raising is based on, assumptions of insecurity, assumptions of willingness to write the check. One assumption that fund raisers work meticulously is the assumption that the gift will somehow give the contributor "access" to the candidate. Thus the best of fund raisers will either have access to the top man, or at least the appearance of that access. Another assumption is that the giving of the money will provide status for the contributor. Craving for status, of course, is the most visible manifestation of the insecurity of the Jewish contributor. Wyman once said, in pointed reference to his refusal to support McGovern in 1972, that "A fund raiser can't be successful unless he's got a commitment, unless people know he has a commitment, and unless the candidate publicly recognizes that commitment." Translated, that meant that McGovern, among other failings, did not know how—or disdained—to give the appearance of access to Wyman and to massage the egos of his Jewish fund raisers, something at which Humphrey had been grand national champion. Humphrey has understood the trembling psyche of the Jewish contributor. He eagerly has learned their names (their first ones), has flattered them by inviting them to go campaigning with him, has made them feel they truly have had an input into his thinking. While some candidates have tended to closet themselves with strategists and counselors at the end of a hard day of handshaking and speechmaking, Humphrey unfailingly found time and energy to philosophize until late into the night with his big contributors, as if *they* were the strategists. Further, his discussions never dipped into small talk—he encouraged deep conversation about policies and national issues. Often, his partners in conversation would be talked out by the gregarious candidate. Humphrey's contributors have considered him a friend, which he has been.

"What a whole lot of people don't understand about political contributing," said finance expert Alexander, "is, first of all, it is an index for participation. For a wealthy person, it's easier to sign a check than it is to give time. As hard as it is for the average person to believe, for a guy to sign a check for $3,000 or $5,000 is easy for a wealthy person. Secondly, a lot of contributing is not for a preferment or favors, but for status. People like to get invited to the White House, to the governor's mansion. They like to be on the dais when the political person is speaking. They like to be on the inside. This kind of contributor is likely to think: 'I like to have him call me by my first name.' Now, all of these things are status symbols— 'when I had dinner at the White House' kinds of things. And for Jews, who maybe traditionally have felt excluded, not accepted, to be accepted at the very highest levels by political figures in the news all the time, by government leaders, is important, and gives them a sense of belonging and acceptance that they might not otherwise get or that they aren't satisfied with merely in the business world. In other words, they've got to prove something to themselves beyond that they can make a dollar."

Said Willen: "It's like giving to the arts. That gave you status even if it didn't give you acceptance in the golf clubs. The court Jew has a long history." Shorenstein put it even more directly: "For a long while, I would contribute, but no one even knew I existed. Everybody goes through that, and I've talked to a lot of people on this.

When you're involved in business you have to be almost like—well, Vince Lombardi, I think, expressed it, about the many, many ways of psyching yourself up, and so forth. And then you get like Babe Ruth: after you've hit so many home runs, how much of a thrill do you get out of each new home run, in no matter what you do, in business and so forth? So you look for other outlets. And when you look for other outlets, you do the thing that you feel most comfortable and happiest doing. I was on the board of Mount Sinai Hospital and I was on the Cancer Society and the Chamber of Commerce and president of the Recreation and Parks Commission, but the thing that I always got a bigger fascination out of and enjoyed doing is being around good political people. They're gregarious. They're fun. You go to a Cancer Society meeting, who you gonna meet there? And what fun do you have with it, or what enjoyment or what thrill do you get? And you do get a tremendous thrill if you've been involved in a person's campaign and they've won. You've had a lot of enjoyment out of it."

In substance, many of the Jewish political givers have ended up as political "groupies," hangers-on of a very special nature, needing—almost desperately needing—to know someone in power. As Willen said, they have craved the security of being near power, "of having parties for important people, of picking up the phone to call a governor or somebody like that." Muskie's former aide, Stewart, commented that many of the Jewish contributors to that campaign "would ask, 'Will you pick up the phone when I call you in the White House? Will you be there for me? That's all I want to know.'" This is a very important feeling to a Jew, to say he knows somebody in power. Perhaps, someday, it could save his life.

IX

The myth of "liberalism"
The Jewish voter

WHEN ANALYZING the "Jewish vote," academicians tend to agree that Jews' "liberal" voting often is inimical to their own best interests and almost inevitably conclude that this voting behavior must emanate from the strong ethical tradition of Judaism. Their overwhelming attachment to progressive causes over the last four decades in America often is cited as proof per se that Jews are the most selfless voters in the American polity; that a Jew, when he steps inside a voting booth, is cloaked in a history and tradition of social justice, humanism, and charity that virtually preordain his voting posture. Jews do have a sturdy tradition of charity, love for fellow man—particularly if fellow man is downtrodden, oppressed and disadvantaged. But other religious and ethnic groups have such traditions too; the humanitarian ethic is neither the invention nor the exclusive property of Jews.

Jews' distinctive voting history suggests something else: that the Jew in America may be motivated not so much by Isaiah's ancient call to "seek justice and relieve the oppressed" beating a tattoo inside his subconscious as he is by the fear of a tattoo on his forearm. While sociologists have striven to trace patterns, the politicians—actually the most perceptive students of behavior in America—have known all along the core fact: the Jew is an insecure, frightened voter. Thus those politicians who have captured the "Jewish vote" have played to Jews with hardly any effort at subtlety. As long ago as the 1870s, Rutherford B. Hayes was protesting Russia's treatment of its Jewish citizens and making sure that Americans knew of his protests. Theodore Roosevelt did the same later. So did William Howard Taft. Perhaps the most blatantly hypocritical of such acts in those days was that committed by Secretary of State John Hay, who, at the direction of President William McKinley during the off-year congressional campaign of 1902, complained loudly to Rumania over its persecution of Jews. Hay's protest was bruited widely throughout the American Jewish community while he noted privately, "The Hebrews—poor dears! All over the country they think we are bully boys."

For decades, many Jews have insisted that no such thing as a "Jewish vote" exists. Jews, they have maintained, are like all Americans and, as such, vote on all the issues, not just "Jewish" ones. To admit otherwise would, of course, lend credence to the anti-Semites' claim that Jews in America are subversively un-American, are Jews before they are

Americans, before they are editors, before they are stock-brokers. So, while some Jewish agencies have persistently denied the existence of a "Jewish vote," just as persistently the politicians have pandered specifically to "Jewish" interests and issues. The pandering has been especially observable since 1948, when the state of Israel was created. Many appeals have been in the form of accusations against opposing candidates' alleged lack of zeal for Israel's defense. The tactic is employed whether or not the opposing candidate is Jewish. Unsubtle appeals to the "Jewish vote" have been most obvious in New York State, where more than two of every five Jews in America live. In 1956, for example, in Jacob Javits' first race for the United States Senate, his opponent, Robert F. Wagner—then mayor of New York City and a Catholic—bought advertisements in Jewish newspapers that showed Wagner with the chief rabbi of Israel. Another pictured Wagner with fellow Democrat Herbert Lehman's hand on his shoulder. The Jewish Lehman had been a popular governor and senator from New York.

New York Jewish voters were bombarded by similar propaganda in 1970. In the gubernatorial race between Arthur J. Goldberg, the former Supreme Court justice, and the incumbent, Nelson A. Rockefeller, Rockefeller had a particularly delicate problem: not only was Goldberg a Jew, he had been a lifelong, ardent Zionist. Advertisements claimed that Rockefeller was "one of the staunchest supporters of the state of Israel" and always were signed by leading Jewish businessmen and community figures. One pro-Rockefeller letter, over the signature of E. J. Korvettes' Charles Bassine, was mailed to one hundred thousand Jews in "swing" voting districts. Similar appeals were used in the Senate race, where a

Jew, Richard Ottinger, and a Protestant, Charles Goodell, lost to James Buckley, a Catholic, who won 13 per cent of Jews' votes.*

Probably the crudest appeals of that year came in the congressional race in Manhattan between two Jews, Bella Abzug and radio talk show interviewer Barry Farber ("A vote for Farber is a vote for the survival of Israel. A vote for Farber is a vote for the survival of Soviet Jews. A vote for Farber is a vote for my neighborhood and my America."). A major issue of the campaign was whether Ms. Abzug had or had not said that Israel ought not to get more American jets.

Such appeals are used outside New York, as well, in cities and states where Jews compose a significant portion of the vote. They were used, for instance, in Illinois in the 1964 gubernatorial race between two non-Jews, Otto Kerner and Charles Percy. Which of the two was the better friend of the Jews? Kerner, who took 71 per cent of Jews' votes.

One of the appeals to the Jewish vote may even have cost the life of Robert F. Kennedy, whose pro-Israel statements had inflamed the young Arab, Sirhan Sirhan. Before the Democratic presidential primary vote was cast in California in June of 1968, Los Angeles radio stations were beaming a message to California's Jewish voters from Kennedy in which he strongly advocated America's giving more military aid to Israel. Ironically, the broadcast message had been drafted in the Senator's apartment in United Nations Plaza by a delegation of three New York rabbis who had been pressuring him to be a stronger advocate of Jewish causes.

* Statistics for Jewish voting used in this chapter are those generally accepted by both politicians and Jewish organizations. A further explication can be found in an extended note to this chapter.

Appealing to Jewish interests has occurred in all recent presidential campaigns, a notable example coming in 1960. In the race between John Kennedy and Richard Nixon, according to one description of the campaign, "Vice President Nixon's headquarters issued a statement declaring that Israeli newspapers had called for Nixon's election as a reliable friend of Israel. The press release drew the direct implication [of Jews' having dual loyalties], calling for 'two million Jews to cast their vote for the sake of Israel.' The bold tie-in of the 'Jewish vote' with the preferences of a foreign state raised a furor throughout the country. A few days later, Nixon's headquarters repudiated the release as the work of an overzealous subordinate." Nonetheless, the appeals continued, with advertisements in Jewish newspapers saying that Mr. Nixon was a better friend of Israel than was Senator Kennedy and implying that Joseph Kennedy, Sr., was an anti-Semite.

The notable feature of all such appeals is that none are pitched to altruism and progressivism. They are aimed at Jews' insecurity, an insecurity that can, on occasion, make this highly educated group appear incredibly and almost pathetically gullible. Politicians know (because they are told so by the Jewish strategists they hire) that many Jews perceive Israel as their ultimate refuge, as being synonymous with survival.

What politicians also know is that voting decisions are not the result, ordinarily, of the enthusiastic acceptance of a candidate's ideology. In any given election, the majority of voters know remarkably little about the candidates, often not even their names. For example, in 1973, the Eagleton Institute of Politics at Rutgers University randomly sampled 1,224 New Jersey voters about their knowledge of the candidates who were actively seeking their parties' nominations for governor. Of those who said they received most of their information about New Jersey politics from the newspapers, only 10 per cent could identify more than one candidate for governor, with primary day but two months away. Only one in three could even name one candidate. Of those who specified television as their best political source, only 4 per cent could name more than one candidate! Since New Jersey has no commercial television stations, these numbers may be somewhat untypical, but the fact remains—and it is a fact that those involved in politics deeply often tend to forget—that the electorate, in general, cares little for and knows little of politics. The classic political study, *The American Voter,* put it this way:

In the electorate as a whole the level of attention to politics is so low that what the public is exposed to must be highly visible—even stark—if it is to have an impact on opinion.

In effect then, countless voters start with zero information about a political contest. All they have are their biases about issues in general and their professional, ethnic, racial, sexual, regional, or other influences. In terms of particular candidates, they pick up glimpses of candidates over television or radio, or gather snatches of information (often inaccurate) from friends or neighbors. The voter stacks various candidates against his particular set of biases, then rejects those who fail to measure up. The process is, basically, the one by which one arrives at a personal value system—rejecting certain values to arrive at accepted, positive ones. Thus the continual quest for identity seems largely to be a negative process, as is that for political identity. The negative push usually precedes the positive pull. In political terms, although a "conservative" may say he is *for* maintaining the status quo or *for* moving backwards, he arrives at that point after deciding that change is inimical, that it will destroy or threaten something he has or wants. Politicians—successful ones, anyway—plan their campaigns with that in mind.

Public opinion surveys like those by Gallup and Harris are not the ones politicians rely on. The publicized surveys give "horse race" results—who leads whom at X point in time, among X group. Such results make news since elections are, of course, ultimately horse races. Political strategists usually commission their own surveys, choosing from as many as 150 different commercial organizations, or creating their own polling apparatus. They pay great sums of money for such surveys to find out how voters perceive the various candidates, favorably and unfavorably, and why. They are pleased if their candidate is viewed favorably, but often "favorables" are less important than "unfavorables." If a candidate has high unfavorables, it means he is vulnerable, and the details of the unfavorable factors will guide the opposing strategist —who certainly will have his own poll data—as to how and where to attack.

Ideology can contribute to voters' impressions of a candidate, favorable or unfavorable, but ideology is less important than many assume. Many in America distrust ideology altogether and, for that matter, ideology in American politics is fluid and unstable. What was "liberal" yesterday may be "middle of the road" today, "conservative" tomorrow. Voters make decisions in terms of what a candidate can do for them or, more to this writer's point, what a candidate might do *to* them, to hurt them. Such behavior is selfish but, of course, self-interest is what voting in a democracy is supposed to be all about.

The negative input into voting decisions was strikingly evident in the 1972 presidential election, where Nixon's huge victory was not an overwhelming affirmation of him. Rather, his majority was the result of voters' casting ballots *against* George McGovern. Lawrence Goldberg illustrated this when he recalled a chance conversation he had one Sunday morning before the voting. Goldberg, who directed the Jewish voters' section of Nixon's re-election campaign, was having coffee with a friend in a restaurant in Amagansett, Long Island, discussing the campaign:

"A kid sitting next to us leaned over and asked, 'Did I hear you say you work for Nixon?' I said 'yeah.' 'I'm gonna vote for the son of a bitch,' he said. Naturally that way of putting it rather interested me, so I asked why he put it that way, and he said, 'Because I don't like the other son of a bitch more.' And that's the way a lot of people feel. I got to talking with this kid. He was twenty-three years old and was working in his first job, at an advertising agency that specializes in funeral homes and restaurants. At one point this kid said to me, 'McGovern, the bastard, he wants to take it away from me before I even get it.' "

Although the voting behavior of Americans, generally, is affected by such negative factors, Jews add something more: they carry more such baggage than other voters. "We're all familiar, intellectually and even emotionally, with what three hundred years of slavery have done to the black soul and spirit," said Marvin Schick, an orthodox Jew and a political scientist who, for several years, was Jewish affairs assistant to New York Mayor

John Lindsay. "Well, think of what two *thousand* years of being murdered for the simple crime of being Jewish have done to the Jews? It has done something to them. It has made them angry, tired, distrustful of other people —and for good reason, often."

Just how distrustful Jews are has been calculated in a survey conducted by the National Opinion Research Center for Dr. Melvin Kohn of the National Institute of Mental Health. In this survey, Jews almost leaped off the chart in terms of their intrinsic distrust of others. That survey, reported by the center's Andrew Greeley in his book *That Most Distressful Nation*, attempted to assess various white ethnic groups' comparable levels of distrust. The scale went from Plus 4—most trusting—to Minus 4—least trusting:

GROUP	ORDER AND SCORE
Irish Catholic	2.506
Scandinavian Protestant	1.583
Slavic Catholic	1.481
German Protestant	0.767
German Catholic	0.757
Italian Catholic	0.502
White, Anglo-Saxon, Protestant	0.242
Jewish	—3.106

These figures might also suggest that the disparity in general outlook between Jews and non-Jews carries over into political behavior, since voting statistics of Jews compared with non-Jews show the same variant. It has been proven, too, that as other members of society advance up the educational, economic, and professional ladders, their votes become increasingly "conservative," for preserving the status quo. But as Jews move up the same ladders— and they have hurried up them faster than other groups

—their votes become increasingly progressive, more amenable to change.

This syndrome was vividly shown in an unusual series of surveys conducted in 1945 and 1946 by the Office of Public Opinion Research at Princeton University. Seventeen religious groups were sampled as to their approval of "guaranteed economic security," and their responses were charted in relation to the percentage of each group that would benefit from guaranteed security. In each case except one, the percentage employed as urban manual workers corresponded directly to the percentage favoring security. The one group that differed was the Jews:

DENOMINATIONAL GROUPS	PER CENT URBAN MANUAL WORKERS IN DENOMINATION	PER CENT FOR GUARANTEED SECURITY
National	44	44
Catholic	55	58
Baptist	51	51
Lutheran	43	40
Methodist	39	38
Episcopalian	36	33
Presbyterian	31	31
Congregational	28	26
Jewish	27	56

Jews, with the lowest percentage engaged in manual labor, ranked second among those favoring guaranteed security. Milton Himmelfarb, who brought the survey to the attention of this writer, mentioned that, "These people [the Jews] don't live in the same political universe."

"Gentile Republicans don't understand it," said Larry Goldberg. "They're looking at things from an economic and class interest. They'll come up to me and say, 'Gee, this guy makes as much as I do, and why is he such a liberal and I'm not?' and they just don't understand that the Jewish upper class liberal hears a different tune."

The tune they hear is one the gentile American has never heard, because neither he nor his ancestors have ever been stalked by memories such as the pogroms in 1881 in Russia or the *Kristallnacht* all over Germany in 1938 or Hitler's attempt to annihilate all of Jewry a few years later. The European proclivity for Jew-hating has had an inestimable impact on Jews' outlook toward American politics and politicians. It was evident in the call of "Never Again" from Meir Kahane of the Jewish Defense League. Upper-class, highly educated, respectable Jews decried Kahane's extremism, his calls to meet violence with violence. But "Never Again" is imbedded in the psyches of all Jews. It is their different tune.

Interestingly, one reason that "liberal" voting among Jews increases in almost direction relation to a Jew's move up the ladders is that the Jewish elites simply know more; Jews who have been to college learn that anti-Semitism in this world has increased as the years have progressed. The last one hundred years have been the worst for the Jews.*

The upper-class Jews are progressives because they reject what they see as a narrow, parochial route to survival—the one chosen by the more ethnic, more sequestered Jews. The "elite," which moves more in non-Jewish society than the more ethnic Jews, tends to see survival in terms of an America that is open, unauthoritarian, socially concerned. They are *for* civil rights, for "liberal," progressive government. In that kind of America, they

---

* Lawrence Fuchs wrote in 1956:
In the last eighty years anti-Semitism has increased rather than diminished—pogroms in East Europe, the Dreyfus affair, and more recently the monstrous persecutions of Hitler and Stalin.

reason, all Jews as members of the society will thrive. They want a world in which all can live harmoniously, so they view an attack on blacks as an attack on their Harmonious World, an attack on free speech as an attack on their Harmonious World. But this "liberal" stance does not mean the upper-class "elite" is any less defensive or any less protective of Jewish interests than the pious Hasidim with their side curls who want government aid for their Jewish day schools. Their version of defense only sounds more polite than that of the Hasidim. That is why the pattern of Jews' voting in presidential elections is so consistently "liberal." It is in fact not so much liberal as it is *anti* what they fear, as is clear from the record of Jewish voting for the last half century:

PERCENTAGE OF JEWISH VOTE

1916
Republican (Hughes)   45
Democrat (Wilson)   55

1920
Socialist (Debs)   38
Republican (Harding)   43
Democrat (Cox)   19

1924
Progressive (La Follette)   22
Republican (Coolidge)   27
Democrat (Davis)   51

1928
Republican (Hoover)   28
Democrat (Smith)   72

1932
Republican (Hoover)   18
Democrat (Roosevelt)   82

1936
Republican (Landon)   15
Democrat (Roosevelt)   85

1940
Republican (Willkie)   10
Democrat (Roosevelt)   90

1944
Republican (Dewey)   10
Democrat (Roosevelt)   90

1948
Progressive (Wallace)   15
Republican (Dewey)   10
Democrat (Truman)   75

1952
Republican (Eisenhower)   36
Democrat (Stevenson)   64

1956
Republican (Eisenhower)   40
Democrat (Stevenson)   60

1960
Republican (Nixon)   18
Democrat (Kennedy)   82

1964
Republican (Goldwater)   10
Democrat (Johnson)   90

1968
American Independent
  (Wallace)   2
Republican (Nixon)   17
Democrat (Humphrey)   81

1972
Republican (Nixon)   35
Democrat (McGovern)   65

One suspects that one reason why so many analysts of Jewish voting have clung to the notion of consistent "liberalism" is that Jewish voting is usually viewed as a whole—i.e., in terms of all of American history. Most analysts discuss voting from the earliest days of Jewish immigration. The first Jewish immigrants were Sephardic Jews (Spanish and Portuguese) who started arriving in the 1650s and 1660s. They were followed in the mid-1800s by German Jews. The Jews who were in America prior to the huge migration from Eastern Europe after 1880 were a very different kind of Jew. Those who lived in the South went with the prevailing patterns there, including supporting slavery.

Most of America's Jews today are bred of the Eastern Europe immigrants. The previous wave of Jewish immigrants, from Germany, generally had become Republican Progressives, because the Democratic Party had been the party of slavery and because it housed the Populist anti-Semite Tom Watson and William Jennings Bryan, who was perceived to be an anti-Semite. The Republicans "worked" the new Jewish voters assiduously. Further, the political realities that welcomed the Jews in the cities pushed them toward the Republicans. The millions of Irish who had arrived earlier had seized political control of the cities by way of the Democratic Party. They refused to let the Jews in—for jobs, in particular. What the poorer Jews found in America was not that different from what they had left in Europe. In Europe, as Alex Rose pointed out, Jews had to bribe their way to neutrality, to keep from being discriminated against. In New York, "when you had a store and you gave a cop on that beat money, what did you give it to him for?" asked Rose. "All you wanted him to be was neutral—he shouldn't be against you. The Jews were paying graft for neutrality, not for any privileges. Just not to be harassed, not to be annoyed. The unions did the same thing in the early years. The unions were handing out all kinds of gifts to the police department in order to have their neutrality. . . ."

Those Jews in the slums who did vote Democratic were often bribed to do so. The very notion of that turned New York's Jacob Javits into a Republican. His father, Morris, had been a janitor in three Lower East Side tenements ("he never made more than $45 a month in his whole life," said Javits) and the young Jack was appalled by the corruption he witnessed among the Democrats. The Tammany saloonkeeper down the block would give Morris Javits two dollars per voter in the three buildings, and Morris's job was to distribute the money so that the new citizens would vote for all of Tammany's candidates. Until David Dubinsky, Rose, and Sidney Hillman organized the American Labor Party in 1936, says Rose, "if you wanted to be part of an anti-Tammany political organization, then you had to go to the Republicans." Many of the new citizens could stomach neither party and voted not at all, or voted Socialist. To the more ardent reformers, voting for a Democrat or a Republican was selling out their principles. Some of the veteran reformers have never cast a vote for either a Democrat or a Republican, with Rose and Dubinsky as two examples. They have, of course, voted for Democrats and Republicans who have been endorsed by the Labor Party (or, subsequently, the Liberal Party), thus avoiding pulling the lever of a party that was, to them, symbolic of the evils of capitalism.

The hold of Republicans over the majority of Jews began to erode in 1912, when the ultimate internationalist, Woodrow Wilson, was the Democrats' presidential nominee. Jews were internationalists by necessity. But Wilson had other attractions for Jews. As an intellectual (and holder of a doctorate), he appealed to their respect for learning. Perhaps more important, he was—like many of them—a reformer. As governor of New Jersey, he had instituted a primary election system and an employers' liability law.

Eight years later, the Democrats could not hold the Jewish voters. With no more Wilson, in a country weary of war, the Democratic candidate, James M. Cox, could win only 34.1 per cent of the vote nationwide, and 19 per cent of the votes of Jews. Jews voted either for the Republican, Warren Harding, or for the reformer in the race, Socialist Eugene Debs. Again in 1924, many Jews voted reform, for Wisconsin's Bob La Follette, but the internationally minded John W. Davis lured a small majority of Jews' votes to the Democrats again. The big switch came in 1928, with Al Smith as the Democrats' nominee. Not only had he been a reformer as governor of New York, a man who saw government as being responsible for the welfare of the people, he was, also, like the Jews, an ethnic, a poor immigrant from the streets of the big city. And Smith went after Jewish votes. He attacked the Ku Klux Klan. In an age of mounting anti-Semitism, it was important that Al Smith had the courage to have a Jewish campaign manager, Joseph Proskauer. Smith won a resounding 72 per cent of the votes of Jews and set a pattern of Jewish voting that is continuing today.

The seed that Smith planted Franklin Roosevelt nurtured to fruition. Roosevelt, to many American Jews, was the next thing to Moses. To many who had left religion, he was the new Moses. He ended the Depression, which had exacerbated the anti-Semitism of the '20s. From the earliest days of Nazism, he had openly criticized Hitler and his brownshirts as outlaws, and led the political faction urging American intervention in Europe. He brought Jews into government for the first time in America. And his conception of government—the New Deal and its social welfare underpinning—reflected the Jews' own conception of community. Jewish pluralities for Roosevelt the Nazi-fighter rose with each passing election, well after some groups' affections for him were waning, to well over nine of every ten of Jews' votes in 1944. After Roosevelt's death and the end of the war, the aura he had provided for the Democratic Party carried on. Jews did not forget and have not forgotten that it was the Republican Party that harbored the anti-Semites in the '20s and '30s, the Republican Party that was home to those who called the New Deal the "Jew Deal," that it was the Republicans who made up the majority of the membership of New York's Colony Club, where Mrs. Henry Morgenthau had been snubbed, a famous incident that caused Eleanor Roosevelt to cancel her membership. So, in 1948, although Jews had no special trust in Harry S Truman, they voted for him, and for the Progressive, Henry Wallace, and against the Republican, Governor Thomas E. Dewey. Dewey won only 10 per cent of Jews' votes, about what he had received when he had run against Roosevelt in 1944.

If anything should have ended the Jews' hostility to

the Republican Party, it was the G.O.P. nominee in 1952. He was General Dwight David Eisenhower, the commander who led Allied forces to victory over the forces of evil, the liberator of Auschwitz, Dachau, Bergen-Belsen. Eisenhower beat Adlai Stevenson in a landslide, winning 442 electoral votes to Stevenson's 89. But two of every three Jews in America voted for Stevenson, against the Republican, against the party that reminded them of big business, of *noblesse oblige*, of privilege, and of danger.

Certainly by 1956, one might have thought that the Jews would finally yield to the lure of Eisenhower. He had pulled America out of a nasty war in Asia and had fulfilled his promise to bring American boys home from Korea.*

His 1956 landslide was even greater—he won all but seven states, and his electoral total climbed by fifteen. But only 4 per cent of the Jews switched to the G.O.P. Again, at least six of every ten Jews voted against the Republicans. Thus, in the case of Jews, a comment about the tenacity of party allegiance in *The American Voter*—"An individual led to a Democratic orientation by a group membership in 1930 may still be registering a manifestation of that influence in 1956."—is classic understatement.

Four years later, in 1960, the Republicans nominated Nixon. To most Jews, he was an archetypal Jew-baiter, the man who had smeared Helen Gahagan Douglas by calling her "soft on Communism," whose supporters had reminded voters that the real name of her husband, actor

---

* A contrary factor for some Jews, however, was their perception of Eisenhower's Secretary of State, John Foster Dulles, as anti-Israel, and of the administration as following a basically pro-Arabist line.

Melvyn Douglas, was Hesselberg.* He was a member of the House Un-American Activities Committee and Jews perceived him as a go-between for the feared Senator Joseph McCarthy. Jewish antipathy to Nixon was so great that it was politically potent beyond the presidential contest. In the New York Senate race between Javits and Mayor Wagner, Wagner took an advertisement in the *Jewish Daily Forward* picturing Javits' shaking hands with Nixon and captioned, "A vote for Javits is a vote for Nixon." Javits lost the Jewish vote to Wagner, overwhelmingly. In the presidential balloting, more than eight of every ten American Jews voted against Nixon. The near solidarity of anti-Nixon sentiment among Jews in states like New York and Illinois may have resulted in the Kennedy victory.

In 1964, the Republicans did even worse among the Jews by nominating ultra-"Conservative" Barry Goldwater. It did not matter that Goldwater's father was Jewish (Goldwater was raised as an Episcopalian). To most Jews, conservatism equals anti-Semitism. Lucy Dawidowicz, the historian, has written that:

The Jewish experience in the Russian and Austro-Hungarian empires established even more emphatically what Jews had learned in Western Europe: that the political right was at best conservative, avowedly Christian and committed to the preservation of ancient privileges; it could, and often did, become reactionary and even anti-Semitic.

Ernest van den Haag put it another way: "To the Jewish mind, the *Gestalt* of the rightist requires anti-Semitism . . . no matter whether they are: they ought to be."

---

* Gerald L. K. Smith chipped in on Nixon's behalf. "Help Richard Nixon get rid of the Jew-Communists," he said, urging Californians "not to send to the Senate the wife of a Jew."

Sixty-one per cent of all Americans voted against Goldwater; 90 per cent of American Jews voted against him.

In 1968, the Republicans could not have had a better opportunity for finally making sizable inroads into the Jewish vote. The Democrats were in disarray. The National Convention in Chicago had seemed to embody all the divisiveness in the land (war versus antiwar, young versus old, old politics versus the new) and all during a Democratic administration. As angry protesters and angry policemen clashed in the streets, as delegates to the convention were frisked at the doors, as the incumbent Democratic President hid in seclusion, his protégé, Humphrey, supporting his leader's policies in Vietnam, was nominated to succeed him. Of all the ethnic groups in the electorate, Jews were far and away the most opposed to the war in Vietnam. Yet despite strong reasons to vote against the Democrats, more than eight of every ten Jews cast their ballots against the Republicans' nominee, Nixon. The real test was to come four years later—when many Jews would worry over whether they might be turned to pillars of salt if they pulled the Republican lever.

X

Years of turbulence

Fear and the blacks

RELENTLESSLY, America's Jews had migrated again. No longer were they foreign-born, foreign-speaking. Seemingly en masse, they thrust into the middle class, as if their very souls had depended on it. They devoted themselves to symphony associations and to collecting oeuvres of Picasso and Miró, to the Book-of-the-Month Club, to bundling their offspring off to Cambridge or Hanover. They were the epitome of open-mindedness—some even bought Volkswagens or Mercedes-Benzes as if to prove it. They were "liberals" in politics, in economics, in race. They invited their middle-class black friends to their dinner parties. They doted almost religiously on the post-New Deal philosophy expounded by journals like *The New Republic* and *The Saturday Review* (both of which, incidentally, were edited by Jews).

"In the 1930s," said Rabbi Arthur Hertzberg, historian and president of the American Jewish Congress, "American Jews were one of the disadvantaged groups. They faced all kinds of patterns of exclusion—in academia, in the State Department, in big business, et cetera, et cetera. In the expansion of everything in America after the War, the only pool of first-class talent immediately available was Jews. . . . When American society suddenly needed them, in a great burst of expanding capitalism, Jews made hay. Now, in a contracting society, their situation is not so good. . . . And it's right on schedule, just like it was in pre-Nazi Germany. The Jews are saying, 'Look, we've really arrived!' They think it's in their best interests to have stopped the clock. If American Jews could have stopped the clock in 1960, they would have been all right. The social change since has affected them negatively."

"There was very little to disunite the Jews," echoes Bertram Gold, executive vice president of the most "establishment" of the country's Jewish organizations, the American Jewish Committee. "All of them believed in an expanding America, all of them believed in a civil libertarian program, and the Jew became a culture hero in the society—for a while. But 1967 was a watershed, for two major reasons: one was the Six-Day War, and the other was the [New York] teachers' strike. . . . Since 1967, you've begun to see a crisis of confidence in the United States generally and a crisis of confidence in the Jewish community, in particular. It's a questioning of the Jewish

'establishment,' the rich heterodoxy versus the poor or-
thodoxy. There has been a sharp differentiation."

Lawrence Goldberg discovered that differentiation in
spending nearly a year studying the dynamics of Jewish
politics before mounting the Republicans' 1972 effort to
woo Jews away from the Democrats. He sees Jewish political history as following a double-tracked course, "one starting in the revolutions of 1789 and 1848, where Jews were
Leftists because the Left was the only option open to
them. At the same time, on the other track, they were
'liberal' for things like civil liberties and so forth because
it was in their self-interest, and so the self-interest merged
with liberalism. . . . The two tracks were going along
fine until the '60s when, suddenly, their self-interest
didn't jibe with the liberal, social-justice outlook. The two
tracks split. The split showed up domestically on things
like busing, where the Jewish 'liberal' dogma will be to
support busing, that integrated schooling is a good thing.
But the Jewish guy in Detroit, who can't afford to send
his child to a private school, looks forward to the idea that
his school is going to change, that the teaching might be
worse. And you've got to understand that the single most
important fact of life for the Jew in America has been the
public school. So there's been a split between the Jewish
'liberal' ideology and the sacrifices this man will have to
make in his own personal life to live up to that ideology.
You can take housing—look at Forest Hills, the same
thing. The classic 'liberal' Jewish ideology is for integrated housing, integrated neighborhoods, but on the other
hand, Sadie has a friend who just got mugged, and her
children won't come out to live in Forest Hills like they'd
planned, they're going to Hewlett [Long Island] instead.
There's a clash. You can go on down each issue and

there's a clash between the two tracks—on police, on civil rights, on international affairs."

Rabbi Wolfe Kelman, executive vice president of the organization made up of Jewry's Conservative* rabbis, added that, "When the Jews were supporting Roosevelt and the New Deal, they were supporting their own interests—labor unions, the minimum wage, for example. These were of great assistance to many, many Jews. Today, you have a different kind of Jewish community, still voting the same personal interests. The issues have changed, the Jews' social and economic status has changed."

The turning point for Jewry had in fact come before the 1968 election. Although the 1968 presidential vote had been heavily Democratic, it may have been misleading, for the vote had in fact been an anti-Nixon vote, not a pro-Democratic one. A more important indicator of the upheaval in Jewish political attitude was the 1966 referendum on a civilian review board for the New York City Police Department. The police review board vote was in fact a civil rights referendum. New York's Jews had for decades been the mainstays of American "liberalism." They once would have voted almost automatically for any issue that would benefit those less privileged; in this instance, for the review board. Instead, 55 per cent of the Jews voted against it. The old allies, the blacks and the Jews, were falling out. All across the country, perceptive blacks and perceptive Jews read the message of that vote, and its meaning for black-Jewish relationships nationwide. New York City is a kind of focal point for both the black

---

* This does not mean politically conservative. One of the three main branches of Judaism is the Conservative, which is non-Orthodox but which retains many of the traditions.

and Jewish communities in America; it encompasses both Harlem and more Jewish residents than any other city.

Further, blacks were pushing Jews in a way that most Jews did not recognize: the surge of black pride had forced all Americans to examine their roots, and many Jews in America, with such self-examination, suddenly came to the realization that their origins were, indeed, something special. Then, in the space of six days in June 1967, a tiny military force from a tiny Jewish state thousands of miles away accomplished more to heighten Jewish pride than had decades of sermons and implorings from thousands of rabbis. At long last, America's Jews felt they could be Jews openly.

No sooner had the new Jewish ethnicity begun to take root when the wrenching New York school strike occurred. The "liberal" establishment of the city—including the Jewish organizations—had supported an experiment in community control of Brooklyn's Ocean Hill-Brownsville school district. Most of the teachers in that school district, like most of the teachers in the rest of the city school system, were Jewish. Most of the community was black. In the fall of 1968, the new community school board fired thirteen teachers, all of them Jews. The city-wide strike of teachers and the sulfurous black-Jewish relations that surfaced in its wake are simmering still.

"The strike signaled two things, which I think had a crucial impact on many people," said Rabbi Seymour Siegel, a theologian and the foremost intellectual spokesman of the new ethnic ideology that has arisen among Jewry. "One, the black leaders, the spokesmen, were attempting to gain their objectives outside the rules," he said. "And two, the so-called 'liberal' politicians like Lindsay—he was the symbol but by no means the only one, the leaders of the mainline Jewish organizations, too—were aiding and abetting this without any interest or compassion for the people being hurt." "These established Jewish agencies make a great deal of noise whenever Jews overseas are threatened," said Rabbi Kelman. "There was a general feeling that American Jews had no problems. They had no sympathy for the Jewish teachers who were fired in Ocean Hill and Brownsville, but if two Jewish teachers in Bucharest were fired, all the Jewish organizations would have turned the world upside down."

Swiftly, Jews who had once so readily advocated civil rights issues were perceiving the struggle of blacks differently. Marvin Schick, who had been Mayor Lindsay's Jewish affairs adviser, noted that "In many Jews, racism is bringing out the worst in them. There's an inner bone in them that tells them this is not their noblest part speaking." But it is speaking and, Schick said, it is growing because, "one, a mental process has set in within the Jewish community that leads to greater distrust of the outside world, greater insularity and, two, too many things are happening in the real world, resulting from the black revolution and the urban crisis, that guarantee a continuing crisis between blacks and Jews, in things like quotas, housing, community action. I'm very pessimistic."

Nick Kisburg, a Teamster lobbyist in New York, put it more bluntly: "Jews see in Negroes The Enemy. Negroes, and maybe they're quite correct, are challenging the system that served Jews so well. After all, the Jews got there first, and it's the Jews who are holding them down."

"You can't ignore the fact that blacks are pressing Jews in many areas," agreed Schick. "And you have the problem of black crime. There are stories upon stories of relatives hurt in one fashion or another, and the Jewish communications processes deal in a lot of rumors. And a lot of it is understandable, with the conflicts and the rhetoric in the black community, which is totally outrageous."

Many of those within the leadership of Jewish organizations have been trying to soften the growing confrontation, appealing to Jews' old emotional ties to the old "liberalism." One of the most prominent of these old "liberals" is Rabbi Hertzberg, who is, incidentally, a cousin of Rabbi Kelman. "If the crunch ever comes between the 'haves' and the 'have-nots,'" said the rabbi, "the 'haves' are perfectly willing to sell out the Jews to the blacks to save what they have. I still believe there's a natural alliance between the Jews and the blacks against the establishment. What's going on is a sham battle, and it would be disastrous if either Jews or blacks got sucked into it. The organized Jewish community has gone to the right and has allowed itself—at least in the blacks' minds—to become antiblack. It's in the interest of Jews and blacks to work this out together. Let's put it this way: I didn't ship any blacks over here as slaves, I never owned any slaves. But I feel a common responsibility for slavery. If prices ought to be paid, and I believe they should be—I just want [the gentiles'] children to have to pay as well as mine. The truth is that both Jews and blacks are marginal to the power structure of the United States. The goyish world looks at Jews as a pool of brains to be used and at blacks as a pool of backs to be used. The WASP world would be perfectly willing to let the brains and the backs fight it out."

Meanwhile, the intellectual elite of "the brains" turned. Many of the Jewish intellectuals hastened to warn the flock that danger was afoot, that the "liberal" coalition that the Jews had once embraced, and that had embraced them, was growing hostile to the Jews. "The prevailing liberal directions are themselves becoming inhospitable to Jewish life," wrote San Francisco sociologist Earl Raab. "Liberalism is no longer a bridge for the Jews to other groups in society," wrote Harvard's Seymour Martin Lipset. "It may soon become a barrier, particularly since liberals no longer see the Jews as an oppressed minority in need of assistance."

"Old coalitions break apart because the pieces aren't getting what they used to get," said sociologist Irving M. Levine. "Jews are no longer getting out of the liberal coalition what they needed. . . . Blacks tried to break away, too, but they had no place else to go." Levine, who has spent much of his life as a "professional liberal," now says, a bit sadly, that "I've advocated many, many things that have not worked. Why should people listen to me now? They still do. But mostly out of hope. Not out of confidence."

A personification of the change in some Jews is Rabbi Siegel, who, in 1965, was a wholehearted supporter of John V. Lindsay in his first campaign for the mayoralty of New York. In 1968, he helped organize a national committee of theological professors for Humphrey. By 1969, he was through with the old "liberalism." In that year, he served on a committee for the election of Mario Procaccino as New York mayor ("Your vote counts the same whether you hold your nose or sing hallelujah," the rabbi said). A year later he was serving as a key adviser on Jewish matters in the campaign of Conservative James Buckley for the Senate. In 1972 he worked hard in the campaign of President Nixon; and, as a reward, he was invited to give the Jewish blessing at Nixon's second inauguration. In a 1972 issue of *Judaism*, Rabbi Siegel spelled out his new, soured definition of liberalism:

1) a tendency to favor liberty over order; 2) a tendency to favor government intervention over private initiative; 3) a tendency to explain human behavior in terms of environment rather than individual will or heredity; 4) a tendency to favor equality of possession rather than equality of opportunity; 5) a tendency to favor universal characteristics rather than particularistic ones; 6) a tendency to favor left-revolutionary movements and nations; 7) a tendency to relegate religion to the private sphere; 8) a tendency to denigrate tradition in favor of novelty; 9) a tendency to prefer change according to rational principle rather than in accordance with the specific facts; 10) a tendency to believe that all problems are solvable.

"The tragedy of life," said the rabbi, resettling the yarmulke atop his head, "is that some problems are not solvable."

Another Jewish intellectual who turned was Norman Podhoretz, the onetime *wunderkind* of Jewish intellectualism and the editor of *Commentary* magazine. Podhoretz for years was at the forefront of non-Jewish, nonparochial universalism; it was reflected in the often non-Jewish mix of articles in his publication. Podhoretz is downright livid over the growing trend to quotas, the result of affirmative action plans to spur employment of blacks and other minority group members. "Quotas are the most serious threat to Jews since World War II," said Podhoretz, "and anybody who thinks I'm overreacting doesn't understand what a quota system is. There is no more serious challenge to the American ethos than a quota system. In 1957, after the Sputnik panic in the country over excellence and the fact that the Russians were going to beat us, that's when the idea of a meritocracy really took hold. Oh yes, there were pockets of anti-Semitism here and there, as in some industries, but for all practical purposes, between 1957 and 1967, people who thought things were bad in this country [for the Jews] were simply wrong. Yes, there was class discrimination but it was snobbery rather than anti-Semitism. It's not so much a matter of losing jobs. But unless certain of these tendencies are reversed, people who don't have jobs aren't going to get them. And people who have them aren't going to get promoted. It's an inevitable development, and the arithmetic is inexorable here. If the group is 3 per cent, the rest speaks for itself." In a 1971 speech to the annual meeting of the American Jewish Committee, which publishes his magazine, Podhoretz said that

The merit system had neither been invented by Jews, nor had it come into being for the sake of Jews. Yet Jews had prospered under an arrangement which, at least in principle, treated all persons on the basis of the merits as individuals regardless of "race, color, creed, or place of national origin"; in the familiar phrase that has now acquired so quaintly archaic a ring.

His associate Milton Himmelfarb had written two years earlier that

To hear some people talk these days, one would think that the merit principle is a Jewish conspiracy. . . . Here and now, somehow, suddenly, it is hard to find anyone who will defend the anonymous examination. If Jews do disproportionately well in these meritocratical contests, the reasoning goes, then the whole thing is unfair, a Jewish conspiracy in effect if not in original intention.

In an interview, Himmelfarb amplified: "Pure proportionality will mean the death of Jews, and I don't mean physically."

"Quotas are something that is within the current lifetime experiences of people who are still rather young," explained Adam Walinsky, who had trouble finding a job with a good New York law firm after his graduation from Yale. "If it were new, it wouldn't be such a problem. In New York, you get a Jew who's progressed through the school system, and some guy comes up and says he wants his job and he says, 'But you didn't pass the test.' These guys have invested their whole lives in the principle that The Test is everything. What they learned is that, if they wanted to 'make it,' they had to be twice as good as anybody who wasn't Jewish, and the whole ethos and culture was built on being twice as good, and now somebody tells them, 'It doesn't matter if you're twice as good. We're not going to give you the job, anyway.' "

All across the nation Jews have perceived the ultimate result of "affirmative action" programs to be exclusion of Jews: any attempt to include other groups by numbers rather than strictly by merit has to mean that Jews, who tend to overqualify in terms of merit, will lose. It bothers Jews in terms of employment, but perhaps even more in terms of education, the process by which Jews traditionally have been able to escape their origins. "Spend a day at the Bronx High School of Science," said Walinsky. "Here's where you begin to appreciate what Jews want out of politics. For Jews, politics hasn't meant so much who's running the city, but establishing an institution like the Bronx High School of Science, where these struggling young kids from all over the city, like some of these little math wizards, can go. That's what public life has been all about. It's at least the equal or better than any prep school in the country. So that's what politics is really about to the Jews. It gives them a chance to move into a different world entirely, and maybe be a Nobel Prize winner like a Dr. Jonas Salk or maybe be a $100,000-a-year Park Avenue doctor."

Not long ago, an institution like the American Jewish Committee would never have touched an issue that could not but help the disadvantaged. The American Jewish Committee, however, had reacted to the pelting it had been receiving from the more ethnic Jews and from the intellectuals, some within its own establishment. Hyman H. Bookbinder, the committee's representative in Washington, was assigned the task of trying to persuade the federal government to make sure that affirmative action plans did not become anti-Jewish quotas. The committee's defensiveness about what it was trying to do was evident in Bookbinder's justification of the attempt:

"In some way," he said, "I suppose that the degree of our concern and participation is a reflection in fact that the A.J.C., like some other groups, has become somewhat more Jewishly oriented—directly, specifically Jewishly oriented—than was the pattern three, five, ten years ago. It's part of the greater Jewish consciousness. Some of it is defensive, because there are some new kinds of threats or competitions with Jewish achievement or the Jewish role, but greater identification is also part of the culture of our times. . . . There is generally greater Jewish consciousness and a feeling of a threat against the Jewish community. Norman [Podhoretz] and others have written much about the Golden Era having passed. So there is, generally, a greater Jewish consciousness and the quota thing is at least partially that. I prefer to think of it, I *do* think of it, more as an essential aspect of democratic living. I don't want to have a quotaized society. . . . I'm sick and tired, I'm absolutely livid when I'm sitting at a meeting of twenty-five people, called together on some issue or other from all kinds of organizations and, before the meeting is fifteen minutes old, somebody will say, 'I see only three women out of twenty-five' or 'Why are there only two blacks out of twenty-five?' Every meeting, every association, every activity, has got to be a representation of our ethnic mix. I think that's just plain bad. I mean it's a threat to the kind of society I want. So I see the quota thing not as a narrow employment protection activity— it takes that form sometimes—but I see it more generally. Within our organization and some other organizations, we—who are dubbed the universalists—keep resisting what might be considered a narrow, vested-interest kind of thing. And to this day, most of us, I'm happy to say, still look upon the quota thing not in a narrow, protectionist sense, but in the Jewish sense that Jews need kind of an open society, based on quality and merit, rather than the fact that any given program would take X number of jobs away from us. If it were narrow self-interest that motivated us, we couldn't be for better education, nor for college training programs, because anytime you do something to open up opportunities for more groups, blacks and so on, that obviously must mean at some point down the line, Jews will have more competition, therefore there may be fewer Jews in teaching or in law or something else. That obviously is not our position."

All of the issues that had been broiling between Jews and blacks in the 1960s came to a head in 1971, in the donnybrook over a public housing project being built in the Forest Hills section of Queens, New York. The particular area where workmen began digging is not the Forest Hills that many conjure up when they hear the name. This is decidedly not the Forest Hills one associates with the national tennis championships or with graceful, neatly clipped lawns. Instead, this part of Forest Hills is squeezed against the noisy, fumy Long Island Expressway, ringed by high-rise apartments and attached houses and schools already on double sessions and jammed subway platforms and second mortgage payers who often have to hold down second jobs driving cabs at night. And it is a section that is predominantly Jewish, the kind of Jews who have not been to Harvard or Dartmouth but who have just barely migrated out of the Bronx's Grand Concourse or Brownsville in hopes of finding a better life in Forest Hills, one not constantly disrupted by crime and the fear of violence. Into the center of this the city of New York had decided to locate three buildings, each twenty-four stories high, for approximately 2,600 public housing tenants.

Rabbi Siegel called Forest Hills "a classical case" of the failure of American liberals and liberalism. "Here was what everybody agreed was a terrible plan," he maintained, "from every point of view. The land was terribly overpriced. You had a huge number of people already there without adequate services. You would have had economic segregation. It would have stigmatized people. It was against the wishes of the community. . . . The masses of Jews understood it, all over the the city and all over the country. And what happens? The Anti-Defamation League and the American Jewish Congress voted resolutions in favor of the project. The American Jewish Committee fudged. One of them had a meeting at Grossinger's, of all places, in the midst of all this. You can't mention those names today in Forest Hills." Suddenly, the voice of "liberalism" had become the voice of treason.

No argument could salve the Jews of Forest Hills, even reminders that it had been very recently indeed that they had been kept out of many residential areas, even the thought that a child given a new opportunity through better teaching in Forest Hills might someday make a great medical discovery that might even save their lives.

"Forest Hills really shook up everything," said Rabbi Kelman, shaking his head. "Forest Hills voted for Lindsay. Lindsay assumed it was a place where he could safely deposit his housing project. After all, Jews are not given to violence: they wouldn't burn black homes. When the community rose up and said, 'NO,' all the establishment Jewish organizations responded by rebuking the bigotry of the Forest Hills people. It was well known that I was one of the first 'establishment' people who sided with the underclass Jews. They [the establishment people] couldn't understand. How could a relatively intelligent man like me, who had marched with Martin Luther King in Selma, who couldn't be called a bigot, do these things? It was very disturbing to them." Rabbis Kelman and Siegel quickly founded an organization, now called the Jewish Rights Council, to defend Jews in America who become embroiled in problems like the Forest Hills project. "Our little group," said Rabbi Kelman, "was organized in response to a mood, not that we think this is Weimar Germany, but that we think the Jewish public institutions ought to be as sensitive to Jewish issues in the United States as they are to Jewish issues overseas." "If blacks worry about blacks, Italians can worry about Italians, Greeks about Greeks, who's going to worry about the Jews?" asked the rabbi. "We should begin by asking what's good for the Jews. Certainly that's the first question. Of course that should not be the end of the questioning, but we should not be totally oblivious to Jewish interests. Many of the Jews in positions of leadership, who had taken stands in favor of scatter site public housing, were living in Scarsdale or Great Neck. What the hell, there are more Jews living in Forest Hills than in all of Budapest. So how did the 'establishment' react over Forest Hills? 'Oh, those bigoted Jews.' Those Jewish Pavlovian liberals treated me like an ogre. They had an almost hysterical reaction."

One of the more interesting reactions to Forest Hills has been that of the area's own congressman, Benjamin Rosenthal, a "liberal," a universalist and expert on consumer affairs whose constituents increasingly demand that he worry more about crime in their streets than about protecting America from overzealous business practices. The comments of Rosenthal about Forest Hills can be extended to embrace much of what has happened to change the political mood of many Jews in America. First, he says, the Jews of Forest Hills are not racists. "The vast majority of it," he said, "is fear of crime, fear of a disruption of their tranquillity and fear that an infringement of their turf will disrupt their lives. It is fear, fear of the poor—white poor, black poor. The poor have a tendency, simply because they are poor, to be surrounded by problems. They bring problems with them, and many of the people in Forest Hills moved there to get away from a neighborhood that had problems, and to try to survive their own personal problems. Then you ask them to be anointed with solving the ills of society, and many of them reject that. Most of them are willing to pay their dues to society, but they don't want to have to pay the dues of the guy who's living in Scarsdale or Great Neck. They're willing to pay what they deem to be a fair share. . . . It just happens to be an accident that they're living either in Forest Hills or New York City, where the dues may be far heavier than somewhere else.

"None of them will say to you that the blacks or the impoverished or the undernourished aren't entitled to food, housing and education and all these things. They will not use any of the racist arguments—'these people are dirty' or 'these people are not entitled to anything.' Some few will say, 'Why, we pulled *our*selves up by our bootstraps' and so forth. Many of them don't understand the highly complex argument that, in a technological society, the underprivileged are going to suffer worse. . . . When I meet with a lot of these people, they say to me, 'Look, don't bull us on anything. We moved out of Brownsville and Crown Heights. You, Rosenthal, and your ilk don't understand it' and I have to say to myself, 'Maybe the guy does know.' These people are no longer willing to accept my high-sounding rhetoric that crime is caused by the ills of society and if we eradicate the ills of society, we'll eliminate crime. . . . I'm sympathetic with people it doesn't go over with.

"My job is to look at society in the years ahead and the future. They see their role as tomorrow's shopping and this week's salary and getting their kids to school on time. Many people don't see beyond that and they reject long range views because they inhibit or interfere with what they're doing today. When I've spoken like this to some woman in Forest Hills whose daughter was just beaten up in a school, no argument of any kind can carry any bit of persuasion with her. Her daughter was just beaten up because she wouldn't give her twenty-three cents' lunch money to some black kid—and this does happen, and it is happening at Forest Hills High School and throughout the schools. . . . I'm still naive enough to think that much of it can be solved by money—money and programs and leadership. This sounds like liberal bull now. . . . I'm confused myself. What bothers me is that I'm in a leadership position and I'm confused as to what can make it. I know that giving up won't make it and I know that self-fulfilling prophecies of fear won't make it. That much I do know. The protectionists of Forest Hills think that what will make it is building a wall. They know that within that wall, at least in the immediate future, they can have a certain amount of peace and tranquillity and happiness. They're not concerned with the bigger picture that the cancer can spread and somehow breach the wall. Maybe for the ten-year period, they're right. Maybe. But a wall didn't work in 1400 and it won't work now."

Forest Hills, Rosenthal maintained, is not an illustration of the failure of liberalism, but of the failure of bureaucracy. "Bureaucracy," he said, "is not attuned to correcting injustice in a discreet fashion. The reason they went to twenty-four stories was because of bureaucracy, in other words, H.U.D. limitations [on cost per unit] and then they wiped out all the sociological motivation for scatter site housing. The motivation was to spread people out in an acceptable pattern, where they could become a homogeneous neighborhood. But once you go for this warehousing of the poor in a concrete ghetto you've violated all the sociological motivations that you've started out to comply with. Then you've got the other, existing community up in arms, so you've helped neither group. That's the classic example of bureaucracy gone awry when you're trying to correct a social injustice. Jews are entitled to be supersensitive. No other people in history can claim six million killed in one escapade and the Crusaders going through towns like Cologne and wiping out everybody and things like that. So there's considerable merit to their fear of being the weakest link in the social chain. In some cases, these folks see themselves as weaker than the black link. And the blacks, of course, see themselves as totally excluded from power and society. And blacks will say, 'The Jews have all the levers of power—finance, Hollywood, communications, newspapers, radio, everything—and so we're trying to press a little and they're all going hysterical. . . .'"

A large area of the hysteria is fear of crime, fear of disruption of their neighborhood, fear of losing what they have worked so hard for. Ben Wattenberg believes that such Jews are reacting not so much as Jews but "as upset urban Americans. . . . They're behaving more and more similarly to other Americans." Adam Walinsky added that "The crime problem is not just Jewish, but this is true of every group in every city. These are the people of the Democratic Party and, if you can't tell the people of your party that they're going to have safety in their homes, in their streets, that their children aren't going to be wasted by drugs, what *can* you tell them?"

But these Jews are not just like all Americans in their reaction to crime, in their reaction to the threat of neighborhood disruption. There is a sense of *déjà vu*, for disruption of neighborhoods was a part of the pogroms in Europe. Jews had a very special reaction to black riots in the '60s for the same reason. Because of a variety of factors, many of the businesses in black neighborhoods still are owned by Jews. "Liberals" like Patrick V. Murphy, then head of Washington, D.C.'s police force, ordered his men not to shoot at looters who ran amok in April of 1968, to value life over property. This same philosophy came from "liberals" like Cyrus Vance, President Johnson's emissary to local authorities in the Washington and Detroit riots, and from "liberal" John Lindsay in New York. To some Jews, the scenes bore eerie parallels with the pogroms, where mobs destroyed Jewish homes and businesses while police stood by and watched.

Further, Jews—more so than most Americans—live in and around big cities, where crime is most visible. They are painfully aware that "liberal" ideologues have been unable either to stem the rise of crime or, in some instances, even to discuss it in realistic terms. That "conservatives" have not stemmed it either is irrelevant to their thinking. What is relevant to many of the urban ethnics is that the alleged intellectuals of the "liberal" coalition have failed them, have moved to fancy neighborhoods and left in their wake only fancy phrases—and those who couldn't leave quite so easily. "The failure of the elites to understand the relevance of the law and order issue," Father Andrew Greeley, the ethnic specialist, has written, "has been a disastrous political and social mistake."

An interesting facet of the growing "conservatism" among some Jews is that their politics are coming into line with their religion. Judaism is, basically, a conservative religion. "There is a sense in which Jewish liberalism and radicalism in the public sphere has been combined with a conservatism in the social sphere," said Harvard sociologist Nathan Glazer. "For example, Jews might support easing up laws against pornography, but would not necessarily on a social level or a familial level approve of it. The Jew, I think, is going to vote less and less for 'liberal' candidates. . . . Their 'conservatism'—which means that 'We want a stable community in which outlandish things don't happen, in which our children aren't threatened, which is safe and has law and order' and so on—is being threatened by the politically 'liberal' views they have held all along and the politically 'liberal' leaders they have supported."

A move to the right would not be unprecedented, either in America or in the history of Jewry. In America, Jews in the old South were not "liberals," were not progressives. They rather easily managed to ignore Isaiah's call to "relieve the oppressed": many owned slaves and most went along with the idea of a slave-based economy. Not a single Jew has been identified among the abolitionists in Charleston, South Carolina, which had been home to the largest Jewish community in the United States at one time. The man regarded as the "brains of the Confederacy" was Judah P. Benjamin, a Jew. Almost a century later, after the Supreme Court's 1954 decision in *Brown* v. *Board of Education*, in which school segregation was ruled unconstitutional, many Jewish Southerners protested strongly. Some members of the American Jewish Committee who lived in the South pleaded with the committee to back off its active role in promoting civil rights.

Indeed, until 1848, the Jews of Europe were anything but progressive. They were the most conservative of all the disenfranchised members of European society. They lived in dread of democratic revolution: the streets, not the palaces, were their anathema—for the rabble, not the princes, were rock throwers and rioters. The Jews as the tradesmen and moneylenders paid off the czars and kings and princes and barons and popes to protect them from the peasants. Rabbi Gerson Cohen, new chancellor of the Jewish Theological Seminary, said that in feudal Europe, "The Jews always figured you could bargain with a king, you could bargain with a pope, you could bargain with an archbishop or a cardinal. You paid special taxes and you got therefore special protection. But how are you going to bargain with members of the guild? They don't want you." Historian Cohen said that the turning point for the Jews came when the czars and kings wouldn't bargain any longer. Instead, they started initiating the Jew-baiting themselves, plunging all of Jewry into terror. That terror accelerated and then culminated in the insanity of the death camps of the 1940s.

The question implied by all of this is whether the swing to the right of the more ethnic Jews of the later 1960s represents a return to that feudal ideology. No, says analyst Wattenberg. "It is not fair to say this is a conservative trend," he insisted. "In terms of the traditional definitions of conservative, this is not a conservative shift. The people want federal action. They want mass transportation. They want medical care. They want all the things that used to be called 'liberal.' But they are not prepared to pay the price of social disruption for it. If you want to put a word to that phenomenon, fine, but that word, in my judgment, ought not to be conservative. It's liberalizing on the economic and programmatic issues and it's conservative or hard line or tough on the social issues."

Only a decade ago, to have termed America's Jews—any of them—"hard line or tough on the social issues" would have seemed inconceivable. Perhaps only turbulence of the magnitude of the 1960s in America could have produced a transformation of such magnitude.

XI

Year of the Jew
1972

NINETEEN SEVENTY-TWO was the year of the Jew in American politics. Never before had the Jewish community been subjected to such a barrage of campaign propaganda. Never before had a major American political party publicly surfaced a "Jewish strategy," as the Republican Party did in 1972. Never before had the national media devoted so much air time and ink to such a small percentage of the electorate; by comparison, one could hardly find mention of Catholic voters—to mention just one other group—who outnumber Jewish voters by about eight to one.

Until relatively recently, there has been little public discussion or examination of Jewish affairs in the United

Howard Metzenbaum of Ohio *(right)*, shown campaigning for the Senate in 1970, felt anti-Semitism helped cause his defeat then. Although appointed to the Senate to fill a vacancy, Metzenbaum lost again in 1974. *(Photo by Wide World Photos)*

Milton Shapp, first Jewish governor of Pennslyvania, had been warned that a Jew would have an enormous handicap running in a state with so few Jews. And Shapp did face anti-Semitism. *(Photo by Stanley Olds/Scranton Tribune)*

Sam Massell said that when he was a child "I heard over and over again that a Jewish person couldn't be elected to city-wide office in Atlanta. Maybe that was because no Jewish person had ever run." Defying "ghetto mentality," Massell did run and became mayor. *(Photo by United Press International)*

January 1974: It was a historic occasion when Abraham David
Beame was sworn in as the first Jewish mayor of New York, which
has been called "the biggest Jewish city in the world." Until recently, some say, no Jew could be elected mayor of New York
because the Irish-dominated political machines kept good Jews out.
(Photo by The New York Times)

The best-known Jewish fund raiser in American politics is Max Fisher of Detroit, shown here with his friend George Romney. Not coincidentally, Fisher is also the pre-eminent leader of Jewish communal and charitable agencies in America, for —as he says — political and charitable contributions are very closely related among Jews. *(Photo by Wide World Photos)*

Typical of the Jewish "staffer" who plans campaign strategies for others but does not himself seek office is Ben J. Wattenberg. Wattenberg began his professional political career by writing speeches for President Johnson, whose staff had been impressed with *This U.S.A.*, an influential book Wattenberg wrote with Richard Scammon. Wattenberg, now a chief strategist for Senator Henry Jackson's presidential bid, is author of the recently published *The Real America*. *(Photo by Wally McNamee/Newsweek)*

States. The mass media, in particular, had been most reluctant to dip below the surface, as if the media managers were reluctant to impinge on hypersensitive memories or be accused of anti-Semitism, or both. A bit of this was present, as was the practical matter that rarely did a television network or newspaper employ the kind of specialist who could, with delicacy, report with any depth into any religious group in the country. In the case of Jewish affairs, clearly the easier course seemed to let it lie. The first break-throughs in this type of reporting came in the late 1960s, when anti-Semitic rhetoric again became commonplace among certain groups. Some black activists, no longer dissuaded by reminders of six million Jews slain by the Nazis, started directing their rhetoric at Jewish landlords and businessmen who operated in the black slums. The two decades and more since the liberation of Auschwitz, some blacks felt, had been time enough for mourning. It was time again to debate the role of the Jew in society, time to ventilate what was on the minds of some blacks. "To hold an attitude of antagonism or distrust toward Jews, was bred in us from childhood; it was not merely prejudice, it was part of our cultural heritage," the black author Richard Wright wrote. The black rhetoric shook many Jews, not so much in itself, but because the response by non-Jewish whites seemed to condone it; the white majority, they felt, did not refute the renaissance of anti-Semitic talk harshly enough. These same kinds of Jews were upset by the media's attention to Jews in the 1972 election: they believed they detected tinges of anti-Semitism in the eagerness to chronicle a story that had somehow gone uncovered for so many years.

In some cases, they may have been right. But in the main, the television and newspaper reporters were only doing what comes naturally to them—reporting a story

that had lain untouched for too long. And campaign drives
to capture the votes of Catholics, blacks, Italians, and
other groups were, by then, old news. But in their haste
to report the manipulations by the Committee for the
Re-Election of the President and by McGovern for President, Inc., the "scoop"-conscious reporters overlooked
much of what had transpired among America's Jews since
the previous presidential election. They were, for the
most part, still viewing Jews as that distinctive group,
well off and white, that for some reason had cast 81 per
cent of its 1968 vote for Humphrey—and not as a group
feeling itself increasingly isolated, threatened, and frustrated, as its old political alliances were crumbling. And
so when the ballots had all been counted after the November 7, 1972, election, all misread what had happened to
the Jewish vote. Pundit after pundit described 1972 as a
landmark election for the Jews. The Jews' nearly half-
century affinity for the Democratic Party, they said, had
been breached. Just look, they said: Nixon doubled his
Jewish vote over 1968. Jews, they said, were voting less
as Jews and more as Americans, since the four-year difference in their vote was much like that of other Americans.

The facts are that, despite problems with affirmative
action plans-cum-quotas, the "urban fever zone," scatter
site housing, community control of schools, an inept
Democratic presidential campaign—despite all these
things, and more—the Jewish bloc* vote did hold up.
Even more, according to the prestigious Center for Political Studies of the University of Michigan, Jews voted

---

* By bloc, the writer does not intend to imply that Jews hark to
any individual's or organization's orders; rather, individual members of
the group tend to react similarly to issues and events and their in-
common reaction tends to show up in election returns.

more heavily Democratic than they might have been expected to, on the basis of past voting. Poll figures show that McGovern received stronger support from Jews than did Stevenson in 1952 and 1956, when no one had suggested any kind of landmark break-throughs. In 1972, of every three Jews who cast presidential ballots, two voted against the Republican, Nixon. Further, Jewish voting for Democratic candidates for Congress was 85 per cent, as strong—if not stronger—than it had ever been.

Not that the Republicans' highly publicized effort to woo Jews away from the Democrats was worthless or unsuccessful. What most media analysts failed to see was that the GOP's Jewish strategy was designed with one specific goal: to move enough Jews in New York State from the Democratic line to the Republican line to swing that one state's crucial forty-one electoral votes over to Nixon. Four years earlier, he had lost New York by only 370,538 votes. In that year, Jews in that state had voted more than seven to one against Nixon. Because of the size of the Jewish vote in New York (somewhere between 16 and 20 per cent of the voters), even cutting that winning margin in half would, exclusive of shifts of votes among any other groups, throw New York to the Republicans. As events subsequently have shown, the Republicans in 1972 were notably overthorough in most things. In the case of New York's Jewish voters, they exceeded their goal, cutting the margin to 1.56 Democratic votes for every Republican vote (61 per cent to 39 per cent) or 2.4 to 1 (70 per cent to 29 per cent) depending on which poll one prefers to believe. The Republicans' Jewish strategy, then, was successful.

Part of that success came in cutting down the number of Jews who cast votes at all. Any Jewish voters who could be kept at home, or any regular Democratic contributors who could be kept from writing checks, would aid the Republicans' cause. Studies by the American Jewish Committee showed that the normally astronomic voting regularity of some Jewish areas dropped markedly. In Brighton Beach in Brooklyn, for instance, 23 per cent of the registered voters stayed home, up from 8 per cent four years earlier. In Sheepshead Bay, 21 per cent stayed home, doubling the 1968 percentage. A paralysis factor obviously was at work: the Republican campaign against the "McGovernites" that was directed at such areas—areas where fear of crime, fear of blacks, fear of the world were highest—paid off. While those voters could not bring themselves to vote for their traditional enemy, Nixon, they would not vote for the new politics and McGovern, either.

In terms of Jews, if the Democrats had nominated either Humphrey or Henry Jackson, the Republicans would have had great difficulty in moving any Jews to the Republican line—in Humphrey's case because of his long association with and sensitivity to Jews and Jewish causes and, in Jackson's, because of his obsession with the support of Israel and of Soviet Jewry. The campaign these two waged to keep the nomination from McGovern did much of the Republicans' work for them. Long after McGovern had won the nomination, literature produced by Humphrey's campaign was still being circulated, in both California and New York, by the GOP. An example was this column from *The California Jewish Voice* of May 26, 1972, by Stephen E. Steindel, which was used by the Republicans in October:

. . . For the first year of his presidential campaign, George McGovern either ignored or seemingly baited the Jewish vote.

Ed Muskie would visit Jerusalem to show his solidarity

with the Jewish state. George McGovern would speak of the possibility of internationalizing Jerusalem.

Henry Jackson would introduce legislation to provide Israel with military sales credits. George McGovern would declare his belief that Israel should not be allowed to use American planes (as she did in June 1967) over Arab territory.

Hubert Humphrey would, as honorary chairman of the committee to Rescue Syrian Jewry, raise, as he has since 1949, the plight of Jews in Arab lands. George McGovern would take to the floor of the United States Senate to demand that Israel pay reparations to the Palestinians.

And thus the primary season unfolded with expected results in the Jewish community. In Florida and Wisconsin the McGovern forces did not even place a single advertisement in a Jewish newspaper. In New York State they ran delegate selection caucuses on the second night of Passover. In Ohio George McGovern was the only candidate to let Soviet Jewry Solidarity Day go by without a word on it.

But then came California, and the polls showing McGovern grievously behind in the Jewish community. Suddenly the Jewish vote became important to George McGovern. Suddenly there were ringing statements about Israel and Soviet Jewry. Suddenly there was blanket canvassing of Jewish neighborhoods and McGovern literature in Yiddish.

On the one hand we are pleased to see Senator McGovern's support, belated as it may be, for Israel and the plight of Soviet Jewry. On the other hand we are astonished by the candidate's gall in suddenly asking us to forget what he said and did before the California primary.

All of this leaves us with one sobering thought. What would George McGovern be saying to the voters of California if there were 750,000 citizens of Arab rather than Jewish descent in this state?

The weakness of the McGovern camp's response to such attacks points to the most salient feature of Jewish voting behavior in 1972: Jews, on principle, would support the "progressive" candidate against Nixon despite McGovern's ineptitude and despite the unprecedented vigor of the Republicans' effort.

An example of the McGovern campaign's deficiencies with regard to Jews came immediately after the Democratic convention, which had been held early to give the candidate an early start on his campaign. But the early start never materialized. Instead, McGovern and his followers retreated to the hills of South Dakota to plan. While they were there mishandling the Eagleton affair, Nixon fund raisers had instantly moved to lure Humphrey's big financial backers, most of whom were Jews, to the Nixon cause. The Humphrey contributors already were angry over their friend's having lost. The Republicans impressed upon them the "radicalism" of McGovern's candidacy and the threat his candidacy implied to Jews, especially to affluent ones. Their goal was to convince these men to switch or, at the least, to get them to sit on their checkbooks. Perhaps better than the McGovernites, Nixon's men knew how heavily Democrats have depended on Jews' money to finance their presidential campaigns.

The McGovernites not only failed to counteract this pressure, to all appearances they were unaware it was being applied. From the outset, then, the Democrats were in a hole. Soon after the convention, Californians like Gene Wyman, Walter Shorenstein, and Ben Swig had decided to sit out the presidential race. Some others became Republican contributors, men who had been principal donors to Humphrey in the 1972 primaries and in 1968. These included Eugene Klein, Louis Boyar, John Factor, and Danny Schwartz in California, and Meshulam Riklis, Charles Bassine, and Arthur Cohen in New York.

While the Republicans' Jewish strategy was dictated by Max Fisher, Nixon's wealthy Detroit friend, and Fisher's hand-picked administrator, lawyer Lawrence Goldberg (who had started work on the Jews in October of 1971), the McGovern campaign eventually hired a pleasant but ineffective political amateur named Richard Cohen, whose experience had been as public relations director for the American Jewish Congress, a job he reassumed after the campaign. This meant that McGovern's campaign director, the already overburdened Frank Mankiewicz, was forced to handle many of the campaign's duties with regard to Jews. At one point, Mankiewicz had to break away from his duties and go to Grossinger's, a Jewish spa in the Catskills, to speak to a Jewish audience to counter the Nixon man who had been there first—Jacques Torczyner, former president of the Zionist Organization of America, an old friend of Nixon but certainly no major figure in the GOP campaign.

As his principal weapon, Mankiewicz relied almost totally on Jews' historic enmity for Nixon and for the Republican Party (Goldberg figures that only 8 per cent of the nation's Jews are registered as Republicans). For example, when Adam Walinsky wrote a perceptive, twenty-four-page memorandum to McGovern, trying to explain the complexities of the Jewish attitudes in New York and other big cities, and suggesting how McGovern might avoid being considered a "Prairie John Lindsay," McGovern supposedly was never shown the memo, and Mankiewicz shrugged it off as the rantings of a right winger. Mankiewicz, a former employee of the anti-Defamation League of B'nai B'rith, kept insisting that a Jew who called himself a Jew could never vote for Nixon.

During the campaign he explained his view: "Nixon

is the guy who kept referring to Helen Douglas' husband's real name as Hesselberg. He's the guy who's taken the Jew off the Supreme Court. They're not going to vote for Richard Nixon . . . . The whole problem with this administration [is] it's *judenrein* [what Hitler made his occupied territories—Jewless]. That's one of its real troubles. There isn't a bit of *taam* [Yiddish for soul, spirit] in the whole operation. Look at John Mitchell, for Chrissake, and Kleindienst, and Nixon himself, and Albanalp, or whatever his name is, and Rebozo and all these people. Nixon never had a Jewish friend in his life. I'll bet you Murray Chotiner never came upstairs. And the convention? A *judenrein* convention. There's no Jew in this Cabinet, there's no Jew in the Subcabinet, there's no Jew on the White House staff except for Henry Kissinger, and he doesn't work at it. These are court Jews. They don't have anything to do. Leonard Garment? Nixon sends him to the Interlochen Music Festival, maybe, as his representative. Leonard Garment is the Kaganovich of the Nixon administration. You remember when the Bolsheviks took power in Russia? They all took new names, like, 'This is Comrade Molotov, formerly, I don't know, Vassalevsky,' or whatever the hell it is, they all took Communist names. 'This is Comrade Stalin, formerly Yogoslevsky,' or whatever it is, and 'This is Comrade Kaganovich, formerly Jew bastard.' I don't know what Leonard Garment and Billy Safire think of themselves as Jews, but they must hate themselves every night."

The voters, however, never got Mankiewicz's arguments, which might have convinced many Jews to vote against Nixon—or at least to not vote for him. While the Republicans manned dozens of store-front offices in ethnic

Jewish areas, while their banks of telephone and mail campaigners extolled Nixon as a peacemaker and warned of the dangers of a McGovern presidency, the Democrats were largely, and strangely, silent. While the Republicans busily distorted McGovern's positions vis-à-vis Israel's security, hardly any response came from the Democrats. It was as if McGovern were sitting quietly, providing the widest and most easily hittable target, while in fact it was the President who was doing almost no campaigning. So, at a time when McGovern was making frequent trips, always on the defensive, to boards of rabbis to make his positions perfectly clear, his staff had failed to provide the necessary backup materials; in particular, it still had not put out a fact book that tried to set the records straight on McGovern's and Nixon's positions about Israel. At one point, McGovern for President, Inc., decided that the GOP concentration on Israel would backfire as being too patently condescending and obvious, so did nothing to counter the Republicans. Fisher and Goldberg, gloating, quietly took their operation "underground" for a while to let its impact penetrate, then came back with it stronger than ever not long before the election when the McGovern staff had no time to combat it properly.

To those religious and ethnic Jews who devote a great deal of their psychic energy to worrying over Israel—and these are fewer than one sometimes thinks—McGovern never ever really had much of a chance, anyway. The reason he had won the Democratic nomination, after all, was by route of his opposition to an American involvement in a faraway land. As Rabbi Seymour Siegel put it, "McGovern's whole world view didn't fit into his protestations about the defense of Israel. How can you cut down on all these military things, ease the tensions of the Cold War, 'Come Home, America,' and all this, and then say, 'This is the one place in the world we're ready to send in the fleet.' I didn't doubt his sincerity, but I just didn't see how we could rely on it." "McGovern," said Goldberg, "saw the world through Vietnam glasses."

Nixon's public relations and advance men, meanwhile, had pulled off a remarkable transformation of his image, in regard to the issue of Israel's security. Nixon as vice president had backed Dwight Eisenhower's forcing the Israelis to pull back from Arab territories in 1956. Nixon as president had delayed and delayed sending arms to Israel, causing much alarm to the Israelis and their American supporters. Now he was Israel's greatest friend. Yitzhak Rabin, the war hero and Israel's ambassador to the United States, traveled Washington's cocktail party circuit openly plumping for Nixon's re-election. He repeated the message publicly in a radio interview in Jerusalem: Israelis "must see to it that we express our gratitude to those who have done something for Israel and not just spoken on behalf of Israel." The blatant support of Nixon was interpreted by some Jews here as Israel's declaration of independence from American Jewry.

Even though McGovern's House and Senate record in supporting aid for Israel was consistent, he could not shake the image that he was a vacillator. John P. Roche quoted one leading Jewish Democrat as saying, "In a real crisis [in Israel], McGovern would send in a battalion of the Peace Corps, and then go to the U.N. wearing a yarmulke." He did nothing to assuage Jews' fears by keeping Richard G. Stearns in a key campaign position after it was revealed that Stearns, as vice president of the National Student Association five years before, had signed an anti-

Israel advertisement that had appeared in Washington. Over the objections of California Jews involved in the campaign, Stearns was kept as assistant campaign director in charge of the Western states. Such bumblings led some Republicans to ask aloud just whom McGovern might turn to for advice if elected.

For many American Jews who care little about the fate of Israel, the McGovern campaign was not much more alluring. Many were bothered by an aura, which one New York intellectual described in this way: "McGovern reminded the Jew of America's only home-grown anti-Semites, the Populists. And when he went around inveighing against 'the interests,' somehow it sounded to Jews as if he were talking about them. Their concern about McGovern was the simple notion that Jews have figured in the life of big-city goyim, they haven't figured in the life of small-town South Dakota, and so he had no personal stake in Jews. In short, they saw McGovern simply as a dumb goy—a Midwestern preacher—and he gave them bad vibes." Similarly, Morris B. Abram, former president of the American Jewish Committee and of Brandeis University, who voted for McGovern, felt that McGovern came through "as a rural-smalltown man, well-meaning but lacking in a cosmopolitan view; honest but moralistic. He is not in the citified mold of Al Smith or Roosevelt. . . . Some do McGovern the supposed favor of labeling him a Populist. But many recall this as the tradition of Tom Watson and William Jennings Bryan, two politicians whose images do not evoke favorable responses among Jews."

"McGovern's problem," said financing expert Herbert Alexander, was that he had led "a kind of sheltered life. He came from South Dakota and he hadn't been in the middle of liberal politics the way Hubert Humphrey had for twenty years and the way Lyndon Johnson was as Majority Leader and then as President. And McGovern was slow in learning. . . . Somehow, he was not in the swing of the A.D.A. or some of these organizations where you would've had the kind of upbringing that Humphrey had in this community."

An example of McGovern's lacking sensitivity to Jews' concerns was in the area of quotas. En route to the nomination, McGovern was repeatedly promising proportional representation to women, to blacks, to Chicanos, which Jews translated to quotas that would reduce Jewish representation. Before the convention, Hyman Bookbinder, Washington representative of the American Jewish Committee, sent the following letter to Mankiewicz:

. . . There's an aspect of this I must alert you to before more damage is done. The columnists have not yet caught onto this, and I hope they never do. I believe that in the long pull, even more important than the Israel issue, key Jews will be turned off on George because of his statements on appointments to the Administration on a proportional population basis. . . .

In using the language that he has, the Senator is pledged to a policy of rigid quotas along ethnic, racial and religious lines which is actually the antithesis of non-discrimination. It's difficult enough living with excesses in "affirmative action" plans that affect school teachers and civil service workers. But when George elevates this to the highest levels of government, the concern is very great. It has already turned off some very good associates of mine, and I know the alarm is spreading fast. Many of them see this issue as a fundamental threat to the kind of society we have and cherish.

. . . If George doesn't find better ways of discussing this subject, his problems will only increase.

I do *not* suggest that the Senator stop making commitments to the minority groups about appointments, but his language should be modified. . . .

McGovern, nonetheless, continued making his proportional representation pledges, even after the convention and even after he and Nixon sent letters to the American Jewish Committee specifying their objections to quotas. Nixon, meanwhile, was making no pledges similar to McGovern's. Jews all over the nation were talking about McGovern and quotas, despite the fact that it was Nixon's Department of Health, Education and Welfare that had been pressing affirmative action plans in every area that it could.

Nixon's agents also were busy portraying him as the kind of calm, thoughtful internationalist that Jewish voters could admire. Some Jews talked about how much sensitivity about Jews Nixon had picked up during his five years of practicing law in New York between losing the California gubernatorial race in 1962 and running for President again in 1968.

The "sensitivity" included the careful leaking of a false, last-minute report to the presidents of major Jewish organizations that the President had resolved the problem of the education tax that Russia had been imposing on Jewish emigrants. On two occasions, Kissinger was assigned to brief Jewish financial men on the situation in the Middle East. Fisher, chairman of the Concerned Citizens for the Re-Election of President Nixon [a mildly phrased euphemism for Jews for Nixon], calmly said in a New York press conference that "it has been a heart-warming experience to have the support of so many thousands of people in the Jewish community, most of whom are Democrats or independents, who see this election as a time when principle must be placed above party and when the candidates must be looked at from the basis of what is good for America during the next four years. The basic thrust of the campaign has been educational in nature and we have made an honest and effective effort to present the record of the President on all the issues which might be of concern to the Jewish community during this election. A campaign is an opportunity for each citizen to become better informed before he exercises his vote. We feel we have played a constructive role in helping to achieve this. . . ."

When the ballots had been cast, the returns showed that the trend that had been seen in some municipal elections was carrying into the presidential vote. The more ethnic Jews had tended more to the Republican or "conservative" candidate. The bulk of the Jews, the middle-class suburbanites and the well educated, voted—as they always have—against the "conservative" and against the Republican and against Nixon. Nixon's vote was a landslide of major proportion. He had won the votes of 69 per cent of all the white voters in America. He had won the votes of three of every four persons who live in high socioeconomic areas. But only about a third of the Jews, who are white and most of whom live in high socioeconomic areas, voted for him.

"The fact about this election that everybody missed, said the rabbi-historian Arthur Hertzberg, "is that the Jews were still more than 60 per cent for McGovern, and in a very bad year. They were the only white group still for him, which says not how reactionary Jews have become, but says something about the 'liberal' tradition of Jews. The Jews still were the only white 'have' group voting for him, despite the fact that he intimated, in an unguarded moment, that he'd give in with a quota system, that Jews didn't trust what he said about Israel, and so forth. They were willing to swallow even him. I see it as a continuing stability for the kind of Jewish politics that I stand for."

In September of 1973, the Center for Political Studies announced what it thought to be a remarkable study of the 1972 presidential election. For years, the Center emphasized that American voters and political parties, unlike their European counterparts, were pragmatic and unprogrammatic. The two-party system could survive in such an ethos because so little separated them, ideologically. But 1972, the Center said, can "most appropriately be labeled as an ideological election." To political professionals of this country, the Center's analysis was stunning. For generations, David Broder wrote at the time:

. . . the Democrats and Republicans have survived as shifting coalitions of local, regional, economic, ethnic and racial interest groups, held together by shared loyalties to party labels and party heroes, and a shared lust for office.

Whatever else they have been called, no one has ever accused American politicians, parties or voters of being ideologues.

Except for the Jews. They have never viewed the parties as ideological alikes, as their votes over the last half century have shown. The 1972 election was an ideological election for the Jews, just as was 1968's, 1964's, 1960's, 1956's, and every election in which Jews have voted since their enfranchisement. They voted, as they always have, against the right. Some perceived the McGovernites to be that right. Most, as usual, decided it was Richard Nixon.

XII

To run or not to run
Elected officials

"WHEN I LEFT THE WHITE HOUSE," said Myer Feldman, presidential counsel under John F. Kennedy, "I was asked if I would be interested in running for district attorney in Philadelphia, and from there they pictured mayor and then the Senate seat. . . ." Feldman, a lawyer in Washington, said he declined because he felt a Jew couldn't win a state-wide election in Pennsylvania, that a Jew has "an enormous handicap running for public office in a state where you have such a small minority of Jews. . . . I've talked to enough Jews to know that you have a tough job if you're Jewish and running for office.

You have the same problem that a Catholic used to have but doesn't anymore. I say it not because I've taken any polls or surveys. It's part of the conventional wisdom of politics. It would have to be a very unusual race and an unusual constituency to have a Jew run for public office. In New York it's an advantage but, outside of New York, it's a disadvantage. That's the conventional wisdom. . . . When I talk to people or have friends who are not Jewish talk to people . . . somehow or another they identify the Jew who's on the ticket while they wouldn't identify the Protestant or the Catholic. And very often the word 'Jew' to a non-Jew, even if they say they're not bigoted and they're not going to be swayed by it, they have a kind of reaction that seems to favor the other party. I know Howard [Metzenbaum] and what he's told me about it.; I know [Milton] Shapp and what he's told me about it. . . ."

"I have never had a real problem that I can think of in all the years over the fact that I was Jewish in politics," said Marvin Mandel, the Governor of Maryland. Maryland has about the same percentage of Jewish population (4.68) as does Pennsylvania (3.97).

In August of 1971, a sample of 867 voters in Maryland was surveyed as to impressions of seventeen politicians, ranging from President Nixon to newly elected Maryland Senator J. Glenn Beall. Some of the more interesting results of that survey included the fact that John V. Lindsay apparently mishandled a splendid opportunity to win the Democratic nomination for president and that George McGovern, on the other hand, came from nowhere to get it. Perhaps most interesting, however, is that the highest rating of all those tested was for the only Jew on the list:

	FAV.	UNF.	NO OPINION	NOT HEARD OF	NET RATING
Agnew	47.6	39.6	12.4	.4	8.0
Bayh	14.0	14.0	37.2	34.8	.0
Beall	48.8	17.1	27.4	6.7	31.7
Humphrey	51.1	33.8	14.7	.4	17.3
Jackson	14.6	6.4	31.0	48.0	8.2
Kennedy	51.0	35.0	13.9	.1	16.0
Lee	30.9	15.7	41.7	11.7	15.2
Lindsay	56.7	15.7	23.0	4.6	41.0
Mandel	71.6	13.5	14.2	.7	58.1
Mathias	54.2	12.9	25.9	7.0	41.3
McCarthy	38.1	30.9	26.5	4.5	7.2
McCloskey	14.2	11.4	42.7	31.7	2.8
McGovern	29.4	25.0	35.4	10.2	4.4
Mills	20.4	12.3	33.5	33.8	8.1
Muskie	53.6	22.3	21.6	2.5	31.3
Nixon	51.2	36.7	11.8	.3	14.5
Wallace	21.2	62.3	14.2	2.3	—41.1

The statistics tend to indicate an almost remarkable constituent acceptance of a sitting governor, especially in the turbulence of 1971.

A year earlier, this undapper, unsophisticated, short (5 feet 6) man, the graduate of an old-line, big-city political machine, had more than doubled the vote of his Republican opponent, winning a majority in every political subdivision of his state save one, which he lost by 93 votes.

"Marvin Mandel is a special case," said Frank Licht (he pronounces it Leech), the only Jew to have been elected Governor of Rhode Island. "Marvin Mandel is, and I respect him for this, a real pro as far as politics is concerned. He was Speaker of that House. It might be more difficult to become Speaker of the House than to become governor of the state, because that's where you really have to have political know-how, to become leader of a body like that. . . . He had, within his hands, a great deal of the machinery in Maryland, which I think is to his credit. . . . The infighting can sometimes be tougher than when you get out to the general people. . . ."

"When I was Speaker of the House," said Mandel, "whenever it'd be Yom Kippur, if the Legislature was scheduled to meet, they knew I wasn't going to be there. I think the Legislature itself had a great deal more respect because they knew that I was Jewish and I didn't for one minute ever deny it or hide it or in any way evade it or try to use it in any way."

Despite the involvement of Jews in politics in America, few have actually been elected to public office. In the history of the United States, one hundred and eight men and women of Jewish descent have been elected to high office—governor, senator or congressman:

—Eleven Jews have been elected governors.

—Of the 9,433 persons elected to the House of Representatives, 92 have been Jews, or 0.98 per cent.

—Of the 1,684 senators, twelve have been Jews, or 0.7 per cent.*

In sum, while Jews have become an ever larger and

---

* Adding the totals will not yield the number 108; six of the Jews served in more than one of the offices. Also, one of the twelve senators, Howard Metzenbaum, was appointed to fill a vacancy.

more potent force on the periphery of politics, few have
held or, for that matter, will hold primary positions of
power. The causes, as in most matters concerning Jews'
political behavior, are subject to a kaleidoscopic veil of
misinterpretation, stereotypy, mythology, and even para-
noia. One notion is that Jews can't be elected to high
office in an area where Jews are a small minority. Another
persistent one is that Jews make bad politicians. Yet
another is that, for a Jew to be a viable candidate, he has
to appear statesmanlike and dignified—i.e., "un-Jewish."
At the same time, another is that a Jew has to exhibit
pride in his Jewishness and appear to respect and adhere
to Judaic ritual, lest the gentile world think he's ashamed
of being a Jew.

Each of the stereotypes, however, has had highly visible
refutations. Governor Milton Shapp has proved that a
Jew can get elected to high office in Myer Feldman's
Pennsylvania, and Representative Edward Mezvinsky won
election in 1972 in an Iowa district with almost no Jews.
Governor Marvin Mandel shows that a Jew has not had
to hold himself aloof and dignified. Senator Ernest Gruening, who never paid the slightest attention to things
Jewish, proved that Jews do not have to appear to respect
the ritual. City bosses like Abe Ruef of San Francisco,
Jack Pollack of Baltimore, and Jake Arvey of Chicago
disprove the impression that Jews make poor politicians.

However, because so many Jews believe the myths,
they have become integral to American Jewish folklore.
The result is fewer Jews' seeking public offices, proportionately, than members of other ethnic, sociological, economic, and professional groups. Told often enough that
they make better "staff" people than they do "out-fronters,"

after a while Jews begin to believe it. Further, stereotypes in general are not made of whole cloth. Each does have some small basis in truth, which has been inflated into an entire ethos.

The strongest of the impressions is that non-Jewish citizens won't vote for Jews. In some times and in some places and with some candidates, that is true. Twenty-four states have never elected a Jew to high office. Those twenty-four include Ohio, long a center of Jewish communal life, and which has 158,560 Jewish residents.* The others are Arkansas, Delaware, Georgia, Hawaii, Kansas, Kentucky, Maine, Minnesota, Mississippi, Montana, Nebraska, Nevada, New Hampshire, North Carolina, North Dakota, Oklahoma, South Carolina, South Dakota, Tennessee, Vermont, Virginia, Washington, and Wyoming. That listing might give the impression that Southern, Western, and mountain states won't elect Jews. Yet the first Democratic governor of Idaho, Moses Alexander, was a Jew. Joseph Simon was Oregon's United States senator from 1897 to 1903 and later served as mayor of Portland. He was a Jew. So was Richard Neuberger, senator from 1955 until his death in 1960. The new young mayor of Portland, Neil Goldschmidt, is a Jew. David Levy Yulee, the first senator from Florida, was a Jew. So was David Kaufman, one of Texas' first two U.S. representatives.

Anti-Semitism does exist, as well as antipapism, antiunionism, anticapitalism, racism. But because of their history, Jews tend to react more sensitively to anti-Jewish attitudes than members of other groups might react to biases against them. Those few Jews who have stepped

* Howard Metzenbaum hoped to change that in 1974.

out front have had to be thick-skinned, able to look beyond the parochialism of bigotry.

Governor Shapp said that when he first sought the governorship in 1966, Pennsylvania's Republicans conducted "a vicious anti-Semitic campaign in certain parts of the state. On some of their stamps—the ones on the backs of their letters—it would say, 'Don't put Shapp-iro in Harrisburg.'" Shapp changed his name from Shapiro during the Depression because of anti-Semitism. As a salesman, he found that the name Shapiro would not get him beyond the front doors of the places he was supposed to sell to. The name Shapp did. The Milton Shapp who changed his name, however, came out of World War II a different person than the one who went in:

"I went up into Austria at the time we were liberating the victims of the concentration camps outside of Linz, and I spent a lot of time there. . . . I saw then that you can't run away from bigotry, you have to hit it head on. I came back from World War II an entirely different person than when I went over and I resolved when I came back that I was going to fight bigotry any time I found it. And I've done this."

When Shapp's campaign consultant, Joseph Napolitan, found anti-Semitism affecting Shapp's chances in some areas of Pennsylvania—particularly in the Pennsylvania Dutch country—he ordered a special documentary film from Charles Guggenheim. As Napolitan has written:

Shapp, in a voice-over film, was telling about how his army unit released prisoners from a Nazi concentration camp in Austria at the close of World War II. As he was talking, the camera showed rather gruesome concentration-camp footage: bodies of victims heaped like cordwood, a hollow-eyed man with broomstick legs being carried out on a stretcher, a rabbi praying. Powerful stuff! . . . There was, perhaps still is, a fair amount of anti-Semitism in some sections of Pennsylvania, and we knew this was hurting Shapp. We capitalized on this liability to show what it meant to be a Jew during World War II. I'm sure a lot of people voted for Milton Shapp after seeing that film *because* he is Jewish, a sort of reverse discrimination.

The half-hour film was shown repeatedly as election day neared.

"When I lost," said Shapp, "I wanted to determine what impact anti-Semitism really had in the campaign, and so we made a rather detailed analysis of the voting records around the state . . . We could find places where anti-Semitism had been at work. But I would say, at the very worst, anti-Semitism cost me maybe 50,000 votes. And I lost by 240,000. Remember, in 1966, no Democrat running for U.S. senator or for governor from a major state won except for one—Connally in Texas, and the Connally situation is very different. The Democrats were swept down the drain by anti-L.B.J. feeling. That was a much greater factor. For example, in Northampton County, I trailed the ticket by some 8,000 votes. But the top vote-getter was Jeanette Reibman, a Jewish woman who ran for [state] senate and won. You can't therefore say that I trailed the ticket by 8,000 votes because of anti-Semitism because, if I had, why did Jeanette Reibman win? How did she lead the ticket when everybody knows she's Jewish? . . . I think that people today vote more for the person, more for the principles the candidate stands for, than they think about his religion or his ethnic bacground. In 1971, we elected our first Negro to the [state] Supreme Court. If anybody had said that a black could win a state-wide election in Pennsylvania two years before that, everyone would have said they were nuts."

"Political anti-Semitism just isn't a factor," insisted David Brody, Washington representative of the Anti-Defamation League of B'nai B'rith. "I can't recall any instances of anti-Semitism in the 1970 congressional elections when there were five Jewish candidates for the senate. And take Oregon, where Portland just elected a Jewish mayor, where the Neubergers were from, and there are about 9,000 Jews out of two million people there. Or take Connecticut, where Ribicoff has been the outstanding vote-getter. You've got 100,000 Jews out of three million, so that being Jewish is plainly not a handicap. Ed Brooke is another example. The black population of Massachusetts is about 2 per cent. In other words, you get a good candidate, people will vote for him regardless of his religion or race."

Interestingly, voters in some states—Rhode Island and Connecticut, in particular—sometimes seem to tend to vote for a Jew because he is Jewish, as if to prove they are not bigoted. Thus one had the anomaly in Rhode Island in 1970 where the traditionally Democratic state elected a Republican Jew, Richard Israel, as attorney general at the same time as it elected a Democratic Jew, Frank Licht, as governor. Although neither of those men had to appeal to voters to be "good Americans" and vote on the basis of merit, Abe Ribicoff used such an appeal in his first race for state-wide office in 1954. His "American Dream" speech was broadcast throughout Connecticut, by television, and is credited with having proved the decisive factor in his having been the only Democrat elected by Connecticut voters that year. In that speech, Ribicoff summoned up voters' patriotic sentiment by talking about how he, the son of impoverished immigrants who spoke no English, could believe the American Dream and actually aspire to the highest office in the state of Connecticut. Wasn't it wonderful that a man like an Abe Ribicoff—a Jew—could hope for such a thing in such a wonderful land?

In an interview in 1973, Ribicoff said that, "My feeling is that there's no such thing as a 100 per cent bigot. I think that every evil person or every good person has a little bit of both in them. I think if they can find the type of person they can respect, they won't hesitate to vote for a Jew and say, 'That just proves I'm not anti-Semitic, I have nothing against Jews.' I have had people tell me that they would be riding on the commuter train to New York and there would be guys sitting in back of them who they knew were out-and-out anti-Semitic who would be saying, 'That guy, Ribicoff, he's a hell of a guy, I'm gonna cut my ticket for him.' But why should I look a gift horse in the mouth? I've never gone into self-analysis or voter-analysis about why does a certain type of person who generally doesn't have much to do with Jews vote for Abe Ribicoff. If you look at the '54 election, when I was the only Democrat elected and the rest of the Democratic ticket, from lieutenant governor on down, went down, you will find in the towns in Litchfield and Fairfield counties in which there might've been one or two Jews or no Jews, I was running fifty to sixty votes ahead of everybody, ahead of the ticket, and that's what elected me. And there was no question in anybody's mind that I was Jewish."

There was no question in anybody's mind in Ohio, either, that Howard Metzenbaum was Jewish. When asked whether anti-Semitism played any role in his 1970 senate loss to Robert Taft, he replied:

"It just so happens that I carry only one clipping in my pocket," he said as he pulled it out. "November 7, 1970, from the Cleveland *Plain Dealer,* and it says, 'Latent religious bigotry held down Howard M. Metzenbaum's vote in Cuyahoga County in Tuesday's election. While such things cannot be deduced until the Board of Elections has completed its tabulations, it appears that the reason Metzenbaum did not fare better was latent religious bigotry.' I would also tell you that it's no secret that I feel the religious issue only injected itself into the campaign in the last five to ten days, that it was not there previously, that the *Plain-Dealer,* itself, I felt, played out of all context a story on this subject or, rather, played up a statement of Taft's in denying anti-Semitism. They played it up to the point where it injected the religious issue into the campaign. And then on 'Face the Nation,' the very last question asked me was, 'Do you feel that the fact that you're the first Jewish candidate to run for high public office in Ohio will be a factor in this election?' I denied that it would be and said that I felt Kennedy had put such matters to rest and Taft then spoke at some length on the subject. But I think the denial of the issue is equally tantamount to raising the issue in that, that which wasn't an issue was then a factor. In other words, it wasn't on people's minds and I don't accuse my opponent of having injected the issue but, the fact is, the more he spoke about it not being an issue, the more it was an issue. . . .

"It's my strong feeling, however, that it was to the great credit of the people of Ohio that both in the primary as well as the general election, they took a man by the

name of Metzenbaum, some of whom knew my religion
and some did not, and made it possible for me to defeat
a man whose name was far better known than mine,
certainly a national hero [he was talking here of his
primary opponent, astronaut John Glenn] and made it
possible for me to come within 1 percentage point of a
man whose name unquestionably is the strongest name
in Republican politics in Ohio's history. I don't look at
the negatives about it and when I feel it was a factor,
I'm so grateful for the tremendous amount of support,
that it wasn't a matter of getting smashed or clobbered.
I think a John Jones would have had trouble with Robert
Taft. In sum, I think the factor of being Jewish cost me
some votes. But I think the fact that a Jewish millionaire,
who was also called a Communist during the campaign
and whose name was not that well known, who I think
was well-qualified for the job, was able to run against,
unquestionably, two of the biggest names Ohio ever had
—one the all-American hero and the other the most
respected name in the political history of Ohio—and
take the first one and lose the second one by less than a
percentage point is a pretty good indicator to me that
Jews *can* make it in politics."

The role of the press's calling undue attention to a
Jewish background is not unique to the case of Metzenbaum, nor, for that matter, to Jews. The media, particularly newspapers, often identify blacks as blacks when
race has nothing to do with the news item in question.
Blacks often submit that this is a product of racism, and
Jews, when it happens to them, suggest that it is the
product of anti-Semitism. The Baltimore *Sun*, for instance, regularly pointed out that Mandel was the first
Jew to be governor of Maryland in articles where that

fact was wholly ungermane. Sometimes the Sunpapers got even more blatant, as in *The Evening Sun*'s coverage of a fund-raising dinner for Mandel at Baltimore's Civic Center in October of 1969.

"It was the largest affair ever held in Maryland," said Irv Kovens, Maryland's most successful fund raiser and an old friend of Mandel. "The thing raised $600,000. Our ever-loving Sunpapers didn't play up how big it was. They played up two truckloads of kosher food being delivered to the thing. So they started letting them know early [that Mandel was Jewish]. It was the commonest damn thing they could ever do. . . . At the time, this caterer, probably as far back as I can remember—for presidential elections, governors, senators and anything —had always done the catering and never gotten that kind of story before." Kovens said that in the 1970 Mandel campaign, "we never knew what we'd run into or what would happen on election day [in terms of anti-Semitism, particularly in black neighborhoods of Baltimore] and we put on an all-out campaign. We started early, because we felt we'd need more money than was ever needed before, and we probably spent twice as much as had ever been spent in a gubernatorial election before that." The feared anti-Semitism never materialized either on the Eastern Shore or in black neighborhoods, where Mandel won 88 per cent of the vote.

Consultant Napolitan, a non-Jew who has handled a number of Jewish candidates (Mandel, Shapp, Licht, New York's Howard Samuels, Iowa's Edward Mezvinsky) insisted that, no matter what Jews' impressions about anti-Semitism are, he has never been able to find it playing a decisive role in a contest. "We ask questions, sometimes in a survey, something like this: 'I'm going to read you a list of personal characteristics. Please tell me which of these would cause you to vote against an otherwise qualified candidate—he's black, he's Catholic, he's Jewish, he's A.F.L.-C.I.O., etc.' Sometimes you get 2, 3 or 4 per cent of people who won't vote for a candidate because he's Jewish, but I've never had any particular problem working with any Jewish candidates, or any anti-Semitic feelings."

Over the years, the Gallup Organization has tested American opinion on bigotry as it applies to voting attitudes. In 1937, Gallup asked a sample of the population, "Would you vote for a Jew for President who was well qualified for the position?" Less than half of those questioned—49 per cent—said they would. Over the years, that question has been asked repeatedly (phrased slightly differently for the last fifteen years—now it is, "If your party nominated a generally well-qualified man for President who happened to be a Jew, would you vote for him?"), and now only 8 per cent say they would refuse to vote for a well-qualified Jew. But most politicians, especially Jewish ones, distrust surveys like that. It is one thing to cast a vote for or against a person in the privacy of a booth and quite another to tell an interviewer that you are a bigot—which is what pollsters in effect ask people to do when testing for anti-Semitism or racism or anti-Catholicism or antianything else.

Most Jewish politicians say there is some anti-Semitism around, although not as much as some Jews believe there is. What is more important, they say, is that party leaders, those who have a large say in who gets the nomination, tend to be more anti-Semitic than the electorate, or at least believe anti-Semitism to be a larger political fact of life than it is. To win election, of course, one has to get nominated first. Party leaders, who move in the middle and upper levels of society, would be more likely to sense anti-Semitism's prevalence than is the fact. Surveys have indicated repeatedly that anti-Semitism flourishes more among the well to do and better educated than it does among the general population. A factor in this, Morton Keller has noted, is because "that is where a large proportion of the Jews themselves now dwell." John Dean, in studying Jews in medium-sized American communities, found the party leader factor to be one of the reasons accounting for the extremely few Jews in elected offices, pointing out that anti-Semitism

probably operates not so much at the level of the electorate as it does in the party councils that select the candidates or determine political appointments.

Rhode Island's Licht said that the party leader syndrome affected his career. "I was on the bench," he said, referring to his service on Rhode Island's Superior Court, "and some people were going to offer me the candidacy of the Democratic Party [for governor]. I think it was either '64 or '66. A small group of men got together. . . . I was not there, I heard about it later. The Democratic Party was in trouble and the Republicans had a very popular governor, John Chafee, and somebody said, 'You know, Frank Licht would be a good man to run against John Chafee.' One fellow said, 'Yeah, but how could he do it? He's Jewish.' The conversation ended. In 1968, I like to tell the story that they drafted me. That isn't true. Nobody wanted the nomination in '68." Frank Licht did. He grabbed it, ran with it, and upset Chafee.

"You will find in some places in some times the politicians will say what the people think," said Licht, "and since they have the machinery in their hands to determine who may get a nomination, you'll never be able to disprove it. And so you can simply say, 'Well, the guy's Jewish and he can't get elected governor.'"

Licht said the party bosses never were correct about Jews' electability, pointing to the difference in Shapp's fate in Pennsylvania between 1966 and 1970: "Milton Shapp won the nomination but he was not a 'regular.' He was frozen outside. He had to do it the hard way. His problem really was that he didn't help his chances in an election by what he had to do to get the nomination. . . . When he came around the second time, it was then easier. The whole trouble with getting the nomination was not involved . . . and Milton Shapp went in."

The same thing happened to Jacob Javits in 1953 in New York. He wanted the Republican nomination for mayor, but the party bosses turned him down. Javits, ever the politician, told this writer that the rejection was "not so much because I was Jewish, but because I was liberal." But Alex Rose, who was not running for anything in 1974, said he warned Javits at the time not to ask the leaders, just go ahead and announce his candidacy. Instead, said Rose, Javits "went to see Tom Curran, who was the Republican leader of this county. Tom Curran did not want him to run. Tom Curran was a conservative. Tom Curran had no real love for liberals. He had a lot less love for Jewish liberals. I got along with him more or less but I have no doubt in my mind he had no affection for our kind of people. By the way, Cardinal Spellman—and it's no secret—had no special love for Jewish liberals, either, and Cardinal Spellman dominated the political scene here for a very long time."

The practical result of all this is an impression among many American Jews that a Jew just can't make it in politics and in effect they censor themselves out of even trying for elective office. Many Jews interviewed by this writer insisted that "Jews make better staff people." Such limited expectations in politics—and in professional life—are common among upper-middle-class Jews. Studies of law students, for example, have found that Jewish students, even if they do better in school than their non-Jewish classmates, expect to do less well in terms of getting jobs after they graduate. Arthur I. Goldberg in one such study found that only 17 per cent of the Jewish law students who wanted careers in large law firms felt they could be hired, compared with 35 per cent of the Catholics and 46 per cent of the Protestants. Goldberg said that the Jews in the top echelons of their class at better law schools who aspired to careers in "elite" law firms are those "most sensitive to possible career inhibition due to religion." The syndrome of reduced expectations extends back into high school, as indicated in the Council on Education-American Jewish Committee 1969 survey. The Council asked students how many other colleges they had applied to:

NUMBER OF APPLICATIONS TO OTHER COLLEGES	JEWISH STUDENTS	NON-JEWISH STUDENTS
None	22.1	52.3
One	16.5	20.3
Two	18.1	13.8
Three	15.9	7.5
Four	12.6	3.4
Five	8.1	1.5
Six	6.7	1.1

Non-Jewish students, by a large margin, were far more confident than the Jews that they would be admitted to the college of their choice. (The figures here may be slightly misleading in that Jewish students tend to apply to the more elite, harder-to-get-into colleges, which means that they might apply to more schools to insure admittance somewhere. But even with that possible skew to the result, the lower level of confidence of the Jews stands all the more striking in that the Jews applied to college with better grades than the non-Jews: 19.6 per cent of the Jews compiled high school averages of A, compared with 12.3 per cent of the non-Jews.)

The important thing about this ghetto mentality, this feeling of limited expectations and vulnerability, is not just that the feeling might be justified. In terms of Jews' seeking public office, it is not so much a matter of whether or not discrimination exists but that many Jews believe it does. As Atlanta's Sam Massell said, "When I was a kid, I heard over and over again that a Jewish person couldn't be elected to city-wide office in Atlanta. Maybe that was because no Jewish person had ever run for city-wide office in Atlanta." Massell, who is Jewish, did. He was elected vice mayor in 1961, re-elected in 1965, and elected mayor, accumulating one of the largest votes in the city's history, in 1969. He was defeated by a black in a turbulent—some said it was racist—bid for re-election in 1973.

During that 1969 campaign, a cross was burned on Massell's front lawn. But he was already accustomed to that kind of experience. In the 1950s, he had bought a cabin in a small town outside Atlanta, on the border between Fulton and Cherokee counties. A group of the townspeople asked him to run for one of the five seats on the town council, to which he agreed. One day he was in the county clerk's office writing down all the residents' names and addresses for a campaign mailing and "a clerk came up to me and said, 'They've found out you're Jewish.' I said, 'Well, I thought everybody knew I was Jewish.' So I went right to them [the men who had invited him to run] and asked them and, sure enough, they weren't bashful about it. They were now my adversaries. So I went ahead and ran." Massell came in sixth. But when one of the five winners had to move to Florida, "the remaining four elected me to the seat. Right after that, my cabin was burned to the ground, mysteriously. It was a real grass roots experience."

Such experiences tend to keep most Jews out of such exposed positions. The most common reason cited is, "Who needs it?" Paul Jacobs described the syndrome in his *Is Curly Jewish?* in telling how his parents taught him not to encourage *rishis*. This meant not to make too much noise, lest one incur "the potential wrath of the Christian world:"

The world was conceived of as something like a potentially evil sleeping giant who, if awakened by a loud noise, might, and probably would, turn on the disturber of his peace and do him harm.

One finds ghetto mentality varying from city to city among Jews. In Cincinnati, Jews are quite active politically. Three Jews have been mayors of Cincinnati and have, more or less, reacted stoically to the problems of being a Jew in that kind of an exposed position. Murray Seasongood, who was the reformer mayor between 1926 and 1930, told this writer almost nonchalantly that "of course there's anti-Semitism. I think it's been prevalent for over two thousand years and apparently it will be for two thousand more years."

But a hundred miles up the road in Columbus, the "don't rock the boat" mentality is endemic in the Jewish community. The Jews of Columbus were upset when a fellow Jew, attorney Robert Shamansky, tried to unseat ultra-"conservative" Representative Samuel L. Devine in 1966. As one of Shamansky's campaign aides said, "They were just too comfortable. They didn't want anybody spoiling it for them." Shamansky himself first warned that "maybe they just didn't like me," but then said, "It's the old bit of quiet, don't say anything. In the '30s, when Hitler was out after the Jews, you didn't want to call attention to yourself." But things have changed in the last few years. Shamansky said that, "I went to Israel recently and I brought my nephew, who goes to the Columbus Academy—a posh, private school—a yarmulke from Jerusalem. He took it to school to show the kids. Well, my generation didn't do that, we weren't pushing the bit of being Jewish."

No way exists to plumb the depth of political self-effacement among Jews, short of mass psychoanalysis. But one suspects that ghetto mentality is widespread, since Jews have certainly shown an overwhelming interest in participating in all other aspects of politics in America. It also shows up in how Jews react to Jewish candidates whom they perceive as reflecting unfavorably on Jews as a whole. They have tended to vote against Jews who act out unfavorable stereotypes of Jews or who they feel are not "classy" enough to be respectable examples for Jews. Some Jews of Manhattan's West Side voted against Bella Abzug for Congress because they thought she was too much a "pushy Jew" (some articulated this notion in so many words; others would just say, "There's something about her I don't like"). Many Jews in the Bronx voted against James Scheuer (a congressman from a predominantly Jewish district in the Bronx) when he was running against the patrician Jonathan Bingham and started making, they felt, too much noise about being Jewish. Many Jews voted against Abe Beame for mayor in 1965 because they felt he lacked proper "stature," when what they really meant was that if they were going to have a Jewish mayor, they wanted one who was not 5 feet 1 inch tall. Beame likely would have done poorly in 1973, too, had not 6-foot 3-inch John Lindsay given tall mayors a bad image. About half of the Jews could turn around in 1969, however, and cast votes for Mario Procaccino—unclassy, inarticulate, and an Italo-American—who did not reflect on the Jews as a group.

Many Jews strongly believed that ghetto mentality caused Ribicoff to reject McGovern's offer to be his vice presidential running mate. Javits heard—or surmised—that this played a part in Ribicoff's reasoning, and told him of his being upset; after all, Javits himself had tried hard to get the Republican vice presidential nomination in 1968. "I hope no Jew in this country will ever refrain from seeking a public office on the ground that, if he does it badly or wrong, it will hurt the Jewish people," said Javits. "This, I think, is the worst possible thing that any person of the Jewish faith can do to our republic. If you haven't the guts and the conviction in your own faith and its beauty and its truth and its power to decide that one any other way but saying, 'I'll go and I'll take the responsibility and that's my duty under God,' then that's the worst fault of any, in my judgment."

Ribicoff had a different story. "I just didn't want to

be vice-president," he said. "I'm happy being a senator. I don't want to be number two. Further, I don't want to be president, and if a man says he wants to be vice president, that means he wants to be president." Ribicoff denied vigorously any suggestion that he said no three times to McGovern because his candidacy might reflect in any way upon Jewry. "That argument was the same out that was used against me in '54 when I was running for governor," he said. "I think we're beyond that in America, I really do. In '54, when this argument was used to me, I laughed and would say, 'Did you ever stop and think I might do so well it might be a credit to the people?' So then in '58, after I'd done a good job as governor, those same people were saying, 'Oh, Abe Ribicoff, he brings so much credit to us.'"

Jews react very sensitively, indeed, when one of theirs is out front. They watch every move of the out-fronter to see if he will do anything to reflect unfavorably on them. And what might be termed group anguish occurs if the Jewish out-fronter does do something the Jews feel is wrong. An example came in 1973 in Maryland, when Marvin Mandel announced he was planning to divorce his Jewish wife of thirty-two years to marry a non-Jewish divorcee (who later converted to Judaism). Mandel seemed unconcerned, however, that Maryland's Jewish voters would desert him when it came to election day again. Of course he knew before making the announcement that Maryland's Jewish voters regarded him extremely favorably, even more favorably than others. One piece of that 1971 survey showed that his support from Jews far exceeded an already high level of support from others:

	CATHOLICS	JEWS	PROTESTANTS
Mandel is a good gov.	19.3	50.7	17.3
Better than I thought	39.0	37.3	33.8
Tries but hasn't ability	5.3	3.9	7.3
Thot he would be better	6.6	1.5	7.7
Not impressed with him	18.4	—	17.1
No opinion	11.4	7.5	16.8

Maryland is a rarity, however, in terms of numbers of high elected officials who have been Jews. Mandel's 1970 running mate, Louis L. Goldstein, has been elected state comptroller four times. Four Maryland congressmen have been Jews—Harry B. Wolf (1907–9), Daniel Ellison (1943–45), Isidor Rayner (1887–89 and 1891–95), and Samuel N. Friedel (1953–71). Rayner later went on to become United States Senator from 1905 to 1912. Only three states have elected more Jewish congressmen: Illinois (five), Pennsylvania (ten), and, of course, New York (fifty-three).

In the rest of the country, Jewish office-holding is hit-and-miss, probably a reflection more of the values inside the Jewish communities than of non-Jewish society. "I think the Jews themselves are not too prone to run for public office or to seek political careers," noted Javits. "With a person of the Jewish faith, the idealism in terms of a political career is more than the 'making it.' I really think that may be a line of distinction: to 'make it' in terms of position, authority, et cetera, a Jew would more likely seek his way in business, or in the professions, or even in the non-profit organizations."

Indeed, Jews who have distinguished themselves in private careers often consider politics—or at least politics at a relatively low level—to be beneath their status. Martin

Feldman, general counsel of Louisiana's Republican Party, cited that reason when he turned away his party's entreaties in 1972 for him to seek the congressional seat made vacant by the death of Hale Boggs. "I turned them down not because I was afraid a Jew couldn't run," said Feldman. "Frankly, Jews have fared well in New Orleans. But I just didn't want to be a congressman, and I wouldn't be surprised if that isn't an attitude that doesn't exist among many Jews. It's not that I feel safer in the background, although I've always been identified with the background. I just didn't want to be a freshman congressman. . . . I would not have had any hesitation running for Congress as a Jew if I thought I could get a shot at a Senate seat under the right circumstances. In fact, I wanted to run when Ellender died, but the timing was bad."

Many Jews worry about their image, how they look to non-Jews, especially, and they like the fit of the image of the Jew as a prosperous businessman or prestigious specialty doctor or no-nonsense lawyer. They often have a difficult time picturing themselves as local politicians or even as a freshman congressman.

Image is an important factor in the sparsity of Jews in elective offices. Running for office in America is, in effect, the epitome of pushiness. Many Jews who would be viable candidates find it hard to have to act out the stereotype that most worries them—that Jews are too aggressive, too self-promoting. And, to be elected in America, one has to be aggressive and self-promoting. As a result, most Jewish politicans tread an extremely delicate line, balancing the art of politics with what they feel is a proper appearance of dignity. Ribicoff said that Jewish candidates "have a certain combination of personality and characteristics so that people will accept you, up above what they believe the stereotype to be." Ribicoff sees dignity as very, very important. "I've always been dignified," he said. "I've been accused of being aloof. I am what I am. I don't try to be anything but myself. I think I'm approachable, but I'm not a backslapper, a hail fellow well met. I think I'm dignified, and I don't sit around the bars, either. I think my dignity is an asset for me. It's a statesmanlike cast, you've got stature, they respect your dignity and solidity, I think that's a plus. If you weren't that way, you wouldn't make it. I never sat down and figured out that I could only get elected because I'm dignified. I think that the sense of dignity is what people respect in you."

Javits has been known to call columnists to complain when he isn't credited in print when he has been involved in a legislative action. But when queried as to whether that wasn't being a bit pushy, Javits bridled: "Pushiness is a very bad word as far as I'm concerned," he said. "I think indignation and a genuine insistence because it's in the public service is why I do this. I'm not doing this for myself. If I'm given the right attributes and the right recognition, it's a powerful weapon for my state and the people of my state and the causes for which I struggle. There's nothing *in personam* about it. I have all the cachet and all the honors that any one human being is entitled to have. But in the cause in which I fight, I can be very aggressive. I don't call that pushy at all, because it's not to get my wife invited to the opera ball. I couldn't care less. It's the determination to build up the necessary support for the things which I'm fighting for, which I consider to be important. Finally, if I were inhibited because I'm Jewish, I have no business being senator from New York. I represent eighteen and a half million people, of whom, at the most, three million are Jewish. And for the other fifteen million who are not Jewish, they expect me to conduct myself as if I were the WASPiest WASP or the most thorough Catholic or whatever would represent the utmost in dignity and self confidence about what I have to do for them. So I can't be inhibited. I'm not cat-footing around because I'm Jewish. If I were, then I should represent some Jewish state, not the state of New York."

One of Javits' ways of maintaining his sense of dignity has been his seriousness. He pointed out that unlike many politicians, he has never sprinkled his speeches with jokes. "I don't know how to tell jokes when I speak," he said, "and it's unnecessary to tell jokes when you speak. . . . It's not for me. It's just not my style. I don't pretend to be the life of the party. . . . That very seriousness is, I think, my greatest social asset."

In a sense, what Javits was saying is that Jews intent on making it tend to be the antithesis of the image of the successful American politician, the man of the people. Nathan Glazer, the historian, put it this way: "I've always had a rather crude theory, that I think Jews make very poor candidates for elected leadership. They don't have certain kinds of social skills, added to the ability to project and star. I mean they make better staff members. I think it's a social-psychological thing. I mean, why are so many Irishmen running for office and there are so few Irish voting, as a group? The Irish talk better, they project themselves better, they get on better with voters and so on. I think even that very successful Jews very often are rather abrasive types or not really good natural politicians. Now Ribicoff is, Lehman was. But (in general)

I don't think Jews are very affable in a way a politician should be—to project sincerity and the interest in the people they're talking to and so on."

Indeed, the Irish were equipped differently than the Jews to be politicians. William V. Shannon has written that they "had passed a threshold of political conscious-ness that later immigrants from southern Italy, Poland or the Balkans had not reached." The Irish eagerly sought out careers as politicians, enjoying, as Edward Levine has written, "the tempestuousness and color of campaigns and the struggle for position and patronage." Jews, on the other hand, were wary of such activities, and dreaded being considered aggressive politicians, having to promote themselves in the way that politicians must. Morris Abram noticed it in his campaign for Congress in Atlanta in 1954, when he was upset at seeing his picture and name on billboards. "I did it, but I hated it," he said.

Rabbi Seymour Siegel even found it antibiblical. He was asked to run for the state assembly from his West Side New York district and "I told them I wouldn't get the [nominating] petitions signed. They'd have to do it. I wouldn't go door-to-door. I don't know how to do that. I wasn't raised that way. It's imposing yourself on your neighbors. Humility, that's one of the three pillars of religion. It's right there in *Micah*—love justice, do right-eousness and walk humbly with your God."

Milton Shapp perceived that hesitation in himself fre-quently: "At first I found it very embarrassing to go out and try to get a petition. When I first decided to run for office, it was embarrassing, and I found it easier to work behind the scene and have others do it for me. I was very shy, bashful about going out. Well, I shouldn't use either shy or bashful, because I'm not either, but I

found it difficult to go out and face a crowd and ask for
their support. And the first public speech I made, an-
nouncing my candidacy in early January of 1966, that
was the most difficult speech I ever made, because it
was the first time that I got up and lauded myself—
'I can do this, I can do that, I want to do this' and so on.
. . . When I walk down the street, I know people will
recognize me and I still hesitate sometimes to walk up
and shake their hands. It's the same feeling. I never
know whether people want me to or not. I know that
some people want me to, because I can see them moving
toward me specifically, but I never know whether they
want me to. I don't want to be pushy on them, even for
my own position. And so putting out petitions, putting
out all kinds of stuff of this sort is a very straining, very
difficult thing. That barrier was a tough one, but I'm
over the barrier on making speeches. I can go out and
make speeches and talk on the record of the administration. I do this quite often. But to impose upon somebody else is still a difficult thing. The most interesting
thing I've observed in my own self is to see my name or
my picture in the newspapers, as I do so often, and I
become a third person. . . . To a certain extent, there's
a detachment as if it's another person. It's a very strange
thing."

What Shapp described, of course, is not unique to Jews.
The late Robert Kennedy used to say that he found the
aggressiveness required of him to ask contributors for
money to be the hardest single facet of politics for him.
But the difference between a non-Jew's having to act
aggressively and a Jew's having to do so is marked; the
gentile, obviously, cannot then be labeled a pushy Jew.

From all indications, Jews' reluctance to stand out in

public roles is more prevalent in the South than in other areas of the country. Up to and just after the Civil War, a number of Jews were prominent in Southern politics. David Levy Yulee was the first man to represent Florida in the Senate. In Louisiana, Judah P. Benjamin was elected to the Senate in 1852 as a Whig and again in 1858 as a Democrat. His cousin, Henry M. Hyams, was elected Louisiana's lieutenant governor, and another Jew, Dr. Edwin Warren Moise, was elected speaker of the legislature and later became attorney general. In 1878, Benjamin Franklin Jonas, another Jew, was elected senator.

But from 1908, when Louisiana's Adolph Meyer left Congress, until the swearing-in of Florida's William Lehman as a Congressman in January of 1973, no Jew was elected to high office in the South. A few have served in state offices. Solomon Blatt, for instance, was speaker of South Carolina's House for thirty-four years, beginning in 1939. Two of the seven elected cabinet members in Florida in 1974—Robert L. Shevin, the attorney general, and Richard Stone, the secretary of state—are Jews. But these men are the exceptions. The Jews of the South have, over the years, tended to become "honorary white Protestants" in what—in the past—have occasionally been rather hostile surroundings for them, and a more hospitable environment for the Ku Klux Klan. Thus Southern Jewry has tended to keep in its place. Morris Abram recalled his father's being absolutely appalled when Abram had the temerity to run for Congress in Georgia, and stopped making his regular weekly visits up to Atlanta to see his son.

Although Jews in the South have tended to be in the upper economic strata of their communities, they are well aware of their minority status. In most Southern states,

Jews make up tiny minorities of the populations (0.26 per cent in Alabama; 0.16 in Arkansas; 0.55 in Georgia; 0.33 in Kentucky; 0.44 in Louisiana; 0.19 in Mississippi; 0.20 in North Carolina; 0.30 in South Carolina; 0.44 in Tennessee; 0.87 in Virginia) and still face the little daily discriminations that Jews in the South more or less take for granted. Jews are still not considered good enough, for instance, to be members of the Boston, Louisiana, Pickwick, or Stratford clubs in New Orleans or the Louisville Country Club and River Valley Club in supposedly more Midwestern-oriented Louisville.

In the Northeast, through sheer numbers, Jews tend to feel differently about themselves. Not that anti-Semitism is nonexistent in the North. But Jews tend to reinforce other Jews to stand taller. A Jew who might attempt to blend in and vanish in Mobile, Alabama, can be very ethnic, indeed, in Crown Heights, Brooklyn, or Brookline, Massachusetts.

New York is a special case. Because New York is home to so many Jews, party leaders seek out Jews to balance tickets. But that still does not mean that Jews have any kind of hegemony over New York politics. Although they make up the single largest ethnoreligious bloc in New York City, where one of every five residents is Jewish, the Irish got there first. They and Italian Catholics have dominated the internal politics of the city and, while Cardinal Spellman was alive, politicians used to consider the real city hall to be his headquarters, at Fiftieth Street and Madison Avenue, and not the picturesque city hall building downtown.

One of the principal reasons that no Jew was elected to the mayoralty of New York until 1973, according to Alex Rose, was that the Irish-dominated political machines kept good Jews out, so that when it came time to put forward Jewish candidates, no "good" Jews were of sufficient standing in the party organization to nominate. This was true up until 1973, anyway, when a confluence of factors enabled Abraham David Beame to become New York's 104th mayor, and its first Jewish one:* Beame, a product of the Brooklyn political machine, persisted in his ambitions. His persistence, the turbulence of the changing times, and John V. Lindsay combined to make an elderly, old-time machine politician look attractive in 1973, especially when he was compared with the other candidates in the race.

"Professional politics does not always attract good Jews," said Alex Rose, boss of his own machine, "does not always attract good Italians, does not always attract good Irishmen. Machine politics attracts only the bad ones. If you'll examine the Irish politicians, they're not typical of the Irish people. If you'll examine the Italian politicians, you'll find they're not typical of the Italian people. You will find that, until the Jews became more pronounced in their progressive and liberal politics, up to, maybe, twenty-five years ago, the Jewish politicians were the same. . . . The first leading, important Jew who became prominent in political life [in New York] was Herbert Lehman and he came in as lieutenant governor. If he had to be nominated at first as governor, he'd have never got it. They gave him the lieutenant governorship be-

---

* Under technical rabbinic law, Fiorello La Guardia—whose mother was Jewish—would be considered New York's first Jewish mayor. The Yiddish-speaking La Guardia, however, regarded himself as Italian rather than Jewish and was perceived as an Italo-American by the electorate. Under this writer's definition, then, he is not the first Jewish mayor.

cause that was supposed to be an innocuous office; and that was supposed to gild the ticket; he was an outstanding Jew, a banker, a good name in the Jewish community. So they were going to exploit that name. They never intended to make him the powerful governor of New York State that he turned out to be. But even then, there was a big fight not to give him the lieutenant governorship. Roosevelt had to lay down the law."

The sleazy image of the machine politician may indeed have turned some Jews away from careers in politics. But some other Jews used the machines, and benefited from them, attaining the kind of congressional longevity that machines could help achieve. Adolph J. Sabath of the Chicago machine won twenty-three terms. Julius Kahn of San Francisco won twelve and his widow, Florence, added six on her own. In New York, Emanuel Celler won twenty-five terms, Sol Bloom won fourteen, and Samuel Dickstein twelve. But New York State has had but one Jewish governor (Lehman) and he and Javits have been the only two Jews to serve as New York senators. The general tenor of the limitations on a Jewish New York politician was expressed by Raymond Moley, when he was describing the late Sam Rosenman in his book *After Seven Years*, his version of the early years of F.D.R.'s presidency:

Sam had come up from the hurly-burly of New York City's district politics. Sam had been well educated and, by dint of hard work before, during, and after his service in the state legislature, had acquired an admirably detailed knowledge of state business. He was essentially an "inside" worker. Often brusque and tactless, this capable, conscientious man could obviously never look forward to the kind of political career

Al Smith or Bob Wagner had shaped out of the same be-
ginnings as his, and he had shrewdly cut his ambition to fit
his cloth.

In the folklore, the Jew appears to be a political bumbler
who cannot relate well to the common man, who is unable
somehow to negotiate between groups, cannot act as a
conciliator, lacks the discipline necessary for party order,
feels that the door-knocking minutiae of the effective machine are beneath him. To a degree, each of those things
is true. While an Irishman might delight in a day of hard
"ethnic" campaigning—from eating blintzes and donning
yarmulkes in Jewish neighborhoods to dancing the polka
in a Polish union hall or gobbling up chitterlings and
pizza and won-ton soup, all between 2 and 10 P.M.—the
Jew often will disdain such activities. Arthur J. Goldberg
is perhaps the most obvious of that breed: stiff, awkward,
unaffable. Goldberg acknowledged in an interview in 1973
that "I personally take a dim view of ethnic campaigning,
which probably proves that I am not a good politician since
all politicians engage in this type of campaign. I personally found it demeaning to engage in ethnic appeals."
Partly as a result of that kind of attitude—which is not
unique to Goldberg—he was soundly trounced by Nelson
Rockefeller in the 1970 New York gubernatorial race.

The belief of some Jews that they must adopt a cool,
WASPish posture extends to the fact that, as Milton Himmelfarb noted, "Jews tend to make poor male bonders."
Male bonding describes the attraction of males to males
in brotherhood that is supposed to descend from the primi-
tive hunting band, or from primate association. In Himmelfarb's words, "Jews may tend to be more unclubbable,
as the English would say." One ramification of this extends to the effectiveness of Jewish legislators. One route

to success in any legislative body lies in personal relationships with fellow members of the body. The characteristic
"unclubbability" of some Jews means that some of the
Jewish congressmen spend little time fraternizing with
other politicians in Washington. Further, since seven of
the twelve Jews in the Ninety-third House are New Yorkers, they spend as little of their time in Washington as
possible and as much time as possible in their home districts. In the jet age, often they end up as "Tuesday-to-
Thursday" congressmen, spending Friday through Monday in New York.

The Jewish congressmen-politicians would also tend to
be less affable than their fellows because Jews are inclined
to be far more ideological than non-Jews. To appear ideological can be damning in American politics, since the
American electorate distrusts ideology. Voters often will
cast ballots against a politician who appears too ideological
even if they agree with the ideology he or she espouses.
They want representatives whom they perceive as pragmatic, can-do, professional. More often than not, the Jewish politician who enters politics after "making it" in some
other profession is an ideologue or, at the least, a seeming
intellectual (which can be just as damning to some voters).

Given all these political tendencies about Jews, Marvin
Mandel is nevertheless the antithesis of many of them. He
is a strong male bonder, comes across to voters as a can-do
type of guy and not as an ideologue, he is far from a stiff
candidate—voters tend to call him "Marvin," not "Governor," when they encounter him on the street. (By contrast, when Goldberg was running for governor in New
York, he insisted that his aides call him "Mr. Justice.")
Puffing his way through half a pound of Cherry Blend
pipe tobacco every day, Mandel spends much of his time

mixing it up with the boys—reporters, legislators, state
committeemen, whomever. He is a mixer. As he said,
"There isn't a member of that Legislature that I don't
know by his first name and haven't had a drink with or
sat down with." He is a sports nut (many Jews disdain
sports) and when he missed his first Baltimore Colts game
in a dozen years, the players gave him the game ball.
Mandel loves hunting for bear in Alaska or for birds on
Maryland's Eastern Shore, most "un-Jewish" activities.*

Mandel is, first and last, a politician. When his predecessor as governor, Spiro T. Agnew, became Vice President in 1969, Mandel as Speaker of the House never was
seriously contested as the successor. The legislature voted
159 to 26 to make him the new governor. He collected all
the political chits he had earned over the years: "I was
always helping. They knew if they had a problem, they
could walk in the office and sit down and, if there was any
way of doing it, we'd help them. I used to fight some of
their battles for them when they couldn't fight them. . . ."

By virtue of his office, Mandel "heads" the Episcopal
Church in Maryland. The articles of incorporation of the
church, drawn up before the Revolutionary War, desig-
nated Maryland's governor as honorary Episcopal bishop
of the state. Mandel's handling of that indicates his club-
bable state of mind: "Right after I was elected, the minister
from St. Anne's Church sent me a letter and said, 'inas-
much as you're now the head of the Episcopal Church
and we're having a building program, we'd like to get a
contribution.' So I sent them fifty bucks and said, 'inas-
much as I'm head of the church, I'd like to come over

---

* Judaic law forbids hunting for sport and, as well, forbids causing
animals to suffer. Eating meat of animals killed by hunting also is
forbidden.

and conduct services some Sunday.' And he did. He invited me over and I conducted services with him. And every time now I go any place, if they have an Episcopal giving the benediction or anything, I always tell him, 'You do a good job, because you're working for me,' and they all have the greatest kick in the world out of it."

Mandel got into politics in 1951, when former Maryland Representative, then president of the city council, Samuel N. Friedel, asked him to run for the Democratic state central committee, which, at the time, Mandel didn't even know existed. As a graduate of the door-knocking school of politics, Mandel is a politician before he is a Jew. The concluding words of his inaugural speech of January 20, 1971, perhaps best sum up his philosophy: "To those who seek the simple convenience of labels and causes, I say: I am neither liberal nor conservative, I belong to no cults or cliques, I am not swayed by fad or fashion. I will do what must be done because I believe it is right. And I share the wisdom of Woodrow Wilson's observation that 'The ear of the leader must ring with the voices of the people.' I assure you, your voices will always be heard."

Mandel, who came into politics by way of a rare Jewish big-city machine, may be among the last of the breed, for the assimilation of Jews into non-Jewish society is having its political effect in reducing the number of Jews in Congress. As Jews leave their old neighborhoods—and Jews have "suburbanized" faster than any other group—they dissipate the bloc strength that had been the making earlier of an Adolph Sabath, a Julius Kahn, or a Marvin Mandel. "It's affected not only Jews but other white congressmen," said David Brody, Washington representative of the Anti-Defamation League. "Most notably you had this happen in

Michigan where, for example, Representative Thaddeus Machrowitz, who was Polish, finally left his seat—I think it was back in 1961—to take a judgeship because the district in Detroit was becoming black. I think John Conyers represents that district now. Now Pete Rodino has it in his district [Rodino, an Italo-American, represents Newark]. He won last time, but it's becoming a heavily black district. He'll probably have a real hard fight in 1974. The same thing happened to Sam Friedel when he lost to Parren Mitchell in Maryland. What's happened is that the blacks have gained a vote and the inner cities have become more and more black and they just exercise their demand to have a black representative. It hasn't been directed toward the Jew; it's been directed toward whoever the white incumbent has been."

Brody claims that increasing numbers of Jews have sought office in recent years, pointing to five candidates for various Senate seats in 1970, five candidates for Congress in 1972 in California alone. Yet none of those candidates was successful. In fact, the number of Jews in Congress has been falling rapidly. In the Ninety-first Congress, eighteen Jews served in the House. In the Ninety-third, the number was down to twelve (and had not Representative William Ryan died, allowing Bella Abzug a second chance, the Ninety-third would have had eleven).

Most Jews in politics and in the Jewish organizations do not seem to be worried by the declining number of Jews in Washington. Hyman Bookbinder, Washington representative of the American Jewish Committee, probably summarizes the attitude best when he says that "I do not think the measure of Jewish political effectiveness is to be measured by the number of elected officers. I don't consider this a do-all or be-all. If Jews sat down and decided to, they could get twenty-five to thirty congressmen elected, if that were deemed an important objective. That could be thought out and implemented. I would not participate in such a thing—it would not be appropriate—but it could be done. The only reason I can think of for doing that is that you might get a better quality of men elected to Congress."

ELECTED GOVERNORS OF JEWISH DESCENT

MICHAEL HAHN, Louisiana, 1864–65.

MOSES ALEXANDER, Idaho, 1915–19.

SIMON BAMBERGER, Utah, 1917–21.

ARTHUR SELIGMAN, New Mexico, 1931–33.

JULIUS MEIER, Oregon, 1931–35.

HENRY HORNER, Illinois, 1933–40.

HERBERT H. LEHMAN, New York, 1933–42.

ABRAHAM A. RIBICOFF, Connecticut, 1955–61.

FRANK LICHT, Rhode Island, 1969–73.

MARVIN MANDEL, Maryland, 1961–.

MILTON SHAPP, Pennsylvania, 1971–.

UNITED STATES SENATORS OF JEWISH DESCENT

DAVID LEVY YULEE, Florida, 1845–51 and 1855–61.

JUDAH PHILIP BENJAMIN, Louisiana, 1853–61.

BENJAMIN FRANKLIN JONAS, Louisiana, 1879–85.

JOSEPH SIMON, Oregon, 1897–1903.

ISIDOR RAYNER, Maryland, 1905–1912.

SIMON GUGGENHEIM, Colorado, 1907–13.

HERBERT H. LEHMAN, New York, 1949–57.

RICHARD LEWIS NEUBERGER, Oregon, 1955–60.

ERNEST GRUENING, Alaska, 1959–69.

JACOB K. JAVITS, New York, 1957–.

ABRAHAM A. RIBICOFF, Connecticut, 1963–.

HOWARD METZENBAUM, Ohio, 1974–.*

* Appointed to fill a vacancy in January 1974.

UNITED STATES CONGRESSMEN OF JEWISH DESCENT

BELLA S. ABZUG, New York, 1971–.

MARTIN CHARLES ANSORGE, New York, 1921–23.

ISAAC BACHARACH, New Jersey, 1915–37.

VICTOR LUITPOLD BERGER, Wisconsin, 1911–13 and 1923–29.

SOL BLOOM, New York, 1923–49.

JACOB AARON CANTOR, New York, 1913–15.

EMANUEL CELLER, New York, 1923–73.

EARL CHUDOFF, Pennsylvania, 1949–58.

WILLIAM MICHAEL CITRON, Connecticut, 1935–39.

WILLIAM WOLFE COHEN, New York, 1927–29.

IRWIN DELMORE DAVIDSON, New York, 1955–56.

SAMUEL DICKSTEIN, New York, 1923–45.

ISIDORE DOLLINGER, New York, 1949–59.

MORRIS MICHAEL EDELSTEIN, New York, 1940–41.

JOSHUA EILBERG, Pennsylvania, 1967–.

EDWIN EINSTEIN, New York, 1879–81.

HENRY ELLENBOGEN, Pennsylvania, 1933–38.

DANIEL ELLISON, Maryland, 1943–45.

MARTIN EMERICH, Illinois, 1903–05.

LEONARD FARBSTEIN, New York, 1957–71.

SIDNEY ASHER FINE, New York, 1951–56.

ISRAEL FREDERICK FISCHER, New York, 1895–99.

NATHAN FRANK, Missouri, 1889–91.

SAMUEL NATHANIEL FRIEDEL, Maryland, 1953–71.

JACOB H. GILBERT, New York, 1960–71.

BENJAMIN A. GILMAN, New York, 1973–.

BENJAMIN MARTIN GOLDER, Pennsylvania, 1925–33.

HENRY MAYER GOLDFOGLE, New York, 1901–15 and 1919–21.

JULIUS GOLDZIER, Illinois, 1893–95.

MICHAEL HAHN, Louisiana, 1862–63 and 1885–86.

SEYMOUR HALPERN, New York, 1959–73.

EMANUEL BERNARD HART, New York, 1841–53.
LOUIS BENJAMIN HELLER, New York, 1949–54.
ELIZABETH HOLTZMAN, New York, 1973–.
LESTER HOLTZMAN, New York, 1953–61.
JULIUS HOUSEMAN, Michigan, 1883–85.
LEO ISACSON, New York, 1948–49.
MEYER JACOBSTEIN, New York, 1923–29.
JACOB KOPPEL JAVITS, New York, 1947–54.
CHARLES SAMUEL JOELSON, New Jersey, 1961–69.
FLORENCE PRAG KAHN, California, 1925–37.
JULIUS KAHN, California, 1899–1903 and 1905–24.
DAVID SPANGLER KAUFMAN, Texas, 1846–51.
ARTHUR GEORGE KLEIN, New York, 1941–45 and 1946–56.
EDWARD IRVING KOCH, New York, 1969–.
HERMAN PAUL KOPPLEMANN, Connecticut, 1933–39; 1941–43 and 1945–47.
MILTON KRAUS, Indiana, 1917–23.
WILLIAM LEHMAN, Florida, 1973–.
MONTAGUE LESSLER, New York, 1902–3.
LEWIS CHARLES LEVIN, Pennsylvania, 1845–51.
JEFFERSON MONROE LEVY, New York, 1899–1901 and 1911–15.
LUCIUS NATHAN LITTAUER, New York, 1897–1907.
MEYER LONDON, New York, 1915–19 and 1921–23.
ALLARD KENNETH LOWENSTEIN, New York, 1969–71.
SAMUEL MARX, New York, 1922.*
MITCHELL MAY, New York, 1899–1901.
ADOLPH MEYER, Louisiana, 1891–1908.
EDWARD MEZVINSKY, Iowa, 1973–.
ABNER JOSEPH MIKVA, Illinois, 1969–73.
LEOPOLD MORSE, Massachusetts, 1877–85 and 1887–89.
ABRAHAM JACOB MULTER, New York, 1947–67.
RICHARD LAWRENCE OTTINGER, New York, 1965–71.
NATHAN DAVID PERLMAN, New York, 1920–27.

* Died before taking his seat.

THEODORE ALBERT PEYSER, New York, 1933–37.

HENRY MYER PHILLIPS, Pennsylvania, 1857–59.

PHILIP PHILLIPS, Alabama, 1853–55.

BERTRAM L. PODELL, New York, 1968–.

BENJAMIN J. RABIN, New York, 1945–47.

LEO FREDERICK RAYFIEL, New York, 1945–47.

ISIDOR RAYNER, Maryland, 1887–89 and 1891–95.

JOSEPH YALE RESNICK, New York, 1965–69.

ABRAHAM ALEXANDER RIBICOFF, Connecticut, 1949–53.

BENJAMIN LOUIS ROSENBLOOM, West Virginia, 1921–25.

BENJAMIN STANLEY ROSENTHAL, New York, 1962–.

ALBERT BERGER ROSSDALE, New York, 1921–23.

ADOLPH JOACHIM SABATH, Illinois, 1907–52.

LEON SACKS, Pennsylvania, 1937–43.

JAMES HAAS SCHEUER, New York, 1965–73.

ISAAC SIEGEL, New York, 1915–23.

WILLIAM IRVING SIROVICH, New York, 1927–39.

SAM STEIGER, Arizona, 1967–.

ISIDOR STRAUS, New York, 1894–95.

MYER STROUSE, Pennsylvania, 1863–67.

LUDWIG TELLER, New York, 1957–61.

HERBERT TENZER, New York, 1965–69.

HERMAN TOLL, Pennsylvania, 1959–67.

LESTER DAVID VOLK, New York, 1920–23.

SAMUEL ARTHUR WEISS, Pennsylvania, 1941–46.

HARRY BENJAMIN WOLF, Maryland, 1907–9.

LESTER LIONEL WOLFF, New York, 1965–.

SIDNEY RICHARD YATES, Illinois, 1949–63 and 1965–.

HERBERT ZELENKO, New York, 1955–63.

XIII

Jewish power
Taking a stand as Jews

IN THE WANING SUMMER OF 1654, a bedraggled group of
twenty-three Jews set sail from Recife, Brazil. They were
Dutch emigrants who had done well in Brazil until the
feared Portuguese had invaded and seized Recife. Recife's
Jews hastily departed. In September, a French bark
named the St. Charles deposited the twenty-three—four
men, six women, and thirteen youngsters—in the port of
Nieuw Amsterdam (later to be called New York). Their
welcome was less than hospitable. The Jews' possessions
were immediately auctioned by the captain of the ship,
Jacques de la Motte, to defray the cost of transporting

them. Peter Stuyvesant, governor of the Dutch colony, threw some of the Jews into jail and ordered them all to prepare for deportation. He wrote home to his employer, the Dutch West India Company, for permission to rid his colony of these "repugnant" people, "a deceitful race— such hateful enemies and blasphemers of the name of Christ," so that they "be not allowed to further infect and trouble this new colony." The company, however, rejected the governor's request and its action represents the first recorded instance of "Jewish influence" being applied in America. As the company's directors said in their answering letter:

We would have liked to effectuate and fulfill your wishes and request that the new territories should no more be allowed to be infected by people of the Jewish nation, for we foresee therefrom the same difficulties which you fear, but after having further weighed and considered the matter, we observe that this would be somewhat unreasonable and unfair, especially because of the considerable loss sustained by this nation, with others, in the taking of Brazil, and also *because of the large amount of capital which they still have invested in the shares of the company.* . . .

The italics are this writer's.

In American terms, this was one of the few instances of Jewish influence—or the potentials of influence—for centuries to come. While Jewish influence or power, *as* Jewish influence, has surfaced from time to time in the ensuing three hundred years, it was fleeting, and only in the last half-dozen years has America been witness to any clear, sustained exercise of Jewish effectiveness. For the most part, Jews seemed content with marginal positions in the social and political structure of the nation. In his perceptive essay, "The Deadly Innocences of American Jews," Earl Raab assessed the scene in the late 1960s, writing:

. . . Although the Jews accumulated a great deal of political power in those few big cities in which they were concentrated, it was transmissible to the centers of national power only under special circumstances. The acid test was the extent to which the Jews could exert influence on the most corporate power decisions of the nation: those concerning foreign policy. For the most part they have had and continue to have very little influence beyond what might be called the Rule of Marginal Effect. The sentiment of the American-Jewish community, no matter how strongly pressed, will influence American foreign policy only to the extent that it doesn't make any substantial difference to what are *otherwise* considered the best foreign-policy interests of the United States.

Myer Feldman, who worked in the White House during the Kennedy administration, has insisted that the same applies to *any* group in the polity. He maintained that presidential decisions are affected by so many factors that no single group can influence ultimate decisions.

There is no question as to when the open exercise of Jewish influence began in national politics. It was exploded onto the scene during the presidency of Franklin D. Roosevelt. His impact will go down as one of the stranger dichotomies of American Jewish history. His basic domestic policy thrust appealed strongly to Jews. His strong and early revulsion to the Nazis impelled them to him. Further, he leaned heavily upon Jewish minds and skills in developing his basic programs. Yet he remained always the pragmatic political leader, and some of the inactions during his tenure concerning direct Jewish interests read today as evidence of shocking unconcern.

While publicly scornful of Nazi repression and atrocities, he did little to save Europe's tormented, besieged Jews. He did nothing seriously to adjust the nation's restrictive immigration quotas, nor did he move even after learning of the State Department's obstructionism in the 1930s and early 1940s. Study of the record can lead only to the conclusion that, no matter what he felt privately, Roosevelt the politician was not moved to allow the anguish of dying Jews to interfere with his war effort.

When the war was over, counting began. Before Hitler's rise to Power, Poland had been home to more than three million Jews. By 1945 fewer than a hundred thousand were alive. It was that way in nation after nation across Europe. In all, six million Jews had perished.

The inactivity of the Roosevelt administration in coming to the aid of European Jewry has been documented in two books: the impassioned version of the late Arthur D. Morse, *While Six Million Died,* and the more recent and more reasoned one by Henry L. Feingold, *The Politics of Rescue.* The message of both books is summed up in this passage from *While Six Million Died:*

One might describe the American response to Nazi racism as an almost coordinated series of inactions. The moribund immigration policy of the United States, and America's failure to reassert its traditional defense of humanity, combined to produce total apathy. It was one thing to avoid interference in Germany's domestic policies, quite another to deny asylum to its victims.

State Department bureaucrats put all varieties of barriers between Europe's Jews and the safety of America. Morse noted that

During the entire Hitler period the number of immigrants lagged far behind the total permitted under U.S. law. From

1933 to 1943, there were 1,244,858 unfilled places on U.S. immigration quotas. Of these vacancies, 341,567 had been allotted to citizens of countries dominated or occupied by Germany or her allies.

The most callous of the governmental action-inactions was the refusal to provide harbor to the 936 passengers (930 of whom were Jews) aboard the *St. Louis* in 1939; the passengers had bought visas in Europe to immigrate to Cuba, but, when they got there, Cuban politicians would not honor the visas and refused to let them land. Despite impassioned pleas to the United States government to let them in—and with the ship steaming slowly up the East Coast in hopes for some optimistic word—the United States refused. The Jews were taken back to Europe.

The United States' policies toward Jews were not lost on Adolf Hitler. Only a month after he had seized power in Germany

he issued a statement that American citizens had no right to protest his anti-Semitism in view of the United States' own racial discrimination in its immigration policies. "Through its immigration law," said Hitler, "America has inhibited the unwelcome influx of such races as it has been unable to tolerate in its own midst. . . ."

Thus Feingold noted that "the visa system became literally an adjunct to Berlin's murderous plans for the Jews." In trying to assess blame for American inaction, Feingold also noted that the political impotence of America's Jews themselves played a large role, as did sniping among and between various Jewish groups and personalities:

Much of their formidable organizational resources were dissipated in internal bickering until it seemed as if Jews were more anxious to tear each other apart than to rescue their coreligionists. . . . That a community which desperately needed to speak to Roosevelt with one voice remained in an organizational deadlock is no small tragedy, and when one realizes how appallingly irrelevant the issues and personalities dividing them were, one can only shake one's head in disbelief.

Equally important, he said, was "the Jewish 'love affair' with Roosevelt," which translated to the fact that Jewish leaders "could not gain leverage by threatening a withdrawal of votes and were therefore dependent on less certain rewards for political loyalty."

Walter Laqueur wrote that, "The war in Europe was over, the world had been liberated from Nazi terror and oppression, peace had returned. For the Jewish people it was the peace of the graveyard."

The late David K. Niles, a Jew who was an aide to Roosevelt and, later, to Truman, made the point that, had Roosevelt lived, Israel probably would not have become a state. Laqueur, in his *A History of Zionism*, wrote that

Roosevelt was a consummate politician. He knew that a determined effort on behalf of the Jews would have reaped few tangible rewards, for the Jewish vote was in any case his. At the same time it would have caused a great many difficulties and complications both at home and abroad. Roosevelt's attitude towards the Jews was certainly not unfriendly, he was simply unwilling to go out of his way to help them.

In sum, what Roosevelt and the government of the United States of America did not do in the 1930s and 1940s undoubtedly taught America's Jews something about power or, rather, what the lack of it could mean. What is happening today reflects that painful lesson. And what is happening is that, for the first time in American history, American Jews have felt secure enough in their Jewishness and in their Americanism to challenge major aspects of this country's foreign policy, with regard both to the Middle East and to the Soviet Union. To some American Jews, afraid to stimulate *rishis,* afraid to awaken the sleeping giant of anti-Semitism, the current exercise of Jewish power is insanity, far too great a risk. But in fact what is happening today is but a natural evolution of American Jewish history since World War II, combining the memory of inaction during the Nazi era, the turbulence of the 1960s, the 1967 Arab-Israeli war, and the ensuing ethnic consciousness. No longer are many Jews willing to hang back and defer to the "establishment."

"One of the major developments in the Jewish community," said political scientist Marvin Schick, one of the national leaders of the new ethnic consciousness, "is the fact that the more ethnic Jews have come to dominate politically. They are dominating the 'establishment,' determining the agenda, the issues to be debated in the community. They exert pressure on the 'establishment' leadership to react in their direction. Their major weapon is the charge, at times made explicitly and at times more covertly, that the major Jewish organizations don't give a damn about Jews." The Jewish organizations have historically been the focuses for wielding what little Jewish influence has been exercised in America, and they have wielded whatever influence there was gingerly, as court Jews have always done. Naomi Cohen, in her history of the American Jewish Committee, described the technique it used:

The early responses to crises . . . followed the *Hofjude* or shtadlan approach—intercession with the authorities by a Jew who enjoyed government favor or had the ear of the powerful. When necessary, the mediator would approach leaders and molders of public opinion and, if required, would seek to galvanize the Jewish community into action.

Hyman Bookbinder, Washington representative of the committee, is illustrative of that thought process. When asked about Jewish power, he emphasizes that the Jew must walk and talk softly, never pressing too hard. The Jews, after all, are only 3 per cent. "It's idiotic to deny that there are powerful American Jews," he said. "But it doesn't add up to power for Jews *as* Jews. Americans who are Jews have a significant amount of influence. They're aggregate personal successes. There is, I say, an important Jewish influence on social policy that derives, for the most part, from Jewish ideology, Jewish commitment to social justice. . . . But as for Jewish political power—large P partisan Power—there is relatively little organized Jewish political Power." In another interview, Bookbinder emphasized that he felt that "The only way one supports a Jewish issue is to show that, even though it is a Jewish matter, it is really a broader human interest thing. . . . Jewish issues have to be supported in terms of broad American national and human interests and human justification. . . . Take parochial aid. It's basically a Catholic thing. But when we resist parochial aid, we're careful, or at least we should be careful, to say that it is not an anti-Catholic position we're taking but a prodemocratic society position we're taking. . . ." In a speech to members of the committee in March of 1972, Bookbinder amplified even further: ". . . Considering the numbers that we are in a country of two hundred million, I think we pull our weight nicely. We use our resources effectively and thank God we've learned how to use them effectively. That is, for the number that we are, we get pretty good results. But it would be a terrible oversimplification and it

would be very much a disservice to the things we believe
if we felt that in fact we controlled or we determined what
our government wants. At any time when our government
or our country believes that our interests in the Middle
East are not consistent with our American interests, we
don't have that much power that we can keep America
from making that judgment. So our objective is always to
help . . . Americans understand that the things we believe
in are, in fact, good things, right things and consistent
with the goals of this country. . . ."

This kind of thinking is integral to the *shtadlan*—intermediary type—approach to power, making it look good to
the non-Jews, never pushing too far, too fast. In every
community of size in the United States are Jewish citizens
who command significant local power, but they, too, never
push too far, too fast. It is—or has been—part of the American Jewish mentality. And a part of the mentality too is
the old "liberalism," the near-automatic reaction against
right and for reform. Irving M. Levine, a sociologist who
heads the National Project on Ethnic America, and who
works in the American Jewish Committee building, explained how this nearly automatic reaction can operate to
lessen Jewish influence. On the issue of reform of the
electoral college system, he said, "I would say that most of
the people in this agency [the committee] would have
rushed—and did—to say that, since it's long-standing reform that is needed, we are for it. But no one wondered,
or even began to smell out, what would happen to reform's
impact on the big states, where Jews live. Their power
would have been diminished. I was in favor of electoral
reform myself, but at least I was asking about what the
things were that you were giving up. It just tells you
about the deadly innocence of the Jews, based on their

classic 'liberalism' and reformism. So the Committee on this one ended up not taking a position—a reflective stand."

The new Jewish activists speak* with contempt of such thought processes. They plunge forward on narrowly Jewish causes with scant regard for the "old liberalism." When once upon a time all Jews in positions of power would have concentrated their attentions on the naming of a new Supreme Court justice for the United States, one of the most important of the new Jewish activists was more concerned with arms for Israel.

"The Jewish organizations are incompetent and unrepresentative, indecisive, preoccupied with other areas," said Richard Perle, an aide to Democratic Senator Henry M. Jackson. "An example of that, and it really does typify the situation, was a few years ago. I had all three of my telephone lines tied up, juggling calls, working on a Jackson amendment on aid to Israel. The telephone rang, and it was the Washington representative of one of the Jewish organizations. I figured he was calling in with a report on the response of some senator to our lobbying efforts. He wanted to talk about Rehnquist. I said, 'Jesus Christ, don't you know we're in the middle of a crisis?' And he said, 'Well, I also wanted to talk about that,' and I said, 'Well, what do you know?' And the other crisis he had in mind was Bangladesh. Here was the son of a bitch running around on Rehnquist and Bangladesh at the crucial moment we were trying to bring on board the necessary support for this rather substantial appropriation, and that's typical. The principal representatives of the Jewish or-

* The activists were interviewed in January and February of 1973 and their comments must, therefore, be weighed in relation to the context of that time.

ganizations in town all are interested in other things. Hy Bookbinder is interested in . . . the genocide convention and civil rights. Dave Brody, who represents the Anti-Defamation League, is interested in being seen with senators and congressmen regardless of their persuasion. The only guy who does any serious lobbying is Kenen [Isaiah L. ('Si') Kenen, publisher of the *Near East Report* and head of the American Israel Public Affairs Committee] and Kenen is getting on in years and his contacts are with an older generation."

"Bookbinder has been good in working on what amounted to very marginal Jewish interests," said Morris J. Amitay, Senator Ribicoff's specialist in Jewish affairs. "These are the traditional liberal interests in civil rights, integration, housing and all that. As far as the gut issues— Israel and Soviet Jewry—are concerned, his input has been zero. Most of the concrete results we've achieved in the last couple of years have been despite the lack of effort by the organized groups. In the drives for Phantom jets, for letters to the President, a letter to [then-Secretary of State William P.] Rogers and everything else, this is basically a well-knit staff operation in which only at the last minute, and on our say-so, do the organized groups come in, and with marginal contributions. So we would've gotten seventy-one [senators] on the Jackson amendment [in 1972] instead of 76. So we would've gotten 68 on the letter to the President instead of 72. . . ."

Bookbinder is stung by that sort of criticism. His interests, he said, are anything but marginally Jewish. "To allege that I'm not serving Jewish interests by being for civil rights, I disagree with," said Bookbinder, "but I can understand that. But genocide, the genocide treaty is a Jewish issue. That's why the treaty was written. . . ."

Bookbinder questioned whether staff work on the Hill was as valuable as the kind of contacts he has built during twenty years of activity in and around the government, and those of Kenen, Brody, and Herman Edelsberg of B'nai B'rith. "You take the average 70 senators who sign pro-Jewish, pro-Israel type of statements," Bookbinder said. "Sixty of them usually require 60 phone calls. It makes no difference whether Perle has made the call on his inside line or Bookbinder or Kenen makes a call, let's say, to Mathias' office or to Scott's office and says, 'Look, there's a letter out. Is it okay to put your guy's name on it?'" As an example, Bookbinder said that when the first Jackson amendment came along, Kenen asked him if the American Jewish Committee had any members in Georgia who might be able to influence Senator Herman Talmadge into becoming a co-sponsor. "I said it happens that our chapter chairman is a law partner of Talmadge," recalled Bookbinder. "Well, I'm sure that Herman Edelsberg has some B'nai B'rith lodge chairmen who are law partners of other guys. I called our guy and educated him on this and he somehow gets word to Talmadge. I'm sure that, while I'm doing that, four or five other things are happening at the same time to move in on Talmadge, because he's a guy we like to have on something. And at some point. Talmadge or his aide says, 'I'm going to co-sponsor that thing' or 'I'm going to vote that way' or maybe he doesn't tell anybody but, when it comes up for a vote, he votes right."

The new approach on Capitol Hill is far different from the one used in 1956, when American Jews' spokesmen in Washington were hesitant. After Israel's campaign in the Sinai in 1956, President Eisenhower demanded that it return to its prewar boundaries. When America's Jews started complaining about that demand, Secretary of State John Foster Dulles calmly threatened to lift the tax exemption of the United Jewish Appeal. Jews narrowly warded off that threat, through use of the old *Hofjude* technique and some political know-how. They cashed political chits, of past and future support from Jews, with the then-Senate Majority Leader, Lyndon B. Johnson, to intervene with President Eisenhower to protect the tax status of gifts to U.J.A. But American Jews were powerless to affect foreign policy; Israel retreated to its borders.

"Look at the difference between the 1956 Suez war and 1972," said Bert Gold, executive vice president of the American Jewish Committee. "The Israelis were almost at Cairo in 1956. Ike had them stop the war and roll back, with only a hint of assurance that we would guarantee Israel's safety. Over a period of just fifteen years, the recognition of ethnicity and group power and the more expressive society has made it possible for Jews to be more demanding about things that are exclusively Jewish. A lot of Jews are kind of pleased with it. They think maybe it's good for the Jews to control some power."

"All of this built from '56," echoed Rabbi Wolfe Kelman of the Rabbinical Assembly. "It exploded in '67. The American Jewish community reacted in one great emotional outburst, practically paralyzing the American government with protests [for the United States to step in on behalf of Israel]. This was the accumulating tradition of Jews' publicly asserting their rights as citizens to put pressure on our government to defend the rights of other Jews." Adam Walinsky pointed to the newness of the muscle-flexing. "It's a late-blooming thing," he said. "After all, John Kennedy's policy toward Israel would be con-

sidered much too even-handed now. The thing has esca-
lated remarkably in the last few years."

Part of that escalation was spelled out by Rabbi Seymour Siegel in a memorandum he wrote justifying his
advocacy of Nixon's re-election:

. . . We have as much interest in fostering Israel as do blacks
in eliminating the ghettoes or union members in maintaining
the integrity of their unions. No one is upset when blacks
announce their intention to vote for the candidate who best
serves their interests; nor are there protests when labor supports only pro-labor candidates. Why then should there be
opposition to Jews who assess candidates on the basis of Jewish interests?

"Every single group in American society not only has a
right, but an obligation, to become as powerful as they
can," said ethnic specialist Levine. "After all, the Catholics
pushed for aid to parochial schools. . . . It's very expected that the Irish should be interested in Irish self-
interest. It's then very legitimate for American Jews to
get excited over Israel. The ultimate survival of the American Jew is right over there."

This does not mean that American Jews want to become Israelis, that they jump to every desire of Golda Meir
and Moshe Dayan. If anything, up until the Yom Kippur
War, relations between Israel and the bulk of America's
Jews had been worsening, especially in the wake of
Israel's having tied itself so blatantly to an administration
that 65 per cent of America's Jews voted to remove from
office. Further, if it ever came to war between Israel and
the United States, while one can only guess, many if not
most American Jews would fight against Israel. While
they may see Israel as an ultimate refuge if a horrifying
form of anti-Semitism erupted in America, America is

their home, the birthplace of the overwhelming majority of them. The reference points of their loyalties are the elementary school down the block in Beverly Wood and the CBS Evening News, not the relics of Jerusalem. They feel as passionately about America, certainly, as did German Jews about their Germany, who considered Hitler an aberration who would quickly disappear and leave their homeland the proud and civilized land they were certain it was. The Americans' desire to remain Americans is evident in that extremely few have immigrated to Israel. Between the state's founding, in 1948, and the Six-Day War nearly twenty years later, only twenty thousand Americans immigrated, and nine of every ten of those later decided they liked the United States better and returned home. Even with the heightened Jewish identity since the Six-Day War, the number of emigrants from North America (including Canada) has remained low:

$$1968: \ 4,298$$
$$1969: \ 5,606$$
$$1970: \ 7,658$$
$$1971: \ 7,243$$
$$1972: \ 5,586$$
$$1973: \ 4,176$$

All of this is not to say, however, that America's Jews—especially the newer, less inhibited ones—are willing to allow Israel to confront its Arab neighbor states and the Soviet bloc alone, or to abandon the millions of Jews in the Soviet Union to the whims of the Politburo. And, interestingly, they are sensing that non-Jewish society in America seems to respect them more for it. The activist Jews in Washington despair, however, at the reluctance of more Jews to step forward in the cause and in what they say is a naïveté in the manipulation of power. "You talk about

Jews in politics," said Perle. "They're a pain in the neck. They're difficult to organize. . . . It's just a great pity that they're not better organized, because there are some crucial issues—whether Israel survives, whether we get the Russian Jews out—and if the American Jewish community were more sophisticated and better organized, if it had some political direction, if there were a commitment to these values, we'd be enormously more successful."

Richard Perle and Morris Amitay command a tiny army of Semitophiles on Capitol Hill and direct Jewish power in behalf of Jewish interests. These young men (Perle is but thirty-two, Amitay is thirty-seven) drafted the Jackson amendments concerning Soviet emigration, denying America's most-favored-nation tariff status to the Soviet Union unless it allows citizens the right to emigrate. These two, working with a network of other Jewish and non-Jewish activists on Capitol Hill, organized support and enlisted seventy-six senators to co-sponsor the amendment on its first appearance.

According to Ribicoff, Amitay has spent 90 per cent of his time on specifically Jewish issues, although Amitay terms it far less. Amitay has been chief of the Israel lobby lately in Washington—not Si Kenen, as widely believed. Amitay comes to his passion about Israel via his family. His father, Albert, was born in Israel and is a seventh-generation Sabra (native-born Israeli).

Perle said he had no interest in Israel or, for that matter, in things Jewish, until he went to work for Senator "Scoop" Jackson. "Scoop got me interested," he said, and, "in fact, put me to work on the first Jackson amendment, which provided five hundred million dollars for Phantoms and other equipment. My perspective is a little different from Morrie's because I'm just very much convinced of

Abraham Feinberg presents an award from the Anti-Defamation League of B'nai B'rith to President Johnson in 1965. Feinberg, a New York banker, was the first Jew to become a prominent money raiser in presidential campaigns, according to Alex Rose. AT RIGHT: the late Eugene Wyman, one of the best-known and most successful Jewish fund raisers. *(Photos by United Press International)*

Many of the issues that had been broiling in the inner city came to a head in 1971 in a donnybrook over a public housing project being built in Forest Hills in the New York City borough of Queens. Jews in Forest Hills feared that the project would bring poverty and crime to their neighborhood. A "Forest Hills mentality" was discernible in the 1972 election returns. The picture above of demonstrators at the site was taken in April of 1972. *(Photo by United Press International)*.

RIGHT: Arthur Waskow, shown protesting in 1968 against the war in Vietnam, is one of a disproportionate number of radicals who are Jews.

The Walinsky family is a good
example of the way that Jewish
political values have been transmitted from generation to generation. Adam Walinsky — above
with Robert Kennedy in 1968,
on the day Kennedy announced
for the presidency — was a top
Kennedy aide, adviser, and
"house radical." *(Photo by The
New York Times)* After Kennedy's death, Walinsky became
a leader in the antiwar movement
and ran for state office in New
York. Walinsky traces his politics
to his grandfather Ossip, shown
at right at the age of eighty-three
proudly wearing Adam's campaign button. Ossip had been
expelled from Russia as a youth
for radical activity and continued
his efforts in America.

the soundness of the foreign policy. I agree with John Roche, who says he'd be for defending Israel even if it were populated with South Vietnamese. There are sound strategic, political, economic reasons for supporting that piece of real estate *per se,* though obviously there's an emotional attachment beyond that." Perle described his attachment as "based largely on the profound respect for the competence and the dedication and the toughness and the skill of the Israelis. They possess those values that Jackson admires and that, through him, at least initially, I've come increasingly to admire."

Amitay and Perle have coalesced key staff people in the Senate to work on behalf of Israel and Soviet Jewry—those areas where the Senate has had some impact. Included have been Richard D. Siegel (an aide to Pennsylvania's Richard Schweiker); Mel Grossman (an aide to Florida's Edward J. Gurney); Albert A. ("Pete") Lakeland (an aide to Javits); Daniel L. Spiegel (an aide to Senator Humphrey); Mel Levine (an aide to California's John V. Tunney); Jay Berman (an aide to Indiana's Birch Bayh), and Kenneth Davis (an aide to Minority Leader Hugh Scott of Pennsylvania). All but Lakeland are Jewish. This group has worked quietly drafting legislation and other materials and mounting "backfires" to insure support of the legislation, while Jackson, in particular, and Javits and Ribicoff have worked "out front" to garner support among fellow senators.

"There are now a lot of guys at the working level up here," said Amitay, "who happen to be Jewish, who are willing to make a little bit of extra effort and to look at certain issues in terms of their Jewishness, and this is what has made this thing go very effectively in the last couple of years. These are all guys who are in a position to make the decisions in these areas for these senators. You don't need that many to get something done in the Senate. All you need is a certain commitment to get something done and, if guys are willing to put time into that instead of a million other things they have to do, if they're willing to make a couple of calls, if they're willing to become involved, you can get an awful lot done just at the staff level. . . . The senators have a million things to do (and) they'll take the recommendation [of their administrative assistants] most times. With a senator from the Far West or a farm senator, we won't bother on something like the Jackson amendment. But if we get a senator from an industrial state, a state with any sizable Jewish population, and he doesn't come out, we don't let him get away with it. That's when we call for outside help."

"Outside help" means direct pressure on senators from their constituents, something Jews have known about for years but have been reluctant to participate in. "What you have in this country," said Amitay, "is a fantastic, untapped reservoir of Jews who are in influential positions, who were never asked to help. And now it's just a matter of finding them and asking them to help. There are so many Jewish organizations, so many Jewish people sitting out in small towns in Iowa and in Oregon, and there are rabbis with congregations, who are just dying to get a call saying, 'We need help with somebody. Can you help?' They understand the issue immediately—you're dealing with very sophisticated people. The point is, when something is going on here on the Hill, there is not a systematic attempt to coordinate, to let these people know that their help is needed, and the response has been very good. . . ."

In the past, Amitay continued, pro-Israeli lobbyists could at most get no more than fifty to fifty-five senators to sign a letter or co-sponsor a bill. "There was no reason why they didn't do better," he said. "There was no reason they weren't getting three-quarters of the Senate. Now we are." They have done so by capitalizing on the kind of constituents Jews are—relatively wealthy, well-educated, professional, politically active. "In most cases," said Amitay, senators don't consider what he and the other new Jewish activists are doing to constitute undue pressure. "In many cases," he said, "they consider it a favor that they know the people are concerned about it, and they have a chance to show their good faith, their *bona fides*, on it. In a lot of these things, a lot of co-sponsorship requests never come to their attention. . . . On the average during the session, I would say we [Ribicoff's office] get a dozen of them a day. On these, I show the senator or get his thinking on, maybe, two or three a day, at the most. So a lot of these senators, if you can't get to them directly, if someone doesn't mention it to them, they hear from the folks back home and they say, 'Gee, why didn't you tell me about it?' We are making more staff people sophisticated in this area, once their bosses have been burned."

What is important, said Amitay, is that nothing in this is untoward: "When you get to one that's big, you use the traditional tactics of the democracy for making elected representatives know of constituents' feelings: letters, calls. It hasn't been used as much in the past as it should have been. You had a great proliferation of Jewish organizations and a great proliferation of Jews who were moving into higher income classes who were becoming active in politics, who *were* interested. Along with that came a coincidence of a few key senators with staff people who were willing to make this commitment in time and in energy, and who informally consult with each other on matters like this now."

Bookbinder agreed with Amitay's assessment of the importance of people back home, but disagreed somewhat on the import of the Capitol staffers. "Political success depends upon a lot of things happening," he said. "The most basic of all is sufficient support back home—that means voters, contributors, editorial support, newspapers. Without that, a half dozen effective operators on the Hill make no difference."

Jews now have three senators with some seniority who care deeply about Jewish affairs and, although neither Ribicoff nor Javits is a member of the Senate "club," Javits has managed to accumulate enough seniority—he now ranks eighth among Republicans—to have placed some sixty of "his" people in key committee jobs around the Senate. Further, said Amitay, "in getting behind things in support of Israel, your arguments are usually pretty good. . . ."

"There are only six million of us and two hundred-odd million of them," said Amitay, sounding much like Bookbinder, for a moment, "and unless you can always translate this in terms of what's in America's interest, you're lost. You're just a tiny voice. I feel, and people up here who are doing this feel, that when you are talking about democracy, well, Israel is a real democracy. When you're talking about free speech, well, they have it there. When you talk about a lot of the values that we had, maybe, in the frontier days, and we seem to be losing now, particularly the idealism of youth, they still have it. So in a sense, it's sort of a model—a smaller model—that exemplifies certain ideals that we like."

Perle put it somewhat differently: that Jewish power

has succeeded of late because of Americans' fear of the
Soviet Union: "If you look at the progression of issues,"
he said, "the controversy surrounding U.S. policy toward
the Middle East in '69 and '70 is very much a question of
the attitude you took toward the Soviet Union, and had it
been simply a Jewish issue, I think the results might have
been different. . . ."

Jewish activists on the Hill used the anti-Communist
tool broadly for maintaining support of Israel during the
1973 crisis; after the fighting ended in the Middle East
and negotiations began, even harder work began, though.
Bookbinder said: "Our problem was what our best friends
on the Hill were telling us was a clear indication of an
erosion of public support, which could have had an impact on the way Congress finally behaved. The people
themselves were writing [to their senators and congress-
men] about the oil situation; they were writing about the
alert and the danger of getting into the war; they were
worried about the costs. Our job was, first, to do what we
could to strengthen public opinion and keep it strong.
And then to keep educating the members of Congress and
reminding them while it was true that their mail was, for
the first time, reflecting a significant amount of 'take it
easy with Israel' messages, that the friends of Israel were
also still there. . . . In my newsletter I never do that
much explicit lobbying . . . but I went all out on it
then . . . telling Jews and non-Jewish friends of Israel
that the Congressmen must be reminded that support for
Israel still exists out there, to undo the other stuff."

On the Soviet Jewry issue, Perle said that he and
Amitay drafted the amendment to force the Soviets to
ease their restrictions on emigration "so that it refers to
all citizens desiring to emigrate, not just to Jews. We

realized of course two things: one is that it's the Jews who principally will come out initially and, two, it's the Jews who are going to have to do most of the lobbying. But then, the Jews did most of the lobbying for civil rights for a long time, too. They've been in the forefront of humanistic causes and this is yet another one. This is both humanistic and particularist. But the amendment refers to everyone and, obviously, the ratio of Jews to non-Jews is going to be very high initially. But once we open things up, that could change. Hopefully, it would change. And I think the Soviets have handled the problem very badly, they've made one mistake after another. . . . The emigration tax, which just smacked of what the Nazis did, was their big mistake. If they hadn't done that, it might've been very difficult to sustain interest in the emigration issue *per se*. Oddly enough, the tax—which was less odious than the denial of the opportunity to leave—produced more ill will, which we certainly didn't hesitate to use."

The Jewish activists in Washington have also not hesitated to use Americans' traditional distaste for being blackmailed, as they have striven to make it clear to all those who hold the power in Washington that, if the Arab nations succeed in changing America's Middle East policies through withholding oil, nothing can stop them from proceeding on to another, different blackmail attempt.

The one question that the Jewish activists tend to tiptoe around is the one concerning Jewish money. As it did in 1654, Jewish money has played a significant role in the current exercise of Jewish power. The fact has been that intercession by Javits or Ribicoff can sometimes play a major factor in whether a senator has won re-election. And it has been of no small importance that one has been Republican and the other a Democrat; they thus have access to financiers on both political fronts. A call from Ribicoff or Javits to solicit support for a senator has been known to result in a handsome bonus for that senator's re-election campaign. More significantly, their urging has also been known to result in bonuses for the opponents of senators who do not go along. This sounds rough, somehow un-American. But that is the way politics are played in America, and have been for years. It is only that the Jews have just recently begun to use the political tools that have long been familiar to other pressure groups in society.

Jews' new confidence in their Americanism and in their use of these tools was spelled out quite specifically, for instance, in an article in the February 1974 issue of *The National Jewish Monthly*, a publication of B'nai B'rith. The article, by Franklin R. Sibley, a congressional aide, blatantly called Jewish contributors' attention to Jews' "friends" and enemies who were up for election in 1974:

One third of the Senate comes up for re-election this coming fall; among them are vigorous friends of Jewish causes, including Birch Bayh (D-Ind.), Frank Church (D-Ida.), Alan Cranston (D-Cal.), Robert J. Dole (R-Kan.), Thomas F. Eagleton (D-Mo.), Daniel K. Inouye (D-Hawaii), Warren G. Magnuson (D-Wash.), Robert Packwood (R-Ore.), Richard S. Schweiker (R-Pa.), and Adlai E. Stevenson III (D-Ill.).

A few senators consistently opposed to Jewish concerns are also up for re-election. Foremost among these is J. W. Fulbright (D-Ark.), who has lent respectability to the Arab cause and given it a voice in the Senate it never enjoyed before. A believer in detente with the Soviets to the detriment of Israel's interests, he has labored diligently against legislation offered by Henry M. Jackson (D-Wash.) linking preferential trade terms to the relief of Soviet Jewry. Other members of the Senate seeking re-election this year who chose not to sponsor the Jackson Amendment are Henry L. Bellmon (R-Okla.) and Gaylord Nelson (D-Wis.).

This kind of direct, public approach probably would have been impossible a decade ago.

The relationship of Jews and their money to power has been generally misunderstood. That many Jews have accumulated fortunes in Wall Street has not meant that they control the politics of the United States. Their business has been making money, not determining national policy. Jews in Wall Street do have political preferences, just like non-Jews in Wall Street. Their peer-group reference, however, tends to be a Wall Street one, however, and not a Jewish one. Most, like their non-Jewish counterparts, are Republicans. Most also are capitalists.

Gustave L. Levy, managing partner of the important Goldman, Sachs & Company investment banking firm, has been an example. Many have regarded Levy as the most powerful single individual in Wall Street, able to make or break men and companies almost casually. He personally controls the movement of billions of dollars. Levy is a proudly professing Jew but, like most Wall Streeters, his prime political interests are in a solid local and national economy in which his firm can do well. He may have an interest beyond the ordinary in fearing a depression, since he has known that Jews tend to suffer inordinately in times of economic travail. In general, Levy has played his "Jewishness" at a low key in Wall Street, much as the American Jewish Committee used to play its Jewishness at a low key.

"Gus is very conscious of being Jewish. He's very conscious of the problems it can cause," said Philip Greer, a onetime stockbroker who has reported on Wall Street for the old New York *Herald-Tribune* and for the Washington *Post.* "When you talk about Jewish muscle, Gus will back off—'Don't make waves. I've got it, and I can use it, and I know how to use it, and I do use it, but I'm not going to talk to you about it because, then that redneck in Alabama is going to get very upset and I don't want him to know about it. . . .' Fifty years ago, the Warburgs were very powerful people, but they didn't use it in the same way. Theirs was in the Jewish end. The Warburgs, the Kahns, the Schiffs were powerful in their part of the business. It was rare, and it was noted, when they moved out of their part of the business. Gus is powerful because there no longer is a Jewish end. He's powerful across the board."

The new ethnicity has affected Levy, too. "In the Six-Day War," said Greer, "Gus was sending money over like crazy. He would have financed that whole war all by himself. And he made no bones about whether you were Jewish or not. 'You need Goldman, Sachs. I need you now. If I don't get you now, you aren't getting me later.' It's as simple as that. He could've raised it from Schwartz or O'Reilly, it didn't make any difference to him and it didn't make any difference to them, because they're both after the money that Gus Levy controls. . . . So, 'Gus says he needs five grand for the Jews, all right. I hope the Arabs drive them into the Mediterranean, but I ain't going to tell Gus, so I'll give him the five grand and go to church and pray the Arabs drive them into the sea.' That's what Wall Street understands, and they admire it and respect it. They accept it—that's the way it's supposed to be done. You've got the muscle, that's what you've got it for. Nobody questions it. I don't know how much he raised in the

Yom Kippur war. But I do know he sent his own check for
$150,000 before most people knew there was a war."

Levy uses the power of his position politically, although
more on the local level than the national one. He was
treasurer of John Lindsay's mayoralty campaign in 1969.
Without Levy, Lindsay might not have had a chance.
Jewish businessmen like Levy can be found in almost
every large city, wielding the power of their money to
affect local elections.

Amitay insisted, however, that the importance of Jewish
money was vastly overemphasized as a pressure tool on
Congress. "The money angle is important. Contributions
are important to politicians," he said. "But it's also a
question of having someone respected in the community,
say a college professor, someone like a Hans Morgenthau
—they've heard of him, they've read his text books on
political science—going around and talking to people on
Soviet Jewry. If a guy like that or a lawyer from downtown
who's been active in other things besides Jewish things
comes in, it has an impact. A lot of these senators are
from the West, Midwest, down South, and these [Jews]
are some of the elite type of people that these senators like
to be with and talk to, besides the pull of actual contributions. I don't think anyone ever likes to be approached at that level, on the very gut political level. You
look around at who the Jewish constituents are from
sparsely inhabited states. They're teachers, they're doctors,
they've invariably been involved some way in politics.
They're usually respected people in the community, so
you don't have to pitch it at the level of, 'I contributed
ten thousand dollars to your campaign—unless you do this
you'll make me unhappy and I'll contribute to your op-

ponent next time.' At most, it's implicit, and it's not even implicit a large percentage of the time."

More to the point, the teachers, doctors, lawyers, businessmen feel, for the first time, that it is worth endangering their reputations for non-Jewish "objectivity" to press —yes, even pushily—for a specifically Jewish cause. Their vigor is an indication of the depth of their feeling about the three million Jews still under Russian rule, and the two and a half million of the European remnant fighting for their survival again, in Israel. There, but for the grace— and luck and courage—of their grandfathers and grandmothers, go they. Their vigor also undoubtedly reflects the feeling that too few Jews risked enough of what they had in America in the 1930s and 1940s. And it may reflect conscious—or even unconscious—response to the implorings for conscience and humanism coming from the New Left.

The new aggressiveness is, of course, not without substantial risk. Americans could decide that détente with the Soviet Union is more important than her acknowledging that her citizens have a right to leave her, or that it is more important than seemingly endless crisis in the Middle East. Americans could decide that enduring another winter with inadequate heating oil is not worth defending a tiny country thousands of miles distant that seems to defend herself reasonably well, anyway. Or an America-on-wheels could decide that rationing, or another twenty-five cents a gallon, is too high a price to pay to placate 3 per cent of the American population.

Most American Jews were immensely affected by the fourth Middle Eastern war in twenty-five years. Some Jewish intellectuals perceived the swift diplomatic abandonment of Israel to be a subtle and dangerous new mutation of the old anti-Semitism. Identification of American Jews with Israel's plight was virtually complete and bordered on intense religious fervor. America's Jews, Norman Podhoretz pointed out, suddenly had become, en masse, "instant Zionists." One might have thought that Israel's defeat* in 1973 might somehow have reversed or at least dampened the pride and assertiveness that the 1967 conquest helped inspire, that Jews in America might consider hanging back, in effect cowering again lest they seem, to the *goyim,* to be causing too much trouble. In a few cases, this was true. Bertram Gold of the American Jewish Committee, for instance, immediately issued a warning to Jews—to be alert for a rise of anti-Semitism. And a few Jews refrained from demanding the removal of President Nixon when his friends conveyed a starkly simple message: either support the President now, when he needs you, or when you (for that, read Israel) need him, his support might not be there. Most Jews, however, did anything but hang back, either in clamoring for impeachment, or in applying pressure on Israel's behalf on the White House or anywhere else it might help. With unprecedented vigor, they brashly and openly spoke up for their fellow Jews in Israel, bombarding the White House and Congress with telegrams, letters, and calls insisting that America continue its stanch support of Israel. They unashamedly raised money in staggering amounts to send to Israel—and then proudly boasted of their fund-raising accomplishments to the national media. No one hid the

* Military analyst Drew Middleton of the New York *Times* wrote in *The Atlantic* that "Israel has lost, perhaps permanently, certainly temporarily, the military superiority she had enjoyed since the 1956 Suez War." In terms of American Jewish pride, that can be considered "defeat."

fact of enormous 1974 U.J.A. pledges of five million dollars each from tycoons like Meshulam Riklis (and a group of his intimates) and Leonard Stern (of Hartz Mountain Foods).

Those Jews who are less bold warn the activists to slow down. In an era of phases, they warn, the age of ethnicity could prove to be so fleeting that all of America's Jews might be left out on a limb with no supportive allies; even the blacks who once might have been there have gone, they say. But the new Jewish activists can turn right around and remind their fellow Jews that they have already been there, have already fought a lonely battle with the oil companies, the auto makers and others who value profits over Jewish lives. In fact, there seems to be no turning back at this point; the new spokesmen for Jewry do seem to be pulling the rest of the flock behind them. What is happening on Capitol Hill and in communities across the nation is indeed a manifestation of an evolutionary change in Jewish history. It appears to be a major phase of the Emancipation that began in the eighteenth century in Europe and even now is part of the continuing process of the deghettoizing of a people; they are suddenly much less afraid of that sleeping giant.

And it is, as well, a developmental stage of the Americanizing of the Jews. Rabbi Eugene Borowitz wrote that, "For most Jews the American way has become the real faith, the effective Torah, by which they lived." After decades of apologizing and deferring, they are expressing themselves openly, enthusiastically and brashly—as Americans are wont to do. That *is* the American way, and the thrust of their political activity is the ultimate proof of their Americanization.

Acknowledgments

THIS BOOK WAS CONCEIVED by Richard Harwood of the Washington *Post,* and the writer is indebted to him for that as well as for innumerable other lessons over the last twenty years. The writer also thanks Howard Simons and Benjamin C. Bradlee of the *Post* for their encouragement.

No book of this type is possible without the generous help of those whose life work is involved with books. Harry J. Alderman and Judith Selakoff, of the Jacob Blaustein Library of the American Jewish Committee, and Ralph Smith of *Newsweek* were of invaluable assistance. Milton Himmelfarb kindly discussed most of the areas of this book with the writer. Morton Yarmon of the American Jewish Committee was generous with his assistance. Herbert E. Alexander was especially helpful with the chapter on Jewish contributing, both for data he provided and for his insight. The following men and women also were extremely helpful: Marvin Schick,

Rabbi Wolfe Kelman, Hyman Bookbinder, Rabbi Arthur Hertzberg, Ben J. Wattenberg, and Marilyn Tanner.

My father, Norman E. Isaacs, steadfastly edited every word of this book more than once; the book could not have been written without his counsel and editing. My sister, Roberta Mathews, helped edit a final draft, as did Estelle S. Bechhoefer. I am especially grateful to Judith Goldstein for her perceptive and incisively detailed help with the final stages.

The writer also appreciates the patient coaching of Thomas Congdon.

Finally, I thank my wife, Diane, for her support, encouragement, and courage.

Chapter notes

FOREWORD
   ix Mills's quote is on p. 22 of *The Power Elite* (London: Oxford University Press, 1956).

CHAPTER I *"Pray for the welfare of the government . . ."*
   1 Others at the dinner included Harold Toppel, chairman of the board of the supermarket chain of Pueblo International; Newton Gleckel, board chairman of Hygrade Food Products Corporation, and his son Jeffrey; Samuel J. Silberman, retired chairman of the board of Consolidated Cigar Company; former Representative Herbert Tenzer, then a successful Manhattan attorney; E. Paul Charlap, board chairman of Savin Business Machines; Nathan C. Halpern, president of TNT Communications, Inc.; Joseph Hofheimer, president of Richard Bauer & Co., a paper manufacturer; John E. Marqusee, president of Consolidated Fine Arts; real estate men Charles B. Benenson and Frederick Rose; advertising men Charles Goldschmidt and David Altman; Jay Wells of Wells National Services Corporation, a television leasing firm; investment bankers Belmont and Robert Towbin; investment executives Bernard Stein, George Heyman, Raymond Frankel, Eugene Lynn, and Donald C. Samuel.
   6 Population statistics used throughout the book come from the *American Jewish Year Book 1972*, Vol. 73 (New York: The

American Jewish Committee, and Philadelphia: The Jewish Publication Society of America, 1972).

For many years, sociologists have used the ratio of one of every four New Yorkers' being Jewish, based on estimates by the Council of Churches of New York City. A relatively recent survey by the Population Health Survey, Center for Social Research, and The Graduate School and University Center of the City University of New York, published in 1973, puts the percentage of Jewish population at 17.9 per cent, as of 1970. The Council of Churches' statistic for 1970 was 24.1 per cent. The writer has taken a broad average of the two.

7 Lest the reader get the impression that the writer was biased toward a Washington *Post* colleague, fifty-seven leading political writers and commentators were surveyed by graduate students under the direction of Associate Professor Lewis W. Wolfson of American University, and asked which political correspondents they respected the most. Broder's name was cited almost three times as many as the next highest. Further, Broder was awarded the 1973 Pulitzer Prize for commentary.

10 The American Council on Education's report is entitled *A Profile of the Jewish Freshman,* by the A.C.E.'s Office of Research, financed by the American Jewish Committee and prepared by David E. Drew. (A.C.E. Research Reports, Vol. 5, No. 4, June 1970.) The two segments of the survey mentioned are on p. 42 and p. 40; those tables are as follows:

PERCENT OF STUDENTS REPORTING THAT DURING THE PAST YEAR THEY	JEWISH STUDENTS	NON-JEWISH STUDENTS
Voted in Student Election	65.8	68.0
Came Late to Class	61.5	58.2
Played a Musical Instrument	47.6	39.7
Studied in the Library	31.2	36.4
Checked out a Library Book	44.5	47.9
Arranged Date for Another Stdt	57.6	50.8
Overslept and Missed a Class	34.2	23.1
Typed a Homework Assignment	28.7	23.5
Discuss Future with Parent	46.2	39.4
Was Late with Homework Assgnt	68.9	73.0
Argued with Teacher in Class	67.2	53.3
Attended Religious Service	79.5	91.1
Protested Racial Policy	26.6	10.5
Protested US Military Policy	20.4	5.6

Protested against H.S. Admin	39.9	22.4
Did Extra Reading for Class	15.9	13.3
Took Sleeping Pills	7.4	6.4
Tutored Another Student	54.6	43.1
Played Chess	43.5	40.4
Read Poetry not Req'd in Course	62.1	57.9
Took a Tranquilizing Pill	11.3	9.4
Discussed Religion	28.1	28.3
Took Vitamins	55.8	61.7
Visited Art Gallery or Museum	82.6	70.8
Part. in H.S. Politic Campaign	43.5	45.1
Part. in Other Politic Campaign	29.3	15.8
Missed Schl becs of Illness	5.3	3.5
Smoked Cigarettes	17.3	15.5
Discussed Politics	37.6	25.3
Drank Beer	52.6	56.8
Discussed Sports	33.7	43.8
Asked Teacher for Advice	27.4	24.1
Had Vocational Counseling	39.1	59.1
Stayed Up All Night	64.9	63.8

OBJECTIVES CONSIDERED TO BE ESSENTIAL OR VERY IMPORTANT	JEWISH STUDENTS	NON-JEWISH STUDENTS
Achieve in a Performing Art	13.8	11.1
Be an Authority in my Field	58.5	59.3
Obtain Recognition from Peers	42.2	41.0
Influence Political Structure	23.7	15.8
Influence Social Values	38.9	33.7
Raise a Family	75.5	71.7
Have Active Social Life	66.1	59.2
Have Friends different from Me	70.9	66.5
Be an Expert in Finance	12.8	16.8
Be Administratively Responsible	19.7	24.2
Be Very Well-off Financially	44.4	44.5
Help Others in Difficulty	66.7	65.7
Become a Community Leader	16.6	17.8
Contribute to Scientific Theory	12.1	10.1
Write Originial Works	19.2	13.2
Not be Obligated to People	23.4	24.3
Create Works of Art	19.2	15.2
Keep up with Political Affairs	60.6	51.2

| Succeed in my own Business | 42.6 | 45.9 |
| Develop a Philosophy of Life | 84.6 | 82.0 |

11 The religious breakdown of the Ninety-third Congress was published by *Christianity Today* on December 6, 1972.

That Jews still rank well down on the social scale has been proved repeatedly by survey data. A recent major study of anti-Semitism, by Gertrude J. Selznik and Stephen Steinberg, points out that "the social discrimination of the educated shows that an aura of social undesirability still stigmatizes Jews." P. 187 of *The Tenacity of Prejudice* (New York: Harper & Row, 1969).

CHAPTER II *Pursuing salvation*

19 The Wilson-Brandeis story is recounted on p. 277 of Robert St. John's *Jews, Justice and Judaism* (Garden City, N.Y.: Doubleday & Company, Inc., 1969).

21 Gold's quote is from his introduction to *"Kikel"*, ed. by Michael Selzer (New York: World Publishing, 1972), p. xi.

22 Fuchs's important book, *The Political Behavior of American Jews* (Glencoe, Ill.: The Free Press, 1956), has held up remarkably since its publication. He mentions the religious differences on p. 191.

Levine's quote is from p. 51 of his *The Irish and Irish Politicians, A Study of Cultural and Social Alienation* (Notre Dame and London: University of Notre Dame Press, 1966).

23 The percentage of Jewish lawyers is on p. 1506 of Vol. 10 of the *Encyclopaedia Judaica* (New York: The Macmillan Company, 1972; and Jerusalem: Keter Publishing House Ltd., 1971).

24 Novak's book is *The Rise of the Unmeltable Ethnics; Politics and Culture in the Seventies* (New York: The Macmillan Company, 1972), p. 72.

27 Charles S. Liebman, in a survey of Jewish leaders for his article, "Reconstructionism in American Jewish Life" (*American Jewish Year Book 1970*, Vol. 71 (New York: The American Jewish Committee, and Philadelphia: The Jewish Publication Society of America, 1970), found that as an American Jewish value: "Separation of church and state is an absolute essential. It protects America from being controlled by religious groups; it protects Judaism from having alien standards forced upon it, and, most importantly, it protects the Jew from being continually reminded of his minority status." P. 68.

CHAPTER III *Room near the top*

39 The concept of "priorization" is discussed by Norman L. Friedman in "Jewish or Professional Identity? The Priorization Process in Academic Situations," in *Sociological Analysis*, Vol. 32, No. 3, Fall, 1971, p. 149. Friedman notes that " 'priorization' will mean that definitional process whereby an actor, in regard to a given situation, gives precedence to one of his role, identity, self, or membership/reference orientations, over another or others."

The two quotations from Sklare are from p. 68, then p. 66 of *America's Jews* (New York: Random House, 1971).

Yaffe's is on pp. 305–6 of *The American Jews* (New York: Random House, 1968).

CHAPTER IV *Modern scribes*

43 Sidney Goldstein and Calvin Goldscheider note that "Perhaps no other people in world history has functioned in so many languages as have the Jews." See p. 225 of their *Jewish Americans—Three Generations in a Jewish Community* (Englewood Cliffs, N.J.: Prentice-Hall, Inc., 1968).

47 The *Times*' hypersensitivity is discussed on p. 92–93 of Gay Talese's *The Kingdom and the Power* (New York: World Publishing Company, 1969). The Bernstein line is on p. 110.

49 Lindbergh's Des Moines remarks are noted on p. 120 of *Jews in the Mind of America*, by Charles Herbert Stember and others (New York: Basic Books, 1966).

50 The *U.S. News & World Report* mentioned is of August 24, 1970.

54 Seymour Martin Lipset and Everett Carll Ladd, Jr., in "Jewish Academics in the United States: Their Achievements, Culture and Politics," *American Jewish Year Book 1971*, Vol. 72 (New York: The American Jewish Committee, and Philadelphia: The Jewish Publication Society of America, 1971), wrote that Thorstein Veblen pointed out that the secularized Jew was "an 'outsider' in gentile societies. The Jew was disproportionately successful as an intellectual precisely because his social position made him a discontented skeptic. . . ." Pp. 111–12.

Berlin's article, entitled "Jewish Slavery and Emancipation," is on pp. 52–68 of *Forum for the Problems of Zionism, World Jewry and the State of Israel* (Jerusalem: Information Department of the Jewish Agency, December 1953).

56 The Talmud passage is quoted on p. 47 of Rabbi Morris N. Kertzer's *What Is a Jew?* (New York: The Macmillan Company, 1965, and World Publishing Company, 1960). Rabbi Kertzer said it comes from Seder Eliyahu Rabbah, Chapter 23, based on Taanit 11a.

57 Regarding the theme of polluting morals, see John Higham's chapter, "American Anti-Semitism Historically Reconsidered," in *Jews in the Mind of America* (*op. cit.*), p. 247.

57 Schrag's comment comes on p. 108 of *The Decline of the Wasp* (New York: Simon and Schuster, 1971).

59 Van den Haag's quote is from *The Jewish Mystique* (New York: Stein & Day, 1969), p. 231.

CHAPTER V *Avoiding bureaucracy*

61 The figures cited on the number of Jews in Senate staff positions are conservative. They were obtained from reliable sources on Capitol Hill and were carefully verified.

62 The property quote is from Milton R. Konvitz's "Judaism and the Democratic Idea," in his *Judaism and Human Rights* (New York: W. W. Norton & Company, Inc., 1972, c. 1972, B'nai B'rith Commission on Adult Jewish Education), p. 133.

64 The Rosen-velt comment is mentioned in memoranda in the files of the American Jewish Committee. The pamphlet, published by Pelley Publishers of Asheville, N.C., mentioned more than four hundred persons who were Jews whom Roosevelt had appointed to government posts. An American Jewish Committee analysis showed that twenty of the four hundred-plus were not F.D.R. appointees and had been in government before he became President, nineteen were not Jews and fifty were dead or had resigned from the government.

The 121 organizations are mentioned on p. 410 of the Second Edition of *Minorities in American Society,* by Charles F. Marden and Gladys Meyer (New York: American Book Company, 1962), quoting Donald S. Strong's *Organized Anti-Semitism in America* (Washington, D.C.: American Council on Public Affairs, 1941).

The April 1939 survey is cited on pp. 8–9 of Henry Feingold's *The Politics of Rescue: The Roosevelt Administration and the Holocaust 1938–1945* (New Brunswick, N.J.: Rutgers University Press, 1970).

65 Among those upset with the Frankfurter appointment was Arthur Hays Sulzberger, who, according to Talese, "was among a group

of influential Jews who urged President Roosevelt not to appoint Felix Frankfurter to the Supreme Court because they believed that it would intensify anti-Semitism in America," p. 91, *The Kingdom and the Power, op. cit.*

Glazer's observations are in his article "Social Characteristics of American Jews" on p. 1714 of *The Jews—Their History, Culture and Religion,* Third Edition, edited by Louis Finkelstein, Vol. II (New York: Harper and Brothers, 1959).

67 The parallel between NASA and the insurance industry was drawn by Milton Himmelfarb.

See the New Hampshire Sunday *News,* p. 34, of September 2, 1973, and p. 2, the Jewish *Press* October 5, 1973.

CHAPTER VI   *Progeny of the pogroms*

74 Rockefeller's speech on November 29, 1973, was at an Anti-Defamation League dinner honoring the late Jennie Grossinger.

75 The quote is from p. 153 of *Life Is with People: The Culture of the Shtetl,* by Mark Zborowski and Elizabeth Herzog, Eighth Printing, 1971 (New York: Schocken Books, 1962, 1952 copyright by International Universities Press, Inc.). The book came out of a project funded by the Office of Naval Research, conducted under the auspices of Columbia University Research in Contemporary Cultures.

81 Cohn's discussion of marginality is on p. 617, and the quotation on p. 621, of Cohn's article "The Politics of American Jews," in *The Jews: Social Patterns of an American Group,* edited by Marshall Sklare (Glencoe, Ill.: The Free Press, 1958).

82 Feingold's comment is on p. 96 of "The Jewish Radical in His American Habitat," *Judaism,* Issue No. 85, Vol. 22, No. 1, Winter, 1973, published by the American Jewish Congress.

85 Much of the information on the Jewish labor movement here comes from Will Herberg's "The Jewish Labor Movement in the United States," *American Jewish Year Book 1952,* Vol. 53 (New York: The American Jewish Committee, and Philadelphia: The Jewish Publication Society of America, 1952).

88 Glock's remark is on pp. 117–18 of *Christian Beliefs and Anti-Semitism* (New York: Harper & Row, 1966), by Charles Y. Glock and Rodney Stark.

See p. 245 of Hirsch's chapter, "There Shall Be No Poor," in

Judaism and Human Rights, ed. by Milton R. Konvitz (W. W. Norton & Company, Inc., 1972, c. 1972 by the B'nai B'rith Commission on Adult Jewish Education).

89 Konvitz's line is from p. 134 of *Judaism and Human Rights* (*Ibid.*).

Herberg's comment is from p. 28 of his article on the labor movement; the statistic on the garment workers in 1913 also is in his article.

CHAPTER VII *Opposing the powerful*

94 The quote is from p. 19 of *The Freedom Seder, A New Haggadah for Passover* (Washington: The Micah Press, and New York: Holt, Rinehart and Winston, 1969, 1970).

97 Porter's comment is from "Jewish Student Activism," in *Jewish Currents* (May 1970, Vol. 24, No. 5—264), p. 30. Yaffe's is from p. 255 of *The American Jews* (*op. cit.*). The Canadian situation is described on p. 395 of the *American Jewish Year Book 1972* (*op. cit.*). Kenneth Keniston also said that "a disproportionate number of New Leftists are Jewish" on p. 197 of *Young Radicals: Notes on Committed Youth* (New York: Harvest Books, Harcourt, Brace & World, 1968).

98 The Simpson-Yinger quote is on p. 298 of *Racial and Cultural Minorities: An Analysis of Prejudice and Discrimination* (New York: Harper & Row, Fourth Edition, 1972).

Saxbe's comments were reported in the New York *Times.* See the article on p. 13 of April 6, 1974, and the editorial (p. 40) of April 10, 1974.

Podhoretz's comment was in a speech delivered in the spring of 1971 to the sixty-fifth annual meeting of the American Jewish Committee, subsequently published in *Commentary,* p. 10, August, 1971, Vol. 52, No. 2.

99 Fenster's comments are on p. 26 of *Negro and Jew—An Encounter in America,* ed. by Shlomo Katz, a symposium compiled by *Midstream* magazine (New York: The Macmillan Company, 1966).

The chart is from p. 41 of the A.C.E. study (*op. cit.*).

100 Feingold's observation is on p. 94 of his *Judaism* article (*loc. cit.*).

Kahn's story is on pp. 248–49 of *The Passionate People* (New York: William Morrow & Co., Inc., 1968).

The Vietnam war survey was conducted by Stanford and is cited by the Rev. Andrew M. Greeley on p. 215 of his article "Political Attitudes Among American White Ethnics," *The Public Opinion Quarterly*, Vol. 36, No. 2, Summer, 1972. He identified the survey as coming from a forthcoming paper by Norman Nie and Barbara Currie.

101 The Waskow quote is on pp. 84–85 of *The Bush Is Burning* (New York: The Macmillan Company, 1971).

102 This Keniston quote is on p. 8 of *The Uncommitted: Alienated Youth in American Society* (New York: Harcourt, Brace & World, Inc., 1965).

The Feingold quote is on p. 104 of his *Judaism* article.

104 Lipset's observation is from " 'The Socialism of Fools'—The Left, the Jews and Israel," p. 25 of an article pamphlet published by the Anti-Defamation League of B'nai B'rith, 1969, also published in *Encounter*, December 1969.

106 The Feingold comment is also from *Judaism*, p. 98.

109 Feingold, p. 97 (*Ibid.*).

110 Keniston's remark is on p. 69 of *The Uncommitted* (*op. cit*).

111 Feingold again, pp. 101–2.

112 Feingold, pp. 99–100.

113 The first Lewin quote is from p. 181, the second from pp. 181–82 of *Resolving Social Conflicts* (New York: Harper & Row Publishers, 1948).

114 This Keniston quote is on p. 286 of *Young Radicals* (*op. cit.*).

CHAPTER VIII *"Paying a little back . . ."*

117 Fuchs's quote is on p. 182 of *The Political Behavior of American Jews* (*op. cit.*), in quoting Arthur Ruppin, *The Jews in the Modern World* (London: Macmillan & Co. Ltd., 1934), p. 352.

117 The *shtetl* description is from p. 194 of *Life Is with People* (*op. cit.*).

118 The "philanthropy was regarded . . ." line is by David G. Mandelbaum in "Change and Continuity in Jewish Life," the last half of a lecture and booklet printed by the Oscar Hillel Plotkin Library of the North Shore Congregation Israel, Glencoe, Ill., reprinted in Sklare's *The Jews* (*op. cit.*), p. 516.

122 The universities' plans were described in an article on p. 25 of the New York *Times*, December 24, 1972.

123 The writer is grateful to the Citizens' Research Foundation, Princeton, N.J., for its compilations of contributors. Also see

Financing the 1968 Election, by Herbert E. Alexander (Lexington, Mass.: Heath Lexington Books, D. C. Heath and Company, 1971).

123 Kahn's remark is from p. 19 of *The Passionate People* (*op. cit.*).

The description of Jews as America's most affluent group is based on the American Council on Education-American Jewish Committee survey of the 1969 class. Howard Yagerman of the committee staff, at this writer's request, obtained print-outs on income of Jews' parents and of Episcopalians' parents (in all research this writer has been able to find to date, Episcopalians were the only group more affluent than the Jews). Comparisons of the data showed that Jews had moved past the Episcopalians (who also send their children to college in high proportions) and one suspects that the gap has widened since 1969.

126 Statistics support what Wyman and Strauss say, if bank deposits are any indication. An article on p. 30 of the New York *Times,* January 14, 1973, said that the *New York Statistical Yearbook* fixed total deposits at New York banks at $91.5 billion, compared with California's $36 billion.

Singer's article, "The Jewish Gangster: Crime as 'Unzer Shtik,'" is in *Judaism,* Winter 1974, Vol. 23, No. 1 (pp. 70–77).

CHAPTER IX   *The myth of "liberalism"*

140 Some people unfamiliar with survey research wonder how one can talk of the "Jewish vote" or the "Catholic vote" or any other "vote." Some others are angered when writers try to lump them with an ethnic or age or other group; they consider this stereotyping and unfair. This writer considers most of the carefully executed surveys valid, although they vary considerably in quality. The pollsters argue among themselves about whose method is or is not better. In the case of Jewish voters, however, the arguments tend to be splitting hairs, for most results over the years, no matter by which methods, have shown relatively similar patterns.

Several methods are used for measuring group voting. Prior to the establishment of national polling firms like Roper and Gallup, data were gathered by taking relatively "pure" voting wards in various cities around the nation and extrapolating reasonable figures for national averages of a particular group's vote in a particular election. In the case of Jews, areas like the Lower East Side of New York City would give virtually pure data, since few non-Jews lived there. Similar areas in Chicago and Boston and Philadelphia were used. NBC's election-day method of analysis works much the same way. NBC researchers locate voting precincts where most of the voters are known to be Jewish (or, as the case may be for the statistic NBC is seeking, elderly voters, or Italo-Americans, or youths, or blacks). They do this by keeping a constant watch on population trends and by interviewing in the precincts. Normally, a final NBC tally for a particular group would be broad enough, through careful choice in the "pure" precincts, to give a breakdown as to inner-city and suburban, old and young, rich and poor.

Some specialists believe that this method is shoddy, feeling that the research on the purity of the precincts is insufficient. For instance, NBC has used a precinct in Great Neck, Nassau County, New York, not far from the New York City borough of Queens, as one of its "tag" Jewish precincts for election returns, meaning that it considers this particular precinct pure enough to include its results in national Jewish voting data. This writer and two other reporters for the Washington *Post,* Haynes Johnson and Anthony Astrachan, went door-to-door in that precinct in October of 1972. Many of the residents were not Jewish. In fact, half the residents interviewed by this writer were not. One could argue that a peer influence operates on the non-Jews of such a precinct. But this writer's interviews—certainly no definitive sample—tended to refute that. The Jews and non-Jews seemed to diverge sharply.

In 1972, CBS used a different method altogether, much like the method used by Gallup and Harris in their national surveying. CBS has used the sample precinct method in the past. But in 1972, Warren Mitofsky of the CBS Election Unit, working with George Fine Research, Inc., mounted an extensive at-the-polls survey, in which voters were asked as they left their voting place who they had voted for, what religion they considered themselves, and other questions. Nationally, 17,405 persons were queried, 4 per cent of whom identified themselves as being Jewish. Interestingly, the figure for Jewish voting in 1972 was not far different from that obtained by NBC's tag precincts method. CBS's poll showed McGovern's winning 66 per cent of Jews' votes, while NBC's put the figure at 65 per cent. The CBS survey was large enough to give regional breakdowns, whereas NBC keyed on only a few states with large Jewish populations, like New York and Illinois. The writer is grateful to CBS and to Mitofsky for sharing the survey's results.

Nevertheless, some voters may resent reading about themselves as statistical digits rather than as individuals, as if they were somehow devoid of free choice. In fact, such statistics are never applicable to a single individual. They are indicators of group trends and only that.

144 The ancient call is from Isaiah I: 17, p. 533, of *The Holy Scriptures*, according to the Masoretic Text (Philadelphia: The Jewish Publication Society of America, 1917, 1955).

145 The information on Hayes's administration is on p. 63 of Nathaniel Weyl's *The Jew in American Politics* (New Rochelle, N.Y.: Arlington House, 1968).

146 Much of the information on the New York races on this page and p. 147 comes from old issues of *FACTS*, a private publication of the Anti-Defamation League of B'nai B'rith. The Javits-Wagner race is described in *"Our Own Kind"—Voting by Race, Creed or National Origin*, by Moses Rischin, p. 17 (Santa Barbara, Calif.: Center for the Study of Democratic Institutions, 1960).

147 The Kennedy-Nixon campaign description is from *FACTS*, March 1969, Vol. IV, No. 3.

148 *The American Voter* is the product of the Survey Research Center of the University of Michigan. This quote is from p. 28 of the abridged version, by Angus Campbell, Philip E. Converse, Warren E. Miller, and Donald E. Stokes (New York: John Wiley & Sons, Inc., 1964).

148 The table is on p. 152 of *That Most Distressful Nation* (Chicago: Quadrangle Books, 1972).

149 The survey was reported by Wesley and Beverly Allinsmith in *Public Opinion Quarterly*, Fall, 1948.

150 The Fuchs quote is from p. 172 of *The Political Behavior of American Jews (op. cit.)*.

151 The voting statistics are those commonly accepted by Jewish organizations. Much of the later data is reported by Mark R. Levy and Michael S. Kramer in *The Ethnic Factor—How America's Minorities Decide Elections* (New York: Simon and Schuster, 1972), an invaluable source of data on ethnic politics in America.

157 The line is on p. 182 of *The American Voter (op. cit.)*.

158 Smith's comments are discussed by Edward Swayduck in his article "Sabotage—Since 1946, Nixon's Political Stock-in-Trade," p. 4, *Lithopinion* 30, Vol. 8, No. 2, Summer 1973.

158 Mrs. Dawidowicz's quotation is on pp. 80–81 of *Politics in a Pluralist Democracy* (New York: Institute of Human Relations Press, 1963).

Van den Haag's comment is on p. 139 of *The Jewish Mystique* (*op. cit.*).

CHAPTER X *Years of turbulence*

163 The civilian review board voting is analyzed in *Police, Politics and Race*, by David W. Abbott, Louis H. Gold, and Edward T. Rogowsky, a 1969 publication of the American Jewish Committee and the Joint Center for Urban Studies of the Massachusetts Institute of Technology and Harvard University.

167 See Raab's article, "The Deadly Innocences of American Jews," pp. 31–39, *Commentary*, December 1970, Vol. 50, No. 6.

Lipset's comment is on p. 48 of a task force report entitled *Group Life in America* (New York: The American Jewish Committee, 1972).

168 Siegel's analysis is on pp. 24–26 of "An Anatomy of Liberalism —A Conservative View," in *Judaism*, Winter, 1972, No. 81, Vol. 21, No. 1, published by the American Jewish Congress.

169 Podhoretz's speech was reprinted in *Commentary*, August 1971 (*op. cit.*).

169 See p. 36 of Himmelfarb's "Is American Jewry in Crisis?" *Commentary*, March 1969 (Vol. 47, No. 3).

179 Greeley's comment is from p. 162 of *Why Can't They Be Like Us? America's White Ethnic Groups* (New York: E. P. Dutton & Co., Inc., 1971).

180 The absence of Jews among the abolitionists is cited by Fuchs on p. 37 of *The Political Behavior of American Jews* (*op. cit.*).

CHAPTER XI *Year of the Jew*

183 The Richard Wright comment is on p. 86 of Constance Webb's *Richard Wright, a Biography* (New York: G. P. Putnam's Sons, 1968).

185 The voting for Congress in 1972 is described in the Epilogue to the pocketbook edition of Levy and Kramer's *The Ethnic Factor*, p. 244 (a Touchstone Book, 1973).

The New York figures are from CBS (70-29) and NBC (61-39).

The American Jewish Committee's studies were organized by Howard W. Yagerman of the research staff of the committee.

192 Roche quoted the Democrat in his column on the opposite

editorial page of the Washington *Post,* July 13, 1972.

196 The writer is using CBS's figures here.

197 The center's report was described by Broder on p. A1 of the Washington *Post,* September 9, 1973.

CHAPTER XII   *To run or not to run*

200 The writer was assisted by Harry J. Alderman and Judith Selakoff of the American Jewish Committee's Jacob Blaustein Library in ascertaining the names of elected officials. The writer verified data in the *Biographical Directory of the American Congress 1774–1971* (Washington: U. S. Government Printing Office, 1971). Frederick H. Pauls of the Government and Research Division, Congressional Research Service of the Library of Congress, researched the numbers of senators and representatives.

210 Napolitan described his work for Shapp in *The Election Game and How to Win It* (Garden City, N.Y.: Doubleday & Company, Inc., 1972), p. 86.

211 The Gallup surveys on bigotry are reported on pp. 126–27 of Stember's *Jews in the Mind of America* (*op. cit.*).

212 The prevalence of anti-Semitism among those better off is cited by Stember and others, p. 61 (*Ibid.*).

Keller's remark is on p. 269 of his chapter "Jews and the Character of American Life Since 1930" (*Ibid.*).

Dean's article, "Jewish Participation in the Life of Mid-Sized American Communities" originally appeared in *Jewish Social Studies,* Vol. VII, No. 3, 1955, and was reprinted in *The Jews —Social Patterns of an American Group* (*op. cit.*), p. 307.

214 Goldberg's quotes are from pp. 155 and 152 of "Jews in the Legal Profession: A Case of Adjustment to Discrimination" in *Jewish Social Studies,* Vol. 32, No. 2, April 1970.

214 The chart is from p. 37 of the American Council on Education survey.

216 See p. 15 of Jacobs' *Is Curly Jewish?* (New York: Vintage Books, Random House, 1965, 1973).

217 The writer calls Devine "ultraconservative" on the basis of his consistently high ratings from the Americans for Constitutional Action. His 1972 voting record was rated a perfect 100 per cent.

224 Shannon's remark is on p. 15 of *The American Irish* (New York: The Macmillan Company, 1966).

Levine's quote is on p. 134 of *The Irish and Irish Politicians* (*op. cit.*).

229 Moley's description of Rosenman is on p. 8 of *After Seven Years* (New York: Harper & Brothers, 1939).

Wrote Napolitan of Goldberg: "Goldberg has to be one of the poorest candidates who ever came down the pike . . ." on p. 139 of *The Election Game and How to Win It* (*op. cit.*).

In regard to male bonding, Rutgers professor Wilson Carey McWilliams, whose book, *The Idea of Fraternity in America*, was published in 1973, thinks that Himmelfarb is probably correct, for several reasons. One, he says, is that Jewish family lines tend to be strong and "typically, male bonding is across family lines. It's probably an effort to escape the familial orientation. The blood family, part of the whole struggle for identity, is inevitably involved in a kind of cross-pressured situation between your desire for identity and your desire for family and security. Fraternities are a sort of half-way house. What I think tends to happen is, if the moral and psychological hold of the blood family is too strong, it's very hard to form strong fraternal relations. It's not only an ingredient of politics, but the desire for fraternity is a kind of sub rosa theme throughout American letters." Further, McWilliams said in an interview, the relatively unauthoritarian Jewish family structure would tend to discourage male bonding. At least traditionally, he said, the "role of the Jewish father was not overbearing. He underplayed, which meant that boys growing up had less problems with male roles. They didn't feel the need for this tremendous fraternal support against authoritarian fathers. What I think tends to happen now —when you begin to see fraternal feelings among Jews—are feelings of a need to struggle against the mother, and an attempt to become Gentilized."

CHAPTER XIII *Jewish power*

239 The story of the first twenty-three Jews to settle in America is on pp. 48–49 of Oscar and Mary F. Handlin's "The Acquisition of Political and Social Rights by the Jews in the United States," *American Jewish Year Book 1955*, No. 56 (New York: The American Jewish Committee, and Philadelphia: The Jewish Publication Society of America, 1955).

240 The letter from Stuyvesant is on p. 5; the one to him from the directors is on p. 8 of Samuel Oppenheim's *The Early History of the Jews in New York, 1654–1664*. Printed for the author and for the Publications of The American Jewish Historical Society, No. 18 (1909).

Raab's quote is on p. 32 of his *Commentary* article (*op. cit.*).

242 The statistics on Jewish dead are on p. 559 of *A History of Zionism* by Walter Laqueur (New York: Holt, Rinehart & Winston, 1972).

242 The quotes are on p. 129 and pp. 130–31, respectively, of *While Six Million Died, a Chronicle of American Apathy* (New York: Random House, 1967).

See Chapter XV, pp. 270–88 of Morse for a detailed description of the plight of those on the *St. Louis.*

243 The Hitler quote is on p. 145 of Morse (*ibid.*).

Feingold's quote is on p. 299 of *The Politics of Rescue: The Roosevelt Administration and the Holocaust, 1938–1945* (New Brunswick, N.J.: Rutgers University Press, 1970).

Laqueur's comment is on p. 561 of *A History of Zionism* (*op. cit.*). He quotes David Niles on p. 554, with the assessment of Roosevelt that appears on the following page.

245 Professor Cohen's quote is on pp. 5–6 of *Not Free to Desist— The American Jewish Committee 1906–1966* (Philadelphia: The Jewish Publication Society of America, 1972).

253 The statistics on emigration are from the Israel Aliyah Center in New York City.

255 See "Does Jewish Political Philanthropy Serve Jewish Interests?" on pp. 14–17 of *The National Jewish Monthly,* February 1974, Vol. 88, No. 6.

261 See Podhoretz's "Now, Instant Zionism" in the New York *Times* Magazine, February 3, 1974.

266 Middleton's conclusion appeared in his article, "Who Lost the Yom Kippur War?" in *The Atlantic,* March 1974, Vol. 233, No. 3.

267 Rabbi Borowitz's quote is on p. 60 of *The Mask Jews Wear: The Self-Deceptions of American Jewry* (New York: Simon and Schuster, 1973).

Additional bibliography

In addition to those books and articles specifically cited in the chapter notes, the writer used many other books and articles for background and specific use, the major ones of which are cited here:

BOOKS AND PAMPHLETS

E. Digby Baltzell, *The Protestant Establishment—Aristocracy and Caste in America* (New York: Vintage Books, 1964).

Milton L. Barron, ed., *Minorities in a Changing World* (New York: Alfred A. Knopf, 1967).

Francis Chase, Jr., *Sound and Fury, an Informal History of Broadcasting* (New York: Harper and Brothers, 1942).

Richard Cohen, ed., *Let My People Go* (New York: Popular Library, 1971).

Lore and Maurice Cowan, *The Wit of the Jews* (Nashville, Tenn.: Aurora Publishers, Inc., 1970).

Harold Cruse, *The Crisis of the Negro Intellectual* (New York: William Morrow & Co., Inc., 1967).

Isaac Deutscher, *The Non-Jewish Jew and Other Essays*, ed. by Tamara Deutscher (London: Oxford University Press, 1968).

G. William Domhoff, *Fat Cats and Democrats* (Englewood Cliffs, N.J.: Prentice-Hall, Inc., 1972).

Lewis Feuer, *The Scientific Intellectual* (New York: Basic Books, 1963).

John Hope Franklin, Thomas F. Pettigrew, and Raymond W. Mack, *Ethnicity in American Life* (New York: The Anti-Defamation League of B'nai B'rith, 1971).

Murray Friedman, ed., *Overcoming Middle Class Rage* (Philadelphia: The Westminster Press, 1971).

Max Geltman, *The Confrontation: Black Power, Anti-Semitism and the Myth of Integration* (Englewood Cliffs, N.J.: Prentice-Hall, Inc., 1970).

Louis L. Gerson, *The Hyphenate in Recent American Politics and Diplomacy* (Lawrence, Kansas: The University of Kansas Press, 1964).

Nathan Glazer, *American Judaism* (Chicago: The University of Chicago Press, 1964).

Nathan Glazer and Daniel P. Moynihan, *Beyond the Melting Pot* (Cambridge, Mass.: The M.I.T. Press, Second Edition, 1970).

Milton Gordon, *Assimilation in American Life* (New York: Oxford University Press, 1964).

Allen Guttmann, *The Jewish Writer in America* (New York: Oxford University Press, 1971).

Oscar Handlin, *The Uprooted* (New York: Grosset & Dunlap, 1951).

Louis Harris and Bert E. Swanson, *Black-Jewish Relations in New York City* (New York: Praeger Publishers, 1970).

Will Herberg, *Protestant, Catholic, Jew* (Garden City, N.Y.: Doubleday & Company, Inc., Anchor Books, 1955, 1960).

Milton Himmelfarb, *The Jews of Modernity* (New York: Basic Books, 1973).

Morris Janowitz, *Political Conflict—Essays in Political Sociology* (Chicago: Quadrangle Books, 1970).

Oscar I. Janowsky, ed., *The American Jew: A Reappraisal* (Philadelphia: The Jewish Publication Society of America, 1964).

E. J. Kahn, Jr., *The World of Swope* (New York: Simon and Schuster, 1965).

Edwin Kiester, Jr., *The Case of the Missing Executive—How Religious Bias Wastes Management Talent and What Is Being Done About It* (New York: The American Jewish Committee, 1968).

Tina Levitan, *Jews in American Life* (New York: Hebrew Publishing Co., 1969).

Ludwig Lewisohn, *The American Jew—Character and Destiny* (New York: Farrar, Straus and Co., 1950).

Samuel Lubell, *The Future of American Politics* (New York: Harper & Row, Third Edition, 1965).

Eugene Lyons, *David Sarnoff* (New York: Harper & Row, 1966).

Charles A. Madison, *Eminent American Jews* (New York: Frederick Ungar Publishing Company, 1970).

Max L. Margolis and Alexander Marx, *A History of the Jewish People* (New York: Athenaeum, 1969).

Wilson Carey McWilliams, *The Idea of Fraternity in America* (Berkeley: University of California Press, 1973).

Leon Poliakiv, *The History of Anti-Semitism* (New York: The Vanguard Press, 1965).

Jack Nusan Porter and Peter Dreier, eds., *Jewish Radicalism: A Selected Anthology* (New York: Grove Press, Inc., 1973).

Leo Rosten, *The Joys of Yiddish* (New York: McGraw-Hill Book Company, 1968).

Abram Leon Sachar, *A History of the Jews* (New York: Alfred A. Knopf, 1965).

Howard M. Sachar, *The Course of Modern Jewish History* (New York: World Publishing Company, 1958).

Richard M. Scammon and Ben J. Wattenberg, *The Real Majority* (New York: Coward-McCann, Inc., 1970).

Melvin Steinfeld, *Cracks in the Melting Pot—Racism and Discrimination in American History* (Beverly Hills: Glencoe Press, 1970).

W. A. Swanberg, *Pulitzer* (New York: Charles Scribner's Sons, 1967).

Lionel Tiger, *Men in Groups* (New York: Vintage Books, 1970).

Ben J. Wattenberg, in collaboration with Richard M. Scammon, *This U.S.A.* (Garden City, N.Y.: Doubleday & Company, Inc., 1965).

Robert G. Weisbord and Arthur Stein, *Bittersweet Encounter—The Afro-American and the American Jew* (Westport, Conn.: Negro Universities Press, 1970).

ARTICLES, PERIODICALS, ETC.

"The American Jew Today," *Newsweek*, March 1, 1971, cover story.

Ben Zion Bokser, "Democratic Aspirations in Talmudic Judaism," p. 145 in Konvitz's *Judaism in Human Rights* (*op. cit.*).

Elmer E. Cornwell, Jr., "Bosses, Machines and Ethnic Groups," pp. 194–216 in *American Ethnic Politics*, edited by Lawrence H. Fuchs (New York: Harper Torchbooks, 1968).

Lawrence H. Fuchs, "American Jews and the Presidential Vote" (*ibid.*).

Andrew J. Glass, "Nixon Gives Israel Massive Aid but Reaps No Jewish Political Harvest," *The National Journal,* January 8, 1972, Vol. 4, No. 2.

Nathan Glazer, "Blacks, Jews and the Intellectuals," *Commentary,* April 1969.

Nathan Glazer, "Negroes and Jews: The New Challenge to Pluralism," *Commentary,* December 1964.

Nathan Glazer, "Social Characteristics of American Jews," *American Jewish Year Book 1955,* Vol. 56 (New York: The American Jewish Committee, and Philadelphia: The Jewish Publication Society of America, 1955).

Bertram H. Gold, "Who Speaks for the Jews?" an address to the annual meeting of the American Jewish Committee, May 4, 1972.

Milton M. Gordon, "Assimilation in America: Theory and Reality," pp. 263–85, *Daedalus,* Spring, 1961.

Ben Halpern, "America Is Different, the American Jew," in Sklare's *The Jews (op. cit.).*

Will Herberg, "Religious Group Conflict in America," in *Religion and Social Conflict,* edited by Robert Lee and Martin Marty (London: Oxford University Press, 1964) and reprinted in *Ethnic Group Politics,* edited by Harry A. Bailey, Jr., and Ellis Katz (Columbus, O.: Charles E. Merrill Publishing Company, 1969).

Arthur Hertzberg, "The Protestant 'Establishment,' Catholic Dogma and the Presidency," *Commentary,* October 1960.

Milton Himmelfarb and Nathan Glazer, "McGovern and the Jews, a Debate," *Commentary,* September 1972.

Samuel E. Karff, "Jewish Peoplehood—A Signal of Transcendence," in *New Theology No. 9,* edited by Martin E. Marty and Dean G. Peerman (New York: The Macmillan Company, 1972), pp. 59–69.

Walter Kaufmann, "The Future of Jewish Identity," pp. 41–58, *New Theology No. 9 (ibid.).*

Alfred Kazin, "New York Jew," p. 6, *The New York Review of Books,* December 14, 1972.

Wolfe Kelman, "The American Synagogue: Present and Prospects," *Conservative Judaism,* Volume 26, No. 1, Fall, 1971.

Gilbert Kollin, "East Is East and West Is—Different," *Conservative Judaism (ibid.).*

Irving Kristol and Paul Weaver, "Who Knows New York? and Other Notes on a Mixed-up City," *The Public Interest,* No. 16, Summer, 1969.

Bob Kuttner, "White Males and Jews Need Not Apply," *The Village Voice,* August 31, 1972.

Arthur J. Lelyveld, "In Defense of Liberalism," *Judaism*, Winter, 1972 (*op. cit.*).

Irving M. Levine, "New Institutional Responses to Group Differences," speech to San Francisco University Consultation on Ethnicity, November 16, 1971.

George Lichtheim, "Socialism and the Jews," *Dissent*, July–August 1968.

C. Eric Lincoln, Introduction to *Bittersweet Encounter*, by Weisbord and Stein (*op. cit.*).

Jerome K. Myers and Bertram H. Roberts, "Some Relationships Between Religion, Ethnic Origin and Mental Illness," in Sklare's *The Jews* (*op. cit.*).

Jacob Neusner, "Judaism, Jews and the Liberal Outlook," *Judaism*, Winter, 1972 (*op. cit.*).

Jacob Neusner, "Assimilation and Self Hatred in Modern Jewish Life," *Conservative Judaism*, Fall, 1971.

Bernard Postal, "A Minyan of Jewish Governors," *The National Jewish Monthly*, March 1969.

Earl Raab, "Intergroup Relations and Tensions in the United States," *American Jewish Year Book 1970* (*op. cit.*).

Emanuel Rackman, "Judaism and Equality," in *Judaism and Human Rights* (*op. cit.*).

Irwin D. Rinder, "Polarities in Jewish Identification: The Personality of Ideological Extremity," in Sklare's *The Jews* (*op. cit.*).

Bernard C. Rosen, "Race, Ethnicity and the Achievement Syndrome," *American Sociological Review*, Vol. 24, No. 1, February 1959, pp. 47–60.

Richard L. Rubenstein, "Liberalism and the Jewish Interests," *Judaism*, Winter, 1972 (*op. cit.*).

Steven S. Schwarzschild, "The Radical Imperatives of Judaism," *Judaism*, Winter, 1972 (*ibid.*).

Charles R. Snyder, "Culture and Jewish Sobriety: The Ingroup-Outgroup Factor," in Sklare's *The Jews* (*op. cit.*).

Theodore Solotaroff and Marshall Sklare, Introduction to *Jews in the Mind of America* (*op. cit.*).

Fred L. Strodtbeck, "Family Interaction, Values and Achievement," in *The Jews* (*op. cit.*).

U. S. Bureau of the Census, "Religion Reported by the Civilian Population of the United States: March 1957," *Current Population Reports*, Series P-29, No. 79, February 2, 1958.

Anne G. Wolfe, "The Invisible Jewish Poor," presentation to Chicago chapter of the American Jewish Committee, June 8, 1971.

Index